COMMENTARIES ON LIVING

First Series

In this series of commentaries J. Krishnamurti, one of the great thinkers of our time, touches upon many human problems — our hopes, our fears, our illusions, our beliefs, our prejudices — and in the simplest language seems to pierce to their roots.

"The sheer simplicity is breathtaking. The reader is given, in one paragraph, often in one sentence, enough to keep him exploring, questioning, thinking for days." — Anne Morrow Lindbergh.

"The insight, spiritual and poetic, of these commentaries is as simply expressed as it is searching in its demand."—*Times Literary Supplement* **(London)**.

"Krishnamurti is no other than he seems, a free man, one of the first quality, growing older as diamonds do but the gem-like flame not dating, and alive in these COMMENTARIES. It is a treasure." —Francis Hacket, *The New Republic*.

J. Krishnamurti was born in South India and educated in England. Hailed by many from early youth as a spiritual teacher, he rejected adulation and leadership in order to encourage spiritual freedom and the discovery of understanding by each one for himself. He has devoted his life to speaking and counseling, traveling in the U.S.A., Europe, India and other parts of the world, addressing thousands of people, always pointing the way for each man to find himself.

These *Commentaries on Living* are published in three volumes: *First, Second,* and *Third Series.*

OTHER BOOKS

by J. Krishnamurti:
    THE FIRST AND LAST FREEDOM
    EDUCATION AND THE SIGNIFICANCE OF LIFE
    LIFE AHEAD

by J. Krishnamurti, edited by D. Rajagopal
    COMMENTARIES ON LIVING, *Second Series*
    COMMENTARIES ON LIVING, *Third Series*

COMMENTARIES
ON LIVING
First Series

from the notebooks of
J. KRISHNAMURTI

edited by
D. Rajagopal

A QUEST BOOK

Published under a grant from The Kern Foundation

THE THEOSOPHICAL PUBLISHING HOUSE

Wheaton, Ill., U.S.A.

Madras, India / London, England

Copyright © 1956, by Krishnamurti Writings, Inc.

Original edition 1956

Quest Book edition 1967 published by
The Theosophical Publishing House, Wheaton, Illinois,
by arrangement with Krishnamurti Writings, Inc.

Second Quest Book printing 1968

Third Quest Book printing 1970

ISBN: 0-8356-0390-3

Library of Congress Catalog Card Number 67-8405/C.D.

Printed in the United States of America

CONTENTS

Three Pious Egoists

THE OTHER DAY three pious egoists came to see me. The first was a *sannyasi,* a man who had renounced the world; the second was an orientalist and a great believer in brotherhood; and the third was a confirmed worker for a marvellous Utopia. Each of the three was strenuous in his own work and looked down on the others' attitudes and activities, and each was strengthened by his own conviction. Each was ardently attached to his particular form of belief, and all were in a strange way ruthless.

They told me, especially the Utopian, that they were ready to deny or sacrifice themselves and their friends for what they believed. They appeared meek and gentle, particularly the man of brotherhood, but there was a hardness of heart and that peculiar intolerance which is characteristic of the superior. They were the chosen, the interpreters; they knew and were certain.

The *sannyasi* said, in the course of a serious talk, that he was preparing himself for his next life. This life, he declared, had very little to offer him, for he had seen through all the illusions of worldliness and had forsaken worldly ways. He had some personal weaknesses and certain difficulties in concentration, he added, but in his next life he would be the ideal which he had set for himself.

His whole interest and vitality lay in his conviction that he was to be something in his next life. We talked at some length, and his emphasis was always on the tomorrow, on the future. The past existed, he said, but always in relation to the future; the present was merely a passage to the future, and today was interesting only because of tomorrow. If there were no tomorrow, he asked, then why make an effort? One might just as well vegetate or be like the pacific cow.

The whole of life was one continuous movement from the past through the momentary present to the future. We should use the present, he said, to be something in the future : to be wise, to be strong, to be compassionate. Both the present and the future were transient, but tomorrow ripened the fruit. He insisted that today is but a stepping-stone, and that we should not be too anxious or too particular about it; we should keep clear the ideal of tomorrow and make the journey successfully. Altogether, he was impatient of the present.

The man of brotherhood was more learned, and his language more poetic; he was expert in handling words, and was altogether suave and convincing. He too had carved a divine niche for himself in the future. He was to be something. This idea filled his heart, and he had gathered his disciples for that future. Death, he said, was a beautiful thing, for it brought one nearer to that divine niche which was making it possible for him to live in this sorrowful and ugly world.

He was all for changing and beautifying the world, and was working ardently for the brotherhood of man. He considered that ambition, with its attendant cruelties and corruption, was inevitable in a world where you had to get things done; and unfortunately, if you wanted certain organizational activities carried on, you had to be a little bit on the hard side. The work was important because it was helping mankind, and anyone who opposed it had to be put aside—gently, of course. The organization for that work was of the utmost value and must not be hindered. "Others have their paths," he said, "but ours is essential, and anyone who interferes is not one of us."

The Utopian was a strange mixture of the idealist and the practical man. His Bible was not the old but the new. He believed in the new implicitly. He knew the outcome of the future, for the new book foretold what it was to be. His plan was to confuse, organize and carry out. The present, he said, was corrupt, it must be destroyed, and out of this destruction the new would be built. The present was to be sacrificed for the future. The future man was all-important, not the present man.

"We know how to create that future man," he said, "we can shape his mind and heart; but we must get into power to do any good. We will sacrifice ourselves and others to bring about a new state. Anyone who stands in the way we will kill, for the means is of no consequence; the end justifies any means."

For ultimate peace, any form of violence could be used; for ultimate individual freedom, tyranny in the present was inevitable. "When we have the power in our hands," he declared, "we will use every form of compulsion to bring about a new world without class distinctions, without priests. From our central thesis we will never move; we are fixed there, but our strategy and tactics will vary depending upon changing circumstances. We plan, organize and act to destroy the present man for the future man."

The *sannyasi*, the man of brotherhood and the Utopian all live for tomorrow, for the future. They are not ambitious in the worldly sense, they do not want high honours, wealth or recognition; but they are ambitious in a much more subtle way. The Utopian has identified himself with a group which he thinks will have the power to reorient the world; the man of brotherhood aspires to be exalted, and the *sannyasi* to attain his goal. All are consumed with their own becoming, with their own achievement and expansion. They do not see that this desire denies peace, brotherhood and supreme happiness.

Ambition in any form—for the group, for individual salvation, or for spiritual achievement—is action postponed. Desire is ever of the future; the desire to become is inaction in the present. The now has greater significance than the tomorrow. In the now is all time, and to understand the now is to be free of time. Becoming is the continuation of time, of sorrow. Becoming does not contain being. Being is always in the present, and being is the highest form of transformation. Becoming is merely modified continuity, and there is radical transformation only in the present, in being.

IDENTIFICATION

WHY DO YOU identify yourself with another, with a group, with a country? Why do you call yourself a Christian, a Hindu, a

Buddhist, or why do you belong to one of the innumerable sects? Religiously and politically one identifies oneself with this or with that group through tradition or habit, through impulse, prejudice, imitation and laziness. This identification puts an end to all creative understanding, and then one becomes a mere tool in the hands of the party boss, the priest or the favoured leader.

The other day someone said that he was a "Krishnamurti-ite," whereas so-and-so belonged to another group. As he was saying it, he was utterly unconscious of the implications of this identification. He was not by any means a foolish person; he was well read, cultured and all the rest of it. Nor was he senti-mental or emotional over the matter; on the contrary, he was clear and definite.

Why had he become a "Krishnamurti-ite"? He had followed others, belonged to many wearisome groups and organizations, and at last found himself identified with this particular person. From what he said, it appeared that the journey was over. He had taken a stand and that was the end of the matter; he had chosen, and nothing could shake him. He would now com-fortably settle down and follow eagerly all that had been said and was going to be said.

When we identify ourselves with another, is that an indica-tion of love? Does identification imply experimentation? Does not identification put an end to love and to experiment? Identification, surely, is possession, the assertion of ownership; and ownership denies love, does it not? To own is to be secure; possession is defence, making oneself invulnerable. In identifica-tion there is resistance, whether gross or subtle; and is love a form of self-protective resistance? Is there love when there is defence?

Love is vulnerable, pliable, receptive; it is the highest form of sensitivity, and identification makes for insensitivity. Identifica-tion and love do not go together, for the one destroys the other. Identification is essentially a thought process by which the mind safeguards and expands itself; and in becoming something it must resist and defend, it must own and discard. In this process of becoming, the mind or the self grows tougher and more capable; but this is not love. Identification destroys freedom, and only in freedom can there be the highest form of sensitivity.

To experiment, need there be identification? Does not the very act of identification put an end to inquiry, to discovery? The happiness that truth brings cannot be if there is no experimentation in self-discovery. Identification puts an end to discovery; it is another form of laziness. Identification is vicarious experience, and hence utterly false.

To experience, all identification must cease. To experiment, there must be no fear. Fear prevents experience. It is fear that makes for identification—identification with another, with a group, with an ideology, and so on. Fear must resist, suppress; and in a state of self-defence, how can there be venturing on the uncharted sea? Truth or happiness cannot come without undertaking the journey into the ways of the self. You cannot travel far if you are anchored. Identification is a refuge. A refuge needs protection, and that which is protected is soon destroyed. Identification brings destruction upon itself, and hence the constant conflict between various identifications.

The more we struggle for or against identification, the greater is the resistance to understanding. If one is aware of the whole process of identification, outward as well as inner, if one sees that its outward expression is projected by the inner demand, then there is a possibility of discovery and happiness. He who has identified himself can never know freedom, in which alone all truth comes into being.

GOSSIP AND WORRY

How ODDLY SIMILAR are gossip and worry. They are both the outcome of a restless mind. A restless mind must have a changing variety of expressions and actions, it must be occupied; it must have ever-increasing sensations, passing interests, and gossip contains the elements of all these.

Gossip is the very antithesis of intensity and earnestness. To talk about another, pleasantly or viciously, is an escape from oneself, and escape is the cause of restlessness. Escape in its very nature is restless. Concern over the affairs of others seems to occupy most people, and this concern shows itself in the reading of innumerable magazines and newspapers with their gossip columns, their accounts of murders, divorces and so on.

As we are concerned with what others think of us, so we are anxious to know all about them; and from this arise the crude and subtle forms of snobbishness and the worship of authority. Thus we become more and more externalized and inwardly empty. The more externalized we are, the more sensations and distractions there must be, and this gives rise to a mind that is never quiet, that is not capable of deep search and discovery.

Gossip is an expression of a restless mind; but merely to be silent does not indicate a tranquil mind. Tranquillity does not come into being with abstinence or denial; it comes with the understanding of what *is*. To understand what *is* needs swift awareness, for what *is* is not static.

If we did not worry, most of us would feel that we were not alive; to be struggling with a problem is for the majority of us an indication of existence. We cannot imagine life without a problem; and the more we are occupied with a problem, the more alert we think we are. The constant tension over a problem which thought itself has created only dulls the mind, making it insensitive and weary.

Why is there this ceaseless preoccupation with a problem? Will worry resolve the problem? Or does the answer to the problem come when the mind is quiet? But for most people, a quiet mind is a rather fearsome thing; they are afraid to be quiet, for heaven knows what they may discover in themselves, and worry is a preventive. A mind that is afraid to discover must ever be on the defensive, and restlessness is its defence.

Through constant strain, through habit and the influence of circumstances, the conscious layers of the mind have become agitated and restless. Modern existence encourages this superficial activity and distraction, which is another form of self-defence. Defence is resistance, which prevents understanding.

Worry, like gossip, has the semblance of intensity and seriousness; but if one observes more closely one will see that it arises from attraction and not earnestness. Attraction is ever changing, and that is why the objects of worry and gossip change. Change is merely modified continuity. Gossip and worry can come to an end only when the restlessness of the mind is understood. Mere abstinence, control or discipline will not bring about tranquillity, but only dull the mind, making it insensitive and confined.

Curiosity is not the way of understanding. Understanding comes with self-knowledge. He who suffers is not curious; and mere curiosity, with its speculative overtones, is a hindrance to self-knowledge. Speculation, like curiosity, is an indication of restlessness; and a restless mind, however gifted, destroys understanding and happiness.

THOUGHT AND LOVE

THOUGHT, WITH ITS emotional and sensational content, is not love. Thought invariably denies love. Thought is founded on memory, and love is not memory. When you think about someone you love, that thought is not love. You may recall a friend's habits, manners, idiosyncrasies, and think of pleasant or unpleasant incidents in your relationship with that person, but the pictures which thought evokes are not love. By its very nature, thought is separative. The sense of time and space, of separation and sorrow, is born of the process of thought, and it is only when the thought process ceases that there can be love.

Thought inevitably breeds the feeling of ownership, that possessiveness which consciously or unconsciously cultivates jealousy. Where jealousy is, obviously love is not; and yet with most people, jealousy is taken as an indication of love. Jealousy is the result of thought, it is a response of the emotional content of thought. When the feeling of possessing or being possessed is blocked, there is such emptiness that envy takes the place of love. It is because thought plays the role of love that all the complications and sorrows arise.

If you did not think of another, you would say that you did not love that person. But is it love when you *do* think of the person? If you did not think of a friend whom you think you love, you would be rather horrified, would you not? If you did not think of a friend who is dead, you would consider yourself disloyal, without love, and so on. You would regard such a state as callous, indifferent, and so you would begin to think of that person, you would have photographs, images made by the hand or by the mind; but thus to fill your heart with the things of the mind is to leave no room for love. When you are with a friend, you do not think about him; it is only in his absence that thought begins to re-create scenes and experiences that are dead. This revival of the past is called love. So, for most of us, love is death, a denial of life; we live with the past, with the dead, therefore we ourselves are dead, though we call it love.

The process of thought ever denies love. It is thought that has emotional complications, not love. Thought is the greatest hindrance to love. Thought creates a division between what *is* and what *should* be, and on this division morality is based; but neither the moral nor the immoral know love. This moral structure, created by the mind to hold social relationships together, is not love, but a hardening process like that of cement. Thought does not lead to love, thought does not cultivate love; for love cannot be cultivated as a plant in the garden. The very desire to cultivate love is the action of thought.

If you are at all aware you will see what an important part thought plays in your life. Thought obviously has its place, but it is in no way related to love. What is related to thought can be understood by thought, but that which is not related to thought cannot be caught by the mind. You will ask, then what is love? Love is a state of being in which thought is not; but the very definition of love is a process of thought, and so it is not love.

16

We have to understand thought itself, and not try to capture love by thought. The denial of thought does not bring about love. There is freedom from thought only when its deep significance is fully understood; and for this, profound self-knowledge is essential, not vain and superficial assertions. Meditation and not repetition, awareness and not definition, reveal the ways of thought. Without being aware and experiencing the ways of thought, love cannot be.

ALONENESS AND ISOLATION

THE SUN HAD gone down and the trees were dark and shapely against the darkening sky. The wide, strong river was peaceful and still. The moon was just visible on the horizon; she was coming up between two great trees, but she was not yet casting shadows.

We walked up the steep bank of the river and took a path that skirted the green wheat-fields. This path was a very ancient way; many thousands had trodden it, and it was rich in tradition and silence. It wandered among fields and mangoes, tamarinds and deserted shrines. There were large patches of garden, sweet peas deliciously scenting the air. The birds were settling down for the night, and a large pond was beginning to reflect the stars. Nature was not communicative that evening. The trees were aloof; they had withdrawn into their silence and darkness. A few chattering villagers passed by on their bicycles, and once again there was deep silence and that peace which comes when all things are alone.

This aloneness is not aching, fearsome loneliness. It is the aloneness of being; it is uncorrupted, rich, complete. That tamarind tree has no existence other than being itself. So is this aloneness. One is alone, like the fire, like the flower, but one is not aware of its purity and of its immensity. One can truly communicate only when there is aloneness. Being alone is not the outcome of denial, of self-enclosure. Aloneness is the purgation of all motives, of all pursuits of desire, of all ends. Aloneness is not an end-product of the mind. You cannot wish to be alone. Such a wish is merely an escape from the pain of not being able to commune.

Loneliness, with its fear and ache, is isolation, the inevitable action of the self. This process of isolation, whether expansive or narrow, is productive of confusion, conflict and sorrow. Isolation can never give birth to aloneness; the one has to cease for the other to be. Aloneness is indivisible and loneliness is separation. That which is alone is pliable and so enduring. Only the alone can commune with that which is causeless, the immeasurable. To the alone, life is eternal; to the alone there is no death. The alone can never cease to be.

The moon was just coming over the tree tops, and the shadows were thick and dark. A dog began to bark as we passed the little village and walked back along the river. The river was so still that it caught the stars and the lights of the long bridge among its waters. High up on the bank children were standing and laughing, and a baby was crying. The fishermen were cleaning and coiling their nets. A night-bird flew silently by. Someone began to sing on the other bank of the wide river, and his words were clear and penetrating. Again the all-pervading aloneness of life.

PUPIL AND MASTER

"You know, I have been told that I am a pupil of a certain Master," he began. "Do you think I am? I really want to know what you think of this. I belong to a society of which you know, and the outer heads who represent the inner leaders or Masters have told me that because of my work for the society I have been made a pupil. I have been told that I have an opportunity to become a first-degree initiate in this life." He took all this very seriously, and we talked at some length.

Reward in any form is extremely gratifying, especially a so-called spiritual reward when one is somewhat indifferent to the honours of the world. Or when one is not very successful in this world, it is very gratifying to belong to a group especially chosen by someone who is supposed to be a highly advanced spiritual being, for then one is part of a team working for a great idea, and naturally one must be rewarded for one's obedience and for the sacrifices one has made for the cause. If it is not a reward in that sense, it is a recognition of one's spiritual advancement; or, as in a well-run organization, one's efficiency is acknowledged in order to stimulate one to do better.

In a world where success is worshipped, this kind of self-advancement is understood and encouraged. But to be told by another that you are a pupil of a Master, or to think that you are, obviously leads to many ugly forms of exploitation. Unfortunately, both the exploiter and the exploited feel elated in their mutual relationship. This expanding self-gratification is considered spiritual advancement, and it becomes especially ugly and brutal when you have intermediaries between the pupil and the Master, when the Master is in a different country or is otherwise inaccessible and you are not in direct physical contact with him. This inaccessibility and the lack of direct contact opens the door to self-deception and to grand but childish illusions; and these illusions are exploited by the cunning, by those who are after glory and power.

Reward and punishment exist only when there is no humility. Humility is not an end-result of spiritual practices and denials. Humility is not an achievement, it is not a virtue to be cultivated. A virtue that is cultivated ceases to be a virtue, for then it is merely another form of achievement, a record to be made. A cultivated virtue is not the abnegation of the self, but a negative assertion of the self.

Humility is unaware of the division of the superior and the inferior, of the Master and the pupil. As long as there is a division between the Master and the pupil, between reality and yourself, understanding is not possible. In the understanding of truth, there is no Master or pupil, neither the advanced nor the lowly.

Truth is the understanding of what *is* from moment to moment without the burden or the residue of the past moment.

Reward and punishment only strengthen the self, which denies humility. Humility is in the present, not in the future. You cannot *become* humble. The very becoming is the continuation of self-importance, which conceals itself in the practice of a virtue. How strong is our will to succeed, to become! How can success and humility go together? Yet that is what the "spiritual" exploiter and exploited pursue, and therein lie conflict and misery.

"Do you mean to say that the Master does not exist, and that my being a pupil is an illusion, a make-believe?" he asked.

Whether the Master exists or not is so trivial. It is important to the exploiter, to the secret schools and societies; but to the man who is seeking truth, which brings supreme happiness, surely this question is utterly irrelevant. The rich man and the coolie are as important as the Master and the pupil. Whether the Masters exist or do not exist, whether there are the distinctions of Initiates, pupils and so on, is not important, but what is important is to understand yourself. Without self-knowledge, your thought, that which you reason out, has no basis. Without first knowing yourself, how can you know what is true? Illusion is inevitable without self-knowledge. It is childish to be told and to accept that you are this or that. Beware of the man who offers you a reward in this world or in the next.

The Rich and the Poor

IT WAS HOT and humid and the noise of the very large town filled the air. The breeze from the sea was warm, and there was the smell of tar and petrol. With the setting of the sun, red in the distant waters, it was still unyieldingly hot. The large group that filled the room presently left, and we went out into the street.

The parrots, like bright green flashes of light, were coming home to roost. Early in the morning they flew to the north, where there were orchards, green fields and open country, and in the evening they came back to pass the night in the trees of the city. Their flight was never smooth but always reckless, noisy and brilliant. They never flew straight like other birds, but were forever veering off to the left or the right, or suddenly dropping into a tree. They were the most restless birds in flight, but how beautiful they were with their red beaks and a golden green that was the very glory of light. The vultures, heavy and ugly, circled and settled down for the night on the palm trees.

A man came along playing the flute; he was a servant of some kind. He walked up the hill, still playing, and we followed him; he turned into one of the side streets, never ceasing to play. It was strange to hear the song of the flute in a noisy city, and its sound penetrated deep into the heart. It was very beautiful, and we followed the flute player for some distance. We crossed several streets and came to a wider one, better lighted. Farther on, a group of people were sitting cross-legged at the side of the road, and the flute player joined them. So did we; and we all sat around while he played. They were mostly chauffeurs, servants, night watchmen, with several children and a dog or two. Cars passed by, one driven by a chauffeur; a lady was inside, beautifully dressed and alone, with the inside light on. Another car drew up; the chauffeur got out and sat down with us. They were all talking and enjoying themselves, laughing and gesticulating, but the song of the flute never wavered, and there was delight.

Presently we left and took a road that led to the sea past the well-lit houses of the rich. The rich have a peculiar atmosphere of their own. However cultured, unobtrusive, ancient and polished, the rich have an impenetrable and assured aloofness, that inviolable certainty and hardness that is difficult to break down. They are not the possessors of wealth, but are possessed by wealth, which is worse than death. Their conceit is philanthropy; they think they are trustees of their wealth; they have charities, create endowments; they are the makers, the builders, the givers. They build churches, temples, but their god is the god of their gold. With so much poverty and degradation, one must have a very thick skin to be rich. Some of them come to question, to argue, to find reality. For the rich as for the poor, it is extremely difficult to find reality. The poor crave to be rich and powerful, and the rich are already caught in the net of their own action; and yet they believe and venture near. They speculate, not only upon the market, but upon the ultimate. They play with both, but are successful only with what is in their hearts. Their beliefs and ceremonies, their hopes and fears have nothing to do with reality, for their hearts are empty. The greater the outward show, the greater the inward poverty.

To renounce the world of wealth, comfort and position is a comparatively simple matter; but to put aside the craving to be, to become, demands great intelligence and understanding. The power that wealth gives is a hindrance to the understanding of reality, as is also the power of gift and capacity. This particular form of confidence is obviously an activity of the self; and though it is difficult to do so, this kind of assurance and power can be put aside. But what is much more subtle and more hidden is the power and the drive that lie in the craving to become. Self-expansion in any form, whether through wealth or through virtue, is a process of conflict, causing antagonism and confusion. A mind burdened with becoming can never be tranquil, for tranquillity is not a result either of practice or of time. Tranquillity is a state of understanding, and becoming denies this understanding. Becoming creates the sense of time, which is really the postponement of understanding. The "I shall be" is an illusion born of self-importance.

The sea was as restless as the town, but its restlessness had depth and substance. The evening star was on the horizon. We walked back through a street crowded with buses, cars and people. A man lay naked and asleep on the sidewalk; he was a beggar, exhausted, fatally under-nourished, and it was difficult to awaken him. Beyond lay the green lawns and bright flowers of a public garden.

CEREMONIES AND CONVERSION

IN A LARGE enclosure, among many trees, was a church. People, brown and white, were going in. Inside there was more light than in the European churches, but the arrangements were the same. The ceremony was in progress and there was beauty. When it was over, very few of the brown talked to the white, or the white to the brown, and we all went our different ways.

On another continent there was a temple, and they were singing a Sanskrit chant; the *Puja*, a Hindu ceremony, was being performed. The congregation was of another cultural pattern. The tonality of Sanskrit words is very penetrating and powerful; it has a strange weight and depth.

You can be converted from one belief to another, from one dogma to another, but you cannot be converted to the understanding of reality. Belief is not reality. You can change your mind, your opinion, but truth or God is not a conviction : it is an experience not based on any belief or dogma, or on any previous experience. If you have an experience born of belief, your experience is the conditioned response of that belief. If you have an experience unexpectedly, spontaneously, and build further experience upon the first, then experience is merely a continuation of memory which responds to contact with the present. Memory is always dead, coming to life only in contact with the living present.

Conversion is change from one belief or dogma to another, from one ceremony to a more gratifying one, and it does not open the door to reality. On the contrary, gratification is a hindrance to reality. And yet that is what organized religions and religious groups are attempting to do : to convert you to a more reasonable or a less reasonable dogma, superstition or hope. They offer you a better cage. It may or may not be comfortable, depending on your temperament, but in any case it is a prison.

Religiously and politically, at different levels of culture, this

23

conversion is going on all the time. Organizations, with their leaders, thrive on keeping man in the ideological patterns they offer, whether religious or economic. In this process lies mutual exploitation. Truth is outside of all patterns, fears and hopes. If you would discover the supreme happiness of truth, you must break away from all ceremonies and ideological patterns.

The mind finds security and strength in religious and political patterns, and this is what gives stamina to the organizations. There are always the die-hards and the new recruits. These keep the organizations, with their investments and properties, going, and the power and prestige of the organizations attract those who worship success and worldly wisdom. When the mind finds the old patterns are no longer satisfying and life-giving, it becomes converted to other more comforting and strengthening beliefs and dogmas. So the mind is the product of environment, re-creating and sustaining itself on sensations and identifications; and that is why the mind clings to codes of conduct, patterns of thought, and so on. As long as the mind is the outcome of the past, it can never discover truth or allow truth to come into being. In holding to organizations it discards the search for truth.

Obviously, rituals offer to the participants an atmosphere in which they feel good. Both collective and individual rituals give a certain quietness to the mind; they offer a vital contrast to the everyday, humdrum life. There is a certain amount of beauty and orderliness in ceremonies, but fundamentally they are stimulants; and as with all stimulants, they soon dull the mind and heart. Rituals become habit; they become a necessity, and one cannot do without them. This necessity is considered a spiritual renewal, a gathering of strength to face life, a weekly or daily meditation, and so on; but if one looks more closely into this process, one sees that rituals are vain repetition which offer a marvellous and respectable escape from self-knowledge. Without self-knowledge, action has very little significance.

The repetition of chants, of words and phrases, puts the mind to sleep, though it is stimulating enough for the time being. In this sleepy state, experiences do occur, but they are self-projected. However gratifying, these experiences are illusory. The experiencing of reality does not come about through any repetition, through any practice. Truth is not an end, a result, a goal; it cannot be invited, for it is not a thing of the mind.

KNOWLEDGE

WE WERE WAITING for the train, and it was late. The platform was dirty and noisy, the air acrid. There were many people waiting, like us. Children were crying, a mother was suckling her baby, the vendors were shouting their wares, tea and coffee were being sold, and it was an altogether busy and clamorous place. We were walking up and down the platform, watching our own footsteps and the movement of life about us. A man came up to us and began to talk in broken English. He said he had been watching us, and felt impelled to say something to us. With great feeling he promised he would lead a clean life, and that from this moment he would never smoke again. He said he was not educated, as he was only a rickshaw boy. He had strong eyes and a pleasant smile.

Presently the train came. In the carriage a man introduced himself. He was a well-known scholar; he knew many languages and could quote freely in them. He was full of years and knowledge, well-to-do and ambitious. He talked of meditation, but he gave the impression that he was not speaking from his own experience. His god was the god of books. His attitude towards life was traditional and conformatory; he believed in early, pre-arranged marriage and in a strict code of life. He was conscious of his own caste or class and of the differences in the intellectual capacity of the castes. He was strangely vain in his knowledge and position.

The sun was setting, and the train was passing through lovely country. The cattle were coming home, and there was golden dust. There were huge, black clouds on the horizon, and the crack of distant thunder. What joy a green field holds, and how pleasant is that village in the fold of a curving mountain! Darkness was setting in. A big, blue deer was feeding in the fields; he did not even look up as the train roared by.

Knowledge is a flash of light between two darknesses; but knowledge cannot go above and beyond that darkness. Knowledge is essential to technique, as coal to the engine; but it cannot reach out into the unknown. The unknown is not to be caught in the net of the known. Knowledge must be set aside for the unknown to be; but how difficult that is!

We have our being in the past, our thought is founded upon the past. The past is the known, and the response of the past is ever overshadowing the present, the unknown. The unknown is not the future, but the present. The future is but the past pushing its way through the uncertain present. This gap, this interval, is filled with the intermittent light of knowledge, covering the emptiness of the present; but this emptiness holds the miracle of life.

Addiction to knowledge is like any other addiction; it offers an escape from the fear of emptiness, of loneliness, of frustration, the fear of being nothing. The light of knowledge is a delicate covering under which lies a darkness that the mind cannot penetrate. The mind is frightened of this unknown, and so it escapes into knowledge, into theories, hopes, imagination; and this very knowledge is a hindrance to the understanding of the unknown. To put aside knowledge is to invite fear, and to deny the mind, which is the only instrument of perception one has, is to be vulnerable to sorrow, to joy. But it is not easy to put aside knowledge. To be ignorant is not to be free of knowledge. Ignorance is the lack of self-awareness; and knowledge is ignorance when there is no understanding of the ways of the self. Understanding of the self is freedom from knowledge.

There can be freedom from knowledge only when the process of gathering, the motive of accumulation, is understood. The desire to store up is the desire to be secure, to be certain. This desire for certainty through identification, through condemnation and justification, is the cause of fear, which destroys all communion. When there is communion, there is no need for accumulation. Accumulation is self-enclosing resistance, and knowledge strengthens this resistance. The worship of knowledge is a form of idolatry, and it will not dissolve the conflict and misery of our life. The cloak of knowledge conceals but can never liberate us from our ever-increasing confusion and sorrow. The ways of the mind do not lead to truth and its happiness. To know is to deny the unknown.

RESPECTABILITY

HE ASSERTED THAT he was not greedy, that he was satisfied with little, and that life had been good to him, though he suffered the usual miseries of human existence. He was a quiet man, unobtrusive, hoping not to be disturbed from his easy ways. He said that he was not ambitious, but prayed to God for the things he had, for his family, and for the even flow of his life. He was thankful not to be plunged into problems and conflicts, as his friends and relations were. He was rapidly becoming very respectable and happy in the thought that he was one of the *élite*. He was not attracted to other women, and he had a peaceful family life, though there were the usual wrangles of husband and wife. He had no special vices, prayed often and worshipped God. "What is the matter with me," he asked, "as I have no problems?" He did not wait for a reply, but smiling in a satisfied and somewhat mournful way proceeded to tell of his past, what he was doing, and what kind of education he was giving to his children. He went on to say that he was not generous, but gave a little here and there. He was certain that each one must struggle to make a position for himself in the world.

Respectability is a curse; it is an "evil" that corrodes the mind and heart. It creeps upon one unknowingly and destroys love. To be respectable is to feel successful, to carve for oneself a position in the world, to build around oneself a wall of certainty, of that assurance which comes with money, power, success, capacity or virtue. This exclusiveness of assurance breeds hatred and antagonism in human relationship, which is society. The respectable are always the cream of society, and so they are ever the cause of strife and misery. The respectable, like the despised, are always at the mercy of circumstances; the influences of environment and the weight of tradition are vastly important to them, for these hide their inward poverty. The respectable are on the defensive, fearful and suspicious. Fear is in their hearts, so anger is their righteousness; their virtue and piety are their defence. They are as the drum, empty within but loud when beaten. The respectable can never be open to reality, for, like the despised, they are enclosed in the concern for their own self-improvement. Happiness is denied to them, for they avoid truth.

To be non-greedy and not to be generous are closely related. Both are a self-enclosing process, a negative form of self-centredness. To be greedy, you must be active, outgoing; you must strive, compete, be aggressive. If you have not this drive, you are not free of greed, but only self-enclosed. Outgoing is a disturbance, a painful struggle, so self-centredness is covered over by the word non-greedy. To be generous with the hand is one thing, but to be generous of heart is another. Generosity of the hand is a fairly simple affair, depending upon the cultural pattern and so on; but generosity of the heart is of vastly deeper significance, demanding extensional awareness and understanding.

Not to be generous is again a pleasant and blind self-absorption, in which there is no outward-going. This self-absorbed state has its own activities, like those of a dreamer, but they never wake you up. The waking-up process is a painful one, and so, young or old, you would rather be left alone to become respectable, to die.

Like generosity of the heart, generosity of the hand is an outgoing movement, but it is often painful, deceptive and self-revealing. Generosity of the hand is easy to come by; but generosity of heart is not a thing to be cultivated, it is freedom from all accumulation. To forgive, there must have been a wound; and to be wounded, there must have been the gatherings of pride. There is no generosity of heart as long as there is a referential memory, the "me" and the "mine."

POLITICS

HIGH UP IN the mountains it had been raining all day. It was not a soft, gentle rain, but one of those torrential downpours that wash out roads and uproot trees on the hillside, causing landslides and noisy streams which become quiet in a few hours. A little boy, soaked to the skin, was playing in a shallow pool and paying not the least attention to the angry and high-pitched voice of his mother. A cow was coming down the muddy road as we climbed it. The clouds seemed to open and cover the land with water. We were wet through and removed most of our clothing, and the rain was pleasant on the skin. The house was way up on the mountainside, and the town lay below. A strong wind was blowing from the west, bringing more dark and furious clouds.

There was a fire in the room, and several people were waiting to talk things over. The rain, beating on the windows, had made a large puddle on the floor, and the water even came down the chimney, making the fire sputter.

He was a very famous politician, realistic, intensely sincere and ardently patriotic. Neither narrow-minded nor self-seeking, his ambition was not for himself, but for an idea and for the people. He was not a mere eloquent tub-thumper or vote-catcher; he had suffered for his cause and, strangely, was not bitter. He seemed more of a scholar than a politician. But politics was the breath of his life, and his party obeyed him, though rather nervously. He was a dreamer, but he had put all that aside for politics. His friend, the leading economist, was also there; he had intricate theories and facts concerning the distribution of enormous revenues. He seemed to be familiar with the economists of both the left and the right, and he had his own theories for the economic salvation of mankind. He talked easily, and there was no hesitation for words. Both of them had harangued huge crowds.

Have you noticed, in newspapers and magazines, the amount of space given to politics, to the sayings of politicians and their activities? Of course, other news is given, but political news predominates; the economic and political life has become all-important. The outward circumstances—comfort, money, position and power—seem to dominate and shape our existence. The external show—the title, the garb, the salute, the flag—has become increasingly significant, and the total process of life has been forgotten or deliberately set aside. It is so much easier to throw oneself into social and political activity than to understand life as a whole; to be associated with any organized thought, with political or religious activity, offers a respectable escape from the pettiness and drudgery of everyday life. With a small heart you can talk of big things and of the popular leaders; you can hide your shallowness with the easy phrases of world affairs; your restless mind can happily and with popular encouragement settle down to propagate the ideology of a new or of an old religion.

Politics is the reconciliation of effects; and as most of us are concerned with effects, the external has assumed dominant significance. By manipulating effects we hope to bring about order and peace; but, unfortunately, it is not as simple as all that. Life is a total process, the inner as well as the outer; the outer definitely affects the inner, but the inner invariably overcomes the outer. What you are, you bring about outwardly. The outer and the inner cannot be separated and kept in watertight compartments, for they are constantly interacting upon each other; but the inner craving, the hidden pursuits and motives, are always more powerful. Life is not dependent upon political or economic activity; life is not a mere outward show, any more than a tree is the leaf or the branch. Life is a total process whose beauty is to be discovered only in its integration. This integration does not take place on the superficial level of political and economic reconciliations; it is to be found beyond causes and effects.

Because we play with causes and effects and never go beyond them, except verbally, our lives are empty, without much significance. It is for this reason that we have become slaves to political excitement and to religious sentimentalism. There is hope only in the integration of the several processes of which we are made up. This integration does not come into being through any ideology, or through following any particular authority, religious or political; it comes into being only through extensive and deep awareness. This awareness must go into the deeper layers of consciousness and not be content with surface responses.

EXPERIENCING

THE VALLEY WAS in the shadow, and the setting sun touched the far-away mountain tops; their evening glow seemed to come from within. To the north of the long road, the mountains were bare and barren, exposed by the fire; to the south, the hills were green and heavy with bushes and trees. The road ran straight, dividing the long and graceful valley. The mountains on this particular evening seemed so close, so unreal, so light and tender. Heavy birds were circling effortlessly high in the heavens. Ground squirrels were lazily crossing the road, and there was the hum of a distant airplane. On both sides of the road were orange orchards, well ordered and well kept. After the hot day the smell of purple sage was very strong, and so was the smell of sunburnt earth and hay. The orange trees were dark, with their bright fruit. The quail were calling, and a road-runner disappeared into the bush. A long snake-lizard, disturbed by the dog, wriggled off into the dry weeds. The evening stillness was creeping over the land.

Experience is one thing, and experiencing is another. Experience is a barrier to the state of experiencing. However pleasant or ugly the experience, it prevents the flowering of experiencing. Experience is already in the net of time, it is already in the past, it has become a memory which comes to life only as a response to the present. Life is the present, it is not the experience. The weight and the strength of experience shadow the present, and so experiencing becomes the experience. The mind is the experience, the known, and it can never be in the state of experiencing; for what it experiences is the continuation of experience. The mind only knows continuity, and it can never receive the new as long as its continuity exists. What is continuous can never be in a state of experiencing. Experience is not the means to experiencing, which is a state without experience. Experience must cease for experiencing to be.

The mind can invite only its own self-projection, the known. There cannot be the experiencing of the unknown until the mind ceases to experience. Thought is the expression of experience; thought is a response of memory; and as long as thinking intervenes, there can be no experiencing. There is no means, no method to put an end to experience; for the very means is a hindrance to experiencing. To know the end is to know continuity, and to have a means to the end is to sustain the known. The desire for achievement must fade away; it is this desire that creates the means and the end. Humility is essential for experiencing. But how eager is the mind to absorb the experiencing into experience! How swift it is to think about the new and thus make of it the old! So it establishes the experiencer and the experienced, which gives birth to the conflict of duality.

In the state of experiencing, there is neither the experiencer nor the experienced. The tree, the dog and the evening star are not to be experienced by the experiencer; they are the very movement of experiencing. There is no gap between the observer and the observed; there is no time, no spatial interval for thought to identify itself. Thought is utterly absent, but there is being. This state of being cannot be thought of or meditated upon, it is not a thing to be achieved. The experiencer must cease to experience, and only then is there being. In the tranquillity of its movement is the timeless.

32

VIRTUE

THE SEA WAS very calm and there was hardly a ripple on the
white sands. Around the wide bay, to the north, was the town,
and to the south were palm trees, almost touching the water.
Just visible beyond the bar were the first of the sharks, and
beyond them the fishermen's boats, a few logs tied together with
stout rope. They were making for a little village south of the
palm trees. The sunset was brilliant, not where one would expect
it, but in the east; it was a counter-sunset, and the clouds,
massive and shapely, were lit with all the colours of the spectrum.
It was really quite fantastic, and almost painful to bear. The
waters caught the brilliant colours and made a path of exquisite
light to the horizon.

There were a few fishermen walking back to their villages from
the town, but the beach was almost deserted and silent. A single
star was above the clouds. On our way back, a woman joined
us and began to talk of serious things. She said she belonged
to a certain society whose members meditated and cultivated the
essential virtues. Each month a particular virtue was chosen, and
during the days that followed it was cultivated and put into
practice. From her attitude and speech it appeared that she
was well grounded in self-discipline and somewhat impatient
with those who were not of her mood and purpose.

Virtue is of the heart and not of the mind. When the mind
cultivates virtue, it is cunning calculation; it is a self-defence,
a clever adjustment to environment. Self-perfection is the very
denial of virtue. How can there be virtue if there is fear? Fear
is of the mind and not of the heart. Fear hides itself under
different forms : virtue, respectability, adjustment, service and
so on. Fear will always exist in the relationships and activities of
the mind. The mind is not separate from its activities; but it
separates itself, thus giving itself continuity and permanence. As
a child practises the piano, so the mind cunningly practises virtue
to make itself more permanent and dominant in meeting life, or

to attain what it considers to be the highest. There must be vulnerability to meet life, and not the respectable wall of self-enclosing virtue. The highest cannot be attained; there is no path, no mathematically progressive growth to it. Truth must come, you cannot go to truth, and your cultivated virtue will not carry you to it. What you attain is not truth, but your own self-projected desire; and in truth alone is there happiness.

The cunning adaptability of the mind in its own self-perpetuation sustains fear. It is this fear that must be deeply understood, not how to be virtuous. A petty mind may practise virtue, but it will still remain petty. Virtue is then an escape from its own pettiness, and the virtue it gathers will also be petty. If this pettiness is not understood, how can there be the experiencing of reality? How can a petty, virtuous mind be open to the immeasurable?

In comprehending the process of the mind, which is the self, virtue comes into being. Virtue is not accumulated resistance; it is the spontaneous awareness and the understanding of what *is*. Mind cannot understand; it may translate what is understood into action, but it is not capable of understanding. To understand, there must be the warmth of recognition and reception, which only the heart can give when the mind is silent. But the silence of the mind is not the result of cunning calculation. The *desire* for silence is the curse of achievement, with its endless conflicts and pains. The craving to be, negatively or positively, is the denial of virtue of the heart. Virtue is not conflict and achievement, prolonged practice and result, but a state of being which is not the outcome of self-projected desire. There is no being if there is a struggle to be. In the struggle to be there is resistance and denial, mortification and renunciation; but the overcoming of these is not virtue. Virtue is the tranquillity of freedom from the craving to be, and this tranquillity is of the heart, not of the mind. Through practice, compulsion, resistance, the mind may make itself quiet, but such a discipline destroys virtue of the heart, without which there is no peace, no blessing; for virtue of the heart is understanding.

34

SIMPLICITY OF THE HEART

THE SKIES WERE open and full. There were not the big, wide-winged birds that float so easily from valley to valley, nor even a passing cloud. The trees were still and the curving folds of the hills were rich in shadow. The eager deer, consumed with curiosity, was watching, and suddenly darted away at our approach. Under a bush, of the same colour as the earth, was a flat horned toad, bright-eyed and motionless. To the west the mountains were sharp and clear against the setting sun. Far below was a big house; it had a swimming pool, and some people were in it. There was a lovely garden surrounding the house; the place looked prosperous and secluded, and had that peculiar atmosphere of the rich. Farther down a dusty road was a small shack in a dry field. Poverty, squalor and toil, even at that distance, were visible. Seen from that height the two houses were not far apart; ugliness and beauty were touching each other.

Simplicity of the heart is of far greater importance and significance than simplicity of possessions. To be content with few things is a comparatively easy matter. To renounce comfort, or to give up smoking and other habits, does not indicate simplicity of heart. To put on a loin-cloth in a world that is taken up with clothes, comforts and distractions, does not indicate a free being. There was a man who had given up the world and its ways, but his desires and passions were consuming him; he had put on the robes of a monk, but he did not know peace. His eyes were everlastingly seeking, and his mind was riven by his doubts and hopes. Outwardly you discipline and renounce, you chart your course, step by step, to reach the end. You measure the progress of your achievement according to the standards of virtue : how you have given up this or that, how controlled you are in your behaviour, how tolerant and kind you are, and so on and on. You have learnt the art of concentration, and you withdraw into a forest, a monastery or a darkened room to meditate; you pass your days in prayer and watchfulness. Outwardly you have made your life simple, and through this thoughtful and calculated arrangement you hope to reach the bliss that is not of this world.

But is reality reached through external controls and sanctions? Though outward simplicity, the putting aside of comfort, is obviously necessary, will this gesture open the door to reality? To be occupied with comfort and success burdens the mind and the heart, and there must be freedom to travel; but why are we so concerned with this outward gesture? Why are we so eagerly determined to give an outward expression of our intention? Is it the fear of self-deception, or of what another might say? Why do we wish to convince ourselves of our integrity? Does not this whole problem lie in the desire to be sure, to be convinced of our own importance in becoming?

The desire to be is the beginning of complexity. Driven by the ever-increasing desire to be, inwardly and outwardly, we accumulate or renounce, cultivate or deny. Seeing that time steals all things, we cling to the timeless. This struggle to be, positively or negatively, through attachment or detachment, can never be resolved by any outward gesture, discipline or practice; but the understanding of this struggle will bring about, naturally and spontaneously, the freedom from outward and inward accumulation with their conflicts. Reality is not to be reached through detachment; it is unattainable through any means. All means and ends are a form of attachment, and they must cease for the being of reality.

FACETS OF THE INDIVIDUAL

HE CAME TO see us surrounded by his disciples. They were of every kind, the well-to-do and the poor, the high governmental official and the widow, the fanatic and the young man with a smile. They were a pleasant and happy lot, and the shadows were dancing on the white house. In the thick foliage, parrots were screeching, and a noisy lorry went by. The young man was eager and insisted on the importance of the *guru,* the teacher; the others were in accord with him and smiled with delight as he made his points, clearly and objectively. The sky was very blue, and a white-throated eagle was circling just above us with hardly a flutter of the wing. It was a very beautiful day. How we destroy each other, the pupil the *guru,* and the *guru* the pupil! How we conform, break away to take shape again! A bird was pulling out a long worm from the moist earth.

We are many and not one. The one does not come into being till the many cease. The clamorous many are at war with each other day and night, and this war is the pain of life. We destroy one, but another rises in its place; and this seemingly endless process is our life. We try to impose the one on the many, but the one soon becomes the many. The voice of the many is the voice of the one, and the one voice assumes authority; but it is still the chattering of a voice. We are the voices of the many, and we try to catch the still voice of the one. The one is the many if the many are silent to hear the voice of the one. The many can never find the one.

Our problem is not how to hear the one voice but to understand the composition, the make-up of the many which we are. One facet of the many cannot understand the many; one entity cannot understand the many entities which we are. Though one facet tries to control, discipline, shape the other facets, its efforts are ever self-enclosing, narrowing. The whole cannot be understood through the part, and that is why we never understand. We never get the view of the whole, we are never aware of the whole, because we are so occupied with the part. The part divides itself and becomes the many. To be aware of the whole, the conflict of the many, there must be the understanding of desire. There is only one activity of desire; though there are varying and conflicting demands and pursuits, they are all the outcome of desire. Desire may not be sublimated or suppressed; it must be understood without him who understands. If the entity who understands is there, then it is still the entity of desire. To understand without the experiencer is to be free of the one and of the many.

All activities of conformity and denial, of analysis and acceptance, only strengthen the experiencer. The experiencer can never understand the whole. The experiencer is the accumulated, and there is no understanding within the shadow of the past. Dependence on the past may offer a way of action, but the cultivation of a means is not understanding. Understanding is not of the mind, of thought; and if thought is disciplined into silence to capture that which is not of the mind, then that which is experienced is the projection of the past. In the awareness of this whole process there is a silence which is not of the experiencer. In this silence only does understanding come into being.

SLEEP

IT WAS A cold winter and the trees were bare, their naked branches exposed to the sky. There were very few evergreen trees, and even they felt the cold winds and the frosty nights. In the far distance the high mountains were covered with heavy snow, and white billowy clouds hung over them. The grass was brown, for there had been no rain for many months, and the spring rains were still distant. The earth was dormant and fallow. There was no cheery movement of nesting birds in green hedges, and the paths were hard and dusty. On the lake there were a few ducks, pausing on their way to the south. The mountains held the promise of a new spring, and the earth was dreaming of it.

What would happen if sleep were denied to us? Would we have more time to fight, to intrigue, to make mischief? Would we be more cruel and ruthless? Would there be more time for humility, compassion and frugality? Would we be more creative? Sleep is a strange thing, but extraordinarily important. For most people, the activities of the day continue through their nocturnal slumbers; their sleep is the continuation of their life, dull or exciting, an extension at a different level of the same insipidity or meaningless strife. The body is refreshed by sleep; the internal organism, having a life of its own, renews itself. During sleep, desires are quiescent, and so do not interfere with the organism; and with the body refreshed, the activities of desire have further opportunities for stimulation and expansion. Obviously, the less one interferes with the internal organism, the better; the less the mind takes charge of the organism, the more healthy and natural is its function. But disease of the organism is another matter, produced by the mind or by its own weakness.

Sleep is of great significance. The more the desires are strengthened, the less the meaning of sleep. Desires, positive or negative, are fundamentally always positive, and sleep is the temporary suspension of this positive. Sleep is not the opposite of desire, sleep is not negation, but a state which desire cannot penetrate. The quietening of the superficial layers of consciousness takes place during sleep, and so they are capable of receiving the intimations of the deeper layers; but this is only a partial comprehension of the whole problem. It is obviously possible for all the layers of consciousness to be in communication with each other during waking hours, and also during sleep; and of course this is essential. This communication frees the mind from its own self-importance, and so the mind does not become the dominant factor. Thus it loses, freely and naturally, its self-enclosing efforts and activities. In this process the impetus to become is completely dissolved, the accumulative momentum exists no longer.

But there is something more that takes place in sleep. There is found an answer to our problems. When the conscious mind is quiet, it is capable of receiving an answer, which is a simple affair. But what is far more significant and important than all this is the renewal which is not a cultivation. One can deliberately cultivate a gift, a capacity, or develop a technique, a pattern of action and behaviour; but this is not renewal. Cultivation is not creation. This creative renewal does not take place if there is any kind of effort on the part of a becomer. The mind must voluntarily lose all accumulative impulse, the storing up of experience as a means to further experience and achievement. It is the accumulative, self-protective urge that breeds the curve of time and prevents creative renewal.

Consciousness as we know it is of time, it is a process of recording and storing experience at its different levels. Whatever takes place within this consciousness is its own projection; it has its own quality, and is measurable. During sleep, either this consciousness is strengthened, or something wholly different takes place. For most of us, sleep strengthens experience, it is a process of recording and storing in which there is expansion but not renewal. Expansiveness gives a feeling of elation, of inclusive achievement, of having understood, and so on; but all this is not creative renewal. This process of becoming must wholly come to an end, not as a means to further experience, but as an ending in itself.

During sleep, and often during waking hours, when becoming has entirely ceased, when the effect of a cause has come to an end, then that which is beyond time, beyond the measure of cause and effect, comes into being.

LOVE IN RELATIONSHIP

THE PATH WENT by a farm and climbed a hill overlooking the various buildings, the cows with their calves, the chickens, the horses, and many farm machines. It was a pleasant path, wandering through the woods, and it was often used by deer and other wild animals who left their footprints here and there in the soft earth. When it was very still, the voices from the farm, the laughter and the sound of the radio, would be carried to quite a distance. It was a well-kept farm and there was an air of tidiness about it. Often the voices were raised in anger, followed by the silence of children. There was a song among the trees and the angry voices even broke through this song. Suddenly, a woman came out of the house, banging the door; she went over to the cow-shed and began beating a cow with a stick. The sharp noise of this beating came up the hill.

How easy it is to destroy the thing we love! How quickly a barrier comes between us, a word, a gesture, a smile! Health, mood and desire cast a shadow, and what was bright becomes dull and burdensome. Through usage we wear ourselves out, and that which was sharp and clear becomes wearisome and confused. Through constant friction, hope and frustration, that which was beautiful and simple becomes fearful and expectant. Relationship is complex and difficult, and few can come out of it unscathed. Though we would like it to be static, enduring, continuous, relationship is a movement, a process which must be deeply and fully understood and not made to conform to an inner or outer pattern. Conformity, which is the social structure, loses its weight and authority only when there is love. Love in relationship is a purifying process as it reveals the ways of the self. Without this revelation, relationship has little significance.

But how we struggle against this revelation! The struggle takes many forms: dominance or subservience, fear or hope, jealousy or acceptance, and so on and on. The difficulty is that we do not love; and if we *do* love we want it to function in a particular way, we do not give it freedom. We love with our minds and not with our hearts. Mind can modify itself, but love cannot. Mind can make itself invulnerable, but love cannot; mind can always withdraw, be exclusive, become personal or impersonal. Love is not to be compared and hedged about. Our difficulty lies in that which we *call* love, which is really of the mind. We fill our hearts with the things of the mind and so keep our hearts ever empty and expectant. It is the mind that clings, that is envious, that holds and destroys. Our life is dominated by the physical centres and by the mind. We do not love and let it alone, but crave to be loved; we give in order to receive, which is the generosity of the mind and not of the heart. The mind is ever seeking certainty, security; and can love be made certain by the mind? Can the mind, whose very essence is of time, catch love, which is its own eternity?

But even the love of the heart has its own tricks; for we have so corrupted our heart that it is hesitant and confused. It is this that makes life so painful and wearisome. One moment we think we have love, and the next it is lost. There comes an imponderable strength, not of the mind, whose sources may not be fathomed. This strength is again destroyed by the mind; for in this battle the mind seems invariably to be the victor. This conflict within ourselves is not to be resolved by the cunning mind or by the hesitant heart. There is no means, no way to bring this conflict to an end. The very search for a means is another urge of the mind to be the master, to put away conflict in order to be peaceful, to have love, to become something.

Our greatest difficulty is to be widely and deeply aware that there is no means to love as a desirable end of the mind. When we understand this really and profoundly, then there is a possibility of receiving something that is not of this world. Without the touch of that something, do what we will, there can be no lasting happiness in relationship. If you have received that benediction and I have not, naturally you and I will be in conflict. You may not be in conflict, but I will be; and in my pain and sorrow I cut myself off. Sorrow is as exclusive as pleasure, and until there is that love which is not of my making, relationship is pain. If there is the benediction of that love, you cannot but love me whatever I may be, for then you do not shape love according to my behaviour. Whatever tricks the mind may play, you and I are separate; though we may be in touch with each other at some points, integration is not with you, but within myself. This integration is not brought about by the mind at any time; it comes into being only when the mind is utterly silent, having reached the end of its own tether. Only then is there no pain in relationship.

THE KNOWN AND THE UNKNOWN

THE LONG EVENING shadows were over the still waters, and the river was becoming quiet after the day. Fish were jumping out of the water, and the heavy birds were coming to roost among the big trees. There was not a cloud in the sky, which was silver-blue. A boat full of people came down the river; they were singing and clapping, and a cow called in the distance. There was the scent of evening. A garland of marigold was moving with the water, which sparkled in the setting sun. How beautiful and alive it all was—the river, the birds, the trees and the villagers.

We were sitting under a tree, overlooking the river. Near the tree was a small temple, and a few lean cows wandered about. The temple was clean and well swept, and the flowering bush was watered and cared for. A man was performing his evening rituals, and his voice was patient and sorrowful. Under the last rays of the sun, the water was the colour of new-born flowers. Presently someone joined us and began to talk of his experiences. He said he had devoted many years of his life to the search for God, had practised many austerities and renounced many things that were dear. He had also helped considerably in social work, in building a school, and so on. He was interested in many things, but his consuming interest was the finding of God; and now, after many years, His voice was being heard, and it guided him in little as well as big things. He had no will of his own, but followed the inner voice of God. It never failed him, though he often corrupted its clarity; his prayer was ever for the purification of the vessel, that it might be worthy to receive.

Can that which is immeasurable be found by you and me? Can that which is not of time be searched out by that thing which is fashioned of time? Can a diligently practised discipline lead us to the unknown? Is there a means to that which has no beginning and no end? Can that reality be caught in the net of our desires? What we can capture is the projection of the known; but the unknown cannot be captured by the known. That which is named is not the unnamable, and by naming we only awaken the conditioned responses. These responses, however noble and pleasant, are not of the real. We respond to stimulants, but reality offers no stimulant : it *is*.

The mind moves from the known to the known, and it cannot reach out into the unknown. You cannot think of something you do not know; it is impossible. What you think about comes out of the known, the past, whether that past be remote, or the second that has just gone by. This past is thought, shaped and conditioned by many influences, modifying itself according to

43

circumstances and pressures, but ever remaining a process of time. Thought can only deny or assert, it cannot discover or search out the new. Thought cannot come upon the new; but when thought is silent, then there may be the new—which is immediately transformed into the old, into the experienced, by thought. Thought is ever shaping, modifying, colouring according to a pattern of experience. The function of thought is to communicate but not to be in the state of experiencing. When experiencing ceases, then thought takes over and terms it within the category of the known. Thought cannot penetrate into the unknown, and so it can never discover or experience reality.

Disciplines, renunciations, detachments, rituals, the practice of virtue—all these, however noble, are the process of thought; and thought can only work towards an end, towards an achievement, which is ever the known. Achievement is security, the self-protective certainty of the known. To seek security in that which is nameless is to deny it. The security that may be found is only in the projection of the past, of the known. For this reason the mind must be entirely and deeply silent; but this silence cannot be purchased through sacrifice, sublimation or suppression. This silence comes when the mind is no longer seeking, no longer caught in the process of becoming. This silence is not cumulative, it may not be built up through practice. This silence must be as unknown to the mind as the timeless; for if the mind experiences the silence, then there is the experiencer who is the result of past experiences, who is cognizant of a past silence; and what is experienced by the experiencer is merely a self-projected repetition. The mind can never experience the new, and so the mind must be utterly still.

The mind can be still only when it is not experiencing, that is, when it is not terming or naming, recording or storing up in memory. This naming and recording is a constant process of the different layers of consciousness, not merely of the upper mind. But when the superficial mind is quiet, the deeper mind can offer up its intimations. When the whole consciousness is silent and tranquil, free from all becoming, which is spontaneity, then only does the immeasurable come into being. The desire to maintain this freedom gives continuity to the memory of the becomer, which is a hindrance to reality. Reality has no continuity; it is from moment to moment, ever new, ever fresh. What has continuity can never be creative.

The upper mind is only an instrument of communication, it cannot measure that which is immeasurable. Reality is not to be spoken of; and when it is, it is no longer reality.

This is meditation.

THE SEARCH FOR TRUTH

HE HAD COME a very long way, many thousands of miles by boat and plane. He spoke only his own language, and with the greatest of difficulties was adjusting himself to this new and disturbing environment. He was entirely unaccustomed to this kind of food and to this climate; having been born and bred in a very high altitude, the damp heat was telling on him. He was a well-read man, a scientist of sorts, and had done some writing. He seemed to be well acquainted with both Eastern and Western philosophies, and had been a Roman Catholic. He said he had been dissatisfied with all this for a long time, but had carried on because of his family. His marriage was what could be considered a happy one, and he loved his two children. They were in college now in that far-away country, and had a bright future. But this dissatisfaction with regard to his life and action had been steadily increasing through the years, and a few months ago it had reached a crisis. He had left his family, making all the necessary arrangements for his wife and children, and now here he was. He had just enough money to carry on, and had come to find God. He said that he was in no way unbalanced, and was clear in his purpose.

Balance is not a matter to be judged by the frustrated, or by those who are successful. The successful may be the unbalanced; and the frustrated become bitter and cynical, or they find an escape through some self-projected illusion. Balance is not in the

45

hands of the analysts; to fit into the norm does not necessarily indicate balance. The norm itself may be the product of an unbalanced culture. An acquisitive society, with its patterns and norms, is unbalanced, whether it is of the left or of the right, whether its acquisitiveness is vested in the State or in its citizens. Balance is non-acquisitiveness. The idea of balance and non-balance is still within the field of thought and so cannot be the judge. Thought itself, the conditioned response with its standards and judgments, is not true. Truth is not an idea, a conclusion.

Is God to be found by seeking him out? Can you search after the unknowable? To find, you must know what you are seeking. If you seek to find, what you find will be a self-projection; it will be what you desire, and the creation of desire is not truth. To seek truth is to deny it. Truth has no fixed abode; there is no path, no guide to it, and the word is not truth. Is truth to be found in a particular setting, in a special climate, among certain people? Is it here and not there? Is that one the guide to truth, and not another? Is there a guide at all? When truth is sought, what is found can only come out of ignorance, for the search itself is born of ignorance. You cannot search out reality; you must cease for reality to be.

"But can I not find the nameless? I have come to this country because here there is a greater feeling for that search. Physically one can be more free here, one need not have so many things; possessions do not overpower one here as elsewhere. That is partly why one goes to a monastery. But there are psychological escapes in going to a monastery, and as I do not want to escape into ordered isolation, I am here, living my life to find the nameless. Am I capable of finding it?"

Is it a matter of capacity? Does not capacity imply the following of a particular course of action, a predetermined path, with all the necessary adjustments? When you ask that question, are you not asking whether you, an ordinary individual, have the necessary means of gaining what you long for? Surely, your question implies that only the exceptional find truth, and not the everyday man. Is truth granted only to the few, to the exceptionally intelligent? Why do we ask whether we are capable of finding it? We have the pattern, the example of the man who is supposed to have discovered truth; and the example, being elevated far above us, creates uncertainty in ourselves. The example thus assumes great significance, and there is competition between the example and ourselves; we also long to be the record-breaker. Does not this question, "Have I the capacity?", arise out of one's conscious or unconscious comparison of what one is with what one supposes the example to be?

Why do we compare ourselves with the ideal? And does comparison bring understanding? Is the ideal different from ourselves? Is it not a self-projection, a home-made thing, and does it not therefore prevent the understanding of ourselves as we are? Is not comparison an evasion of the understanding of ourselves? There are so many ways of escaping from ourselves, and comparison is one of them. Surely, without the understanding of oneself, the search for so-called reality is an escape from oneself. Without self-knowledge, the god that you seek is the god of illusion; and illusion inevitably brings conflict and sorrow. Without self-knowledge, there can be no right thinking; and then all knowledge is ignorance which can only lead to confusion and destruction. Self-knowledge is not an ultimate end; it is the only opening wedge to the inexhaustible.

"Is not self-knowledge extremely difficult to acquire, and will it not take a very long time?"

The very conception that self-knowledge is difficult to acquire is a hindrance to self-knowledge. If I may suggest, do not suppose that it will be difficult, or that it will take time; do not predetermine what it is and what it is not. Begin. Self-knowledge is to be discovered in the action of relationship; and all action is relationship. Self-knowledge does not come about through self-isolation, through withdrawal; the denial of relationship is death. Death is the ultimate resistance. Resistance, which is suppression, substitution or sublimation in any form, is a hindrance to the flow of self-knowledge; but resistance is to be discovered in relationship, in action. Resistance, whether negative or positive, with its comparisons and justifications, its condemnations and identifications, is the denial of what *is*. What *is* is the implicit;

and awareness of the implicit, without any choice, is the unfold-ment of it. This unfoldment is the beginning of wisdom. Wisdom is essential for the coming into being of the unknown, the inexhaustible.

SENSITIVITY

IT WAS A lovely garden, with sunken lawns and old shady trees. The house was large, with spacious rooms, airy and well pro-portioned. The trees gave shelter to many birds and many squirrels, and to the fountain came birds of every size, some-times eagles, but mostly crows, sparrows and noisy parrots. The house and garden were secluded, the more so as they were enclosed within high, white walls. It was pleasant within those walls, and beyond them was the noise of the road and the village. The road passed the gates, and a few yards along that road was the village, on the outskirts of a large town. The village was foul, with open gutters along its main, narrow lane. The houses were thatched, the front steps decorated, and children were playing in the lane. Some weavers had stretched out long strands of gay-coloured threads to make cloth, and a group of children were watching them at work. It was a cheerful scene, bright, noisy and smelly. The villagers were freshly washed, and they had very little on for the climate was warm. Towards evening some of them got drunk and became loud and rough.

It was only a thin wall that separated the lovely garden from the pulsating village. To deny ugliness and to hold to beauty is to be insensitive. The cultivation of the opposite must ever narrow the mind and limit the heart. Virtue is not an opposite; and if it has an opposite, it ceases to be virtue. To be aware of the beauty of that village is to be sensitive to the green, flowering garden. We want to be aware only of beauty, and we shut our-selves off from that which is not beautiful. This suppression merely breeds insensitivity, it does not bring about the apprecia-tion of beauty. The good is not in the garden, away from the village, but in the sensitivity that lies beyond both. To deny or to identify leads to narrowness, which is to be insensitive. Sensitivity is not a thing to be carefully nurtured by the mind, which can only divide and dominate. There is good and evil; but to pursue the one and to avoid the other does not lead to that sensitivity which is essential for the being of reality.

Reality is not the opposite of illusion, of the false, and if you try to approach it as an opposite it will never come into being. Reality can *be* only when the opposites cease. To condemn or identify breeds the conflict of the opposites, and conflict only engenders further conflict. A fact approached unemotionally, without denying or justifying, does not bring about conflict. A fact in itself has no opposite; it has an opposite only when there is a pleasurable or defensive attitude. It is this attitude that builds the walls of insensitivity and destroys action. If we prefer to remain in the garden, there is a resistance to the village; and where there is resistance there can be no action, either in the garden or towards the village. There may be activity, but not action. Activity is based on an idea, and action is not. Ideas have opposites, and movement within the opposites is mere activity, however prolonged or modified. Activity can never be liberating.

Activity has a past and a future, but action has not. Action is always in the present, and is therefore immediate. Reform is activity, not action, and what is reformed needs further reform. Reformation is inaction, an activity born as an opposite. Action is from moment to moment, and, oddly enough, it has no inherent contradiction; but activity, though it may appear to be without a break, is full of contradiction. The activity of revolution is riddled with contradictions and so can never liberate. Conflict, choice, can never be a liberating factor. If there is choice, there is activity and not action; for choice is based on idea. Mind can indulge in activity, but it cannot act. Action springs from quite a different source.

The moon came up over the village, making shadows across the garden.

WE WERE WALKING along a crowded street. The sidewalks were heavy with people, and the smell of exhaust from the cars and buses filled our nostrils. The shops displayed many costly and shoddy things. The sky was pale silver, and it was pleasant in the park as we came out of the noisy thoroughfare. We went deeper into the park and sat down.

He was saying that the State, with its militarization and legislation, was absorbing the individual almost everywhere, and that worship of the State was now taking the place of the worship of God. In most countries the State was penetrating into the very intimate lives of its people; they were being told what to read and what to think. The State was spying upon its citizens, keeping a divine eye on them, taking over the function of the Church. It was the new religion. Man used to be a slave to the Church, but was now a slave of the State. Before it was the Church, and now it was the State that controlled his education; and neither was concerned with the liberation of man.

What is the relationship of the individual to society? Obviously, society exists for the individual, and not the other way round. Society exists for the fruition of man; it exists to give freedom to the individual so that he may have the opportunity to awaken the highest intelligence. This intelligence is not the mere cultivation of a technique or of knowledge; it is to be in touch with that creative reality which is not of the superficial mind. Intelligence is not a cumulative result, but freedom from progressive achievement and success. Intelligence is never static; it cannot be copied and standardized, and hence cannot be taught. Intelligence is to be discovered in freedom.

The collective will and its action, which is society, does not offer this freedom to the individual; for society, not being organic, is ever static. Society is made up, put together for the convenience of man; it has no independent mechanism of its own. Men may capture society, guide it, shape it, tyrannize over it, depending upon their psychological states; but society is not the master of man. It may influence him, but man always breaks it down. There is conflict between man and society because man is in conflict within himself; and the conflict is between that which is static and that which is living. Society is the outward expression of man. The conflict between himself and society is the conflict within himself. This conflict, within and without, will ever exist until the highest intelligence is awakened.

We are social entities as well as individuals; we are citizens as well as men, separate becomers in sorrow and pleasure. If there is to be peace, we have to understand the right relationship between the man and the citizen. Of course, the State would prefer us to be entirely citizens; but that is the stupidity of governments. We ourselves would like to hand over the man to the citizen; for to be a citizen is easier than to be a man. To be a good citizen is to function efficiently within the pattern of a given society. Efficiency and conformity are demanded of the citizen, as they toughen him, make him ruthless; and then he is capable of sacrificing the man to the citizen. A good citizen is not necessarily a good man; but a good man is bound to be a right citizen, not of any particular society or country. Because he is primarily a good man, his actions will not be anti-social, he will not be against another man. He will live in co-operation with other good men; he will not seek authority, for he has no authority; he will be capable of efficiency without its ruthlessness. The citizen attempts to sacrifice the man; but the man who is searching out the highest intelligence will naturally shun the stupidities of the citizen. So the State will be against the good man, the man of intelligence; but such a man is free from all governments and countries.

The intelligent man will bring about a good society; but a good citizen will not give birth to a society in which man can be of the highest intelligence. The conflict between the citizen and the man is inevitable if the citizen predominates; and any society which deliberately disregards the man is doomed. There is reconciliation between the citizen and the man only when the psychological process of man is understood. The State, the present society, is not concerned with the inner man, but only with the outer man, the citizen. It may deny the inner man, but he always overcomes the outer, destroying the plans cunningly devised for the citizen. The State sacrifices the present for the future, ever safeguarding itself for the future; it regards the future as all-important, and not the present. But to the intelligent man, the present is of the highest importance, the now and not the tomorrow. What *is* can be understood only with the fading of tomorrow. The understanding of what *is* brings about transformation in the immediate present. It is this transformation that is of supreme importance, and not how to reconcile the citizen with the man. When this transformation takes place, the conflict between the man and the citizen ceases.

THE SELF

IN THE OPPOSITE seat sat a man of position and authority. He was well aware of this, for his looks, his gestures, his attitude proclaimed his importance. He was very high up in the Government, and the people about him were very obsequious. He was saying in a loud voice to somebody that it was outrageous to disturb him about some minor official task. He was rumbling about the doings of his workers, and the listeners looked nervous and apprehensive. We were flying far above the clouds, eighteen thousand feet, and through the gaps in the clouds was the blue sea. When the clouds somewhat opened up, there were the mountains covered with snow, the islands and the wide, open bays. How far away and how beautiful were the solitary houses and the small villages! A river came down to the sea from the mountains. It flowed past a very large town, smoky and dull, where its waters became polluted, but a little farther on they were again clean and sparkling. A few seats away was an officer in uniform, his chest covered with ribbons, confident and aloof. He belonged to a separate class that exists all over the world.

Why is it that we crave to be recognized, to be made much

of, to be encouraged? Why is it that we are such snobs? Why is it that we cling to our exclusiveness of name, position, acquisition? Is anonymity degrading, and to be unknown despicable? Why do we pursue the famous, the popular? Why is it that we are not content to be ourselves? Are we frightened and ashamed of what we are, that name, position and acquisition become so all-important? It is curious how strong is the desire to be recognized, to be applauded. In the excitement of a battle, one does incredible things for which one is honoured; one becomes a hero for killing a fellow man. Through privilege, cleverness, or capacity and efficiency, one arrives somewhere near the top—though the top is never the top, for there is always more and more in the intoxication of success. The country or the business is yourself; on you depend the issues, you are the power. Organized religion offers position, prestige and honour; there too you are somebody, apart and important. Or again you become the disciple of a teacher, of a *guru* or Master, or you co-operate with them in their work. You are still important, you represent them, you share their responsibility, you give and others receive. Though in their name, you are still the means. You may put on a loin-cloth or the monk's robe, but it is *you* who are making the gesture, it is *you* who are renouncing.

In one way or another, subtly or grossly, the self is nourished and sustained. Apart from its anti-social and harmful activities, why has the self to maintain itself? Though we are in turmoil and sorrow, with passing pleasures, why does the self cling to outer and inner gratifications, to pursuits that inevitably bring pain and misery? The thirst for positive activity as opposed to negation makes us strive to *be*; our striving makes us feel that we are alive, that there is a purpose to our life, that we shall progressively throw off the causes of conflict and sorrow. We feel that if our activity stopped, we would be nothing, we would be lost, life would have no meaning at all; so we keep going in conflict, in confusion, in antagonism. But we are also aware that there is something more, that there is an otherness which is above and beyond all this misery. Thus we are in constant battle within ourselves.

The greater the outward show, the greater the inward poverty; but freedom from this poverty is not the loin-cloth. The cause of this inward emptiness is the desire to become; and, do what you will, this emptiness can never be filled. You may escape from it in a crude way, or with refinement; but it is as near to you as your shadow. You may not want to look into this emptiness, but nevertheless it is there. The adornments and the renunciations that the self assumes can never cover this inward poverty. By its activities, inner and outer, the self tries to find enrichment, calling it experience or giving it a different name according to its convenience and gratification. The self can never be anonymous; it may take on a new robe, assume a different name, but identity is its very substance. This identifying process prevents the awareness of its own nature. The cumulative process of identification builds up the self, positively or negatively; and its activity is always self-enclosing, however wide the enclosure. Every effort of the self to be or not to be is a movement away from what it is. Apart from its name, attributes, idiosyncrasies, possessions, what *is* the self? Is there the "I," the self, when its qualities are taken away? It is this fear of being nothing that drives the self into activity; but it *is* nothing, it is an emptiness.

If we are able to face that emptiness, to be with that aching loneliness, then fear altogether disappears and a fundamental transformation takes place. For this to happen, there must be the experiencing of that nothingness—which is prevented if there is an experiencer. If there is a desire for the experiencing of that emptiness in order to overcome it, to go above and beyond it, then there is no experiencing; for the self, as an identity, continues. If the experiencer has an experience, there is no longer the state of experiencing. It is the experiencing of what *is* without naming it that brings about freedom from what *is*.

BELIEF

WE WERE HIGH up in the mountains and it was very dry. There had been no rain for many months, and the little streams were silent. The pine trees were turning brown, and some were already dead, but the wind was among them. The mountains stretched out, fold after fold, to the horizon. Most of the wild life had gone away to cooler and better pastures; only the squirrels and a few jays remained. There were other smaller birds, but they were silent during the day. A dead pine was bleached white after many summers. It was beautiful even in death, graceful and strong without the blur of sentiment. The earth was hard and the paths were rocky and dusty.

She said that she had belonged to several religious societies, but had finally settled down in one. She had worked for it, as a lecturer and propagandist, practically all over the world. She said she had given up family, comfort and a great many other things for the sake of this organization; she had accepted its beliefs, its doctrines and precepts, had followed its leaders, and tried to meditate. She was regarded highly by the members as well as by the leaders. Now, she continued, having heard what I had said about beliefs, organizations, the dangers of self-deception, and so on, she had withdrawn from this organization and its activities. She was no longer interested in saving the world, but was occupying herself with her small family and its troubles, and took only a distant interest in the troubled world. She was inclined to be bitter, though outwardly kind and generous, for she said her life seemed so wasted. After all her past enthusiasm and work, where was she? What had happened to her? Why was she so dull and weary, and at her age so concerned with trivial things?

How easily we destroy the delicate sensitivity of our being. The incessant strife and struggle, the anxious escapes and fears, soon dull the mind and the heart; and the cunning mind quickly finds substitutes for the sensitivity of life. Amusements, family,

55

politics, beliefs and gods, take the place of clarity and love. Clarity is lost by knowledge and belief, and love by sensations. Does belief bring clarity? Does the tightly enclosing wall of belief bring understanding? What is the necessity of beliefs, and do they not darken the already crowded mind? The understanding of what *is* does not demand beliefs, but direct perception, which is to be directly aware without the interference of desire. It is desire that makes for confusion, and belief is the extension of desire. The ways of desire are subtle, and without understanding them belief only increases conflict, confusion and antagonism. The other name for belief is faith, and faith is also the refuge of desire.

We turn to belief as a means of action. Belief gives us that peculiar strength which comes from exclusion; and as most of us are concerned with doing, belief becomes a necessity. We feel we cannot act without belief, because it is belief that gives us something to live for, to work for. To most of us, life has no meaning but that which belief gives it; belief has greater significance than life. We think that life must be lived in the pattern of belief; for without a pattern of some kind, how can there be action? So our action is based on idea, or is the outcome of an idea; and action, then, is not as important as idea.

Can the things of the mind, however brilliant and subtle, ever bring about the completeness of action, a radical transformation in one's being and so in the social order? Is idea the means of action? Idea may bring about a certain series of actions, but that is mere activity; and activity is wholly different from action. It is in this activity that one is caught; and when for some reason or other activity stops, then one feels lost and life becomes meaningless, empty. We are aware of this emptiness, consciously or unconsciously, and so idea and activity become all-important. We fill this emptiness with belief, and activity becomes an intoxicating necessity. For the sake of this activity, we will renounce; we will adjust ourselves to any inconvenience, to any illusion.

The activity of belief is confusing and destructive; it may at first seem orderly and constructive, but in its wake there is conflict and misery. Every kind of belief, religious or political, prevents the understanding of relationship, and there can be no action without this understanding.

SILENCE

IT WAS A powerful motor and well tuned; it took the hills easily, without a stutter, and the pick-up was excellent. The road climbed steeply out of the valley and ran between orchards of orange and tall, wide-spreading walnut trees. On both sides of the road the orchards stretched for fully forty miles, up to the very foot of the mountains. Becoming straight, the road passed through one or two small towns, and then continued into the open country, which was bright green with alfalfa. Again winding through many hills, the road finally came out on to the desert.

It was a smooth road, the hum of the motor was steady, and the traffic was very light. There was an intense awareness of the country, of the occasional passing car, of the road signals, of the clear blue sky, of the body sitting in the car; but the mind was very still. It was not the quietness of exhaustion, or of relaxation, but a stillness that was very alert. There was no point from which the mind was still; there was no observer of this tranquillity; the experiencer was wholly absent. Though there was desultory conversation, there was no ripple in this silence. One heard the roar of the wind as the car sped along, yet this stillness was inseparable from the noise of the wind, from the sounds of the car, and from the spoken word. The mind had no recollection of previous stillnesses, of those silences it had known; it did not say, "This is tranquillity." There was no verbalization, which is only the recognition and the affirmation of a somewhat similar experience. Because there was no verbalization, thought was absent. There was no recording, and therefore thought was not able to pick up the silence or to think about it; for the word "stillness" is not stillness. When the word is not, the mind cannot

57

operate, and so the experiencer cannot store up as a means of further pleasure. There was no gathering process at work, nor was there approximation or assimilation. The movement of the mind was totally absent.

The car stopped at the house. The barking of the dog, the unpacking of the car and the general disturbance in no way affected this extraordinary silence. There *was* no disturbance, and the stillness went on. The wind was among the pines, the shadows were long, and a wildcat sneaked away among the bushes. In this silence there was movement, and the movement was not a distraction. There was no fixed attention from which to be distracted. There is distraction when the main interest shifts; but in this silence there was absence of interest, and so there was no wandering away. Movement was not away from the silence but was *of* it. It was the stillness, not of death, of decay, but of life in which there was a total absence of conflict. With most of us, the struggle of pain and pleasure, the urge of activity, gives us the sense of life; and if that urge were taken away, we should be lost and soon disintegrate. But this stillness and its movement was creation ever renewing itself. It was a movement that had no beginning and so had no ending; nor was it a continuity. Movement implies time; but here there was no time. Time is the more and the less, the near and the far, yesterday and tomorrow; but in this stillness all comparison ceased. It was not a silence that came to an end to begin again; there was no repetition. The many tricks of the cunning mind were wholly absent.

If this silence were an illusion the mind would have some relationship to it, it would either reject it or cling to it, reason it away or with subtle satisfaction identify itself with it; but since it has no relationship to this silence, the mind cannot accept or deny it. The mind can operate only with its own projections, with the things which are of itself; but it has no relationship with the things that are not of its own origin. This silence is not of the mind, and so the mind cannot cultivate or become indentified with it. The content of this silence is not to be measured by words.

58

WE WERE SITTING in the shade of a large tree, overlooking a green valley. The woodpeckers were busy and there were ants in a long line scurrying back and forth between two trees. The wind was from the sea, bringing the smell of a distant fog. The mountains were blue and dreamy; often they had seemed so close, but now they were far away. A small bird was drinking from the little pool made by a leaky pipe. Two grey squirrels with large bushy tails were chasing each other up and down a tree; they would climb to the top and come spinning down with mad speed almost to the ground, and then go up again.

He was once a very rich man and had renounced his riches. He had had a great many possessions and had enjoyed the burden of their responsibility, for he was charitable and not too hard of heart. He gave without stint and forgot what he gave. He was good to his helpers and saw to their benefits, and made money easily in a world that was bent on money-making. He was unlike those whose bank accounts and investments are bigger than themselves, who are lonely and afraid of people and their demands, who shut themselves off in the peculiar atmosphere of their wealth. He was not a threat to his family nor did he yield easily, and he had many friends, but not because he was rich. He was saying that he had given up his possessions because it had struck him one day, as he was reading something, how vastly stupid were his money-making and his wealth. Now he had but few things and was trying to lead a simple life to find out what it was all about and whether there was something beyond the appetites of the physical centres.

To be content with little is comparatively easy; to be free from the burden of many things is not difficult when one is on a journey looking for something else. The urgency of inward search clears away the confusion of many possessions, but being free from outer things does not mean a simple life. Outer simplicity and order do not necessarily mean inner tranquillity

59

and innocence. It is good to be simple outwardly, for it does give a certain freedom, it is a gesture of integrity; but why is it that we invariably begin with the outer and not with the inner simplicity? Is it to convince ourselves and others of our intention? Why do we have to convince ourselves? Freedom from things needs intelligence, not gestures and convictions; and intelligence is not personal. If one is aware of all the implications of many possessions, that very awareness liberates, and then there is no need for dramatic assertions and gestures. It is when this intelligent awareness is not functioning that we resort to disciplines and detachments. The emphasis is not on much or little, but on intelligence; and the intelligent man, being content with little, is free from many possessions.

But contentment is one thing and simplicity is quite another. The desire for contentment or for simplicity is binding. Desire makes for complexity. Contentment comes with the awareness of what *is*, and simplicity with the freedom from what *is*. It is well to be outwardly simple, but it is far more important to be inwardly simple and clear. Clarity does not come through a determined and purposeful mind; the mind cannot create it. The mind can adjust itself, can arrange and put its thoughts in order; but this is not clarity or simplicity.

The action of will makes for confusion; because will, however sublimated, is still the instrument of desire. The will to be, to become, however worth while and noble, may give a directive, may clear a way amidst confusion; but such a process leads to isolation, and clarity cannot come through isolation. The action of will may temporarily light up the immediate foreground, necessary for mere activity, but it can never clear up the background; for will itself is the outcome of this very background. The background breeds and nourishes the will, and will may sharpen the background, heighten its potentialities; but it can never cleanse the background.

Simplicity is not of the mind. A planned simplicity is only a cunning adjustment, a defence against pain and pleasure; it is a self-enclosing activity which breeds various forms of conflict and confusion. It is conflict that brings darkness, within and without. Conflict and clarity cannot exist together; and it is freedom from conflict that gives simplicity, not the overcoming of conflict. What is conquered has to be conquered again and again, and so conflict is made endless. The understanding of conflict is the understanding of desire. Desire may abstract itself as the observer, the one who understands; but this sublimation of desire is only postponement and not understanding. The phenomenon of the observer and the observed is not a dual process, but a single one; and only in experiencing the fact of this unitary process is there freedom from desire, from conflict. The question of how to experience this fact should never arise. It must happen; and it happens only when there is alertness and passive awareness. You cannot know the actual experience of meeting a poisonous snake by imagining or speculating about it while sitting comfortably in your room. To meet the snake you must venture out beyond the paved streets and artificial lights.

Thought may record but it cannot experience the freedom from conflict; for simplicity or clarity is not of the mind.

REPETITION AND SENSATION

THE ROAR AND smell of the city came in through the open window. In the large square garden, people were sitting in the shade reading the news, the global gossip. Pigeons strutted about their feet looking for titbits, and children were playing on the green lawns. The sun made beautiful shadows.

He was a reporter, quick and intelligent. He not only wanted an interview, but also wanted to discuss some of his own problems. When the interview for his newspaper was over, he talked of his career and what it was worth—not financially, but its significance in the world. He was a big man, clever, capable and confident. He was climbing rapidly in the newspaper world, and in it there was a future for him.

Our minds are stuffed with so much knowledge that it is almost impossible to experience directly. The experience of pleasure and pain is direct, individual; but the understanding of the experience is after the pattern of others, of the religious and social authorities. We are the result of the thoughts and influences of others; we are conditioned by religious as well as political propaganda. The temple, the church and the mosque have a strange, shadowy influence in our lives, and political ideologies give apparent substance to our thought. We are made and destroyed by propaganda. Organized religions are first-rate propagandists, every means being used to persuade and then to hold.

We are a mass of confused responses, and our centre is as uncertain as the promised future. Mere words have an extraordinary significance for us; they have a neurological effect whose sensations are more important than what is beyond the symbol. The symbol, the image, the flag, the sound, are all-important; substitution, and not reality, is our strength. We read about the experiences of others, we watch others play, we follow the example of others, we quote others. We are empty in ourselves and we try to fill this emptiness with words, sensations, hopes and imagination; but the emptiness continues.

Repetition, with its sensations, however pleasant and noble, is not the state of experiencing; the constant repetition of a ritual, of a word, of a prayer, is a gratifying sensation to which a noble term is given. But experiencing is not sensation, and sensory response soon yields place to actuality. The actual, the what *is*, cannot be understood through mere sensation. The senses play a limited part, but understanding or experiencing lies beyond and above the senses. Sensation becomes important only when experiencing ceases; then words are significant and symbols dominate; then the gramophone becomes enchanting. Experiencing is not a continuity; for what has continuity is sensation, at whatever level. The repetition of sensation gives the appearance of a fresh experience, but sensations can never be new. The search of the new does not lie in repetitive sensations. The new comes into being only when there is experiencing; and experiencing is possible only when the urge and the pursuit of sensation have ceased.

62

The desire for the repetition of an experience is the binding quality of sensation, and the enrichment of memory is the expansion of sensation. The desire for the repetition of an experience, whether your own or that of another, leads to insensitivity, to death. Repetition of a truth is a lie. Truth cannot be repeated, it cannot be propagated or used. That which can be used and repeated has no life in itself, it is mechanical, static. A dead thing can be used, but not truth. You may kill and deny truth first, and then use it; but it is no longer truth. The propagandists are not concerned with experiencing; they are concerned with the organization of sensation, religious or political, social or private. The propagandist, religious or secular, cannot be a speaker of truth.

Experiencing can come only with the absence of the desire for sensation; the naming, the terming must cease. There is no thought process without verbalization; and to be caught in verbalization is to be a prisoner to the illusions of desire.

THE RADIO AND MUSIC

IT IS OBVIOUS that radio music is a marvellous escape. Next door, they kept the thing going all day long and far into the night. The father went off to his office fairly early. The mother and daughter worked in the house or in the garden; and when they worked in the garden the radio blared louder. Apparently the son also enjoyed the music and the commercials, for when he was at home the radio went on just the same. By means of the radio one can listen endlessly to every kind of music, from the classical to the very latest; one can hear mystery plays, news, and all the things that are constantly being broadcast. There need be no conversation, no exchange of thought, for the radio does almost everything for you. The radio, they say, helps students to study; and there is more milk if at milking time the cows have music.

The odd part about all this is that the radio seems to alter so little the course of life. It may make some things a little more convenient; we may have global news more quickly and hear murders described most vividly; but information is not going to make us intelligent. The thin layer of information about the horrors of atomic bombing, about international alliances, research into chlorophyll, and so on, does not seem to make any fundamental difference in our lives. We are as war-minded as ever, we hate some other group of people, we despise this political leader and support that, we are duped by organized religions, we are nationalistic, and our miseries continue; and we are intent on escapes, the more respectable and organized the better. To escape collectively is the highest form of security. In facing what *is*, we can do something about it; but to take flight from what *is* inevitably makes us stupid and dull, slaves to sensation and confusion.

Does not music offer us, in a very subtle way, a happy release from what *is*? Good music takes us away from ourselves, from our daily sorrows, pettiness and anxieties, it makes us forget; or it gives us strength to face life, it inspires, invigorates and pacifies us. It becomes a necessity in either case, whether as a means of forgetting ourselves or as a source of inspiration. Dependence on beauty and avoidance of the ugly is an escape which becomes a torturing issue when our escape is cut off. When beauty becomes necessary to our well-being, then experiencing ceases and sensation begins. The moment of experiencing is totally different from the pursuit of sensation. In experiencing there is no awareness of the experiencer and his sensations. When experiencing comes to an end, then begin the sensations of the experiencer; and it is these sensations that the experiencer demands and pursues. When sensations become a necessity, then music, the river, the painting are only a means to further sensation. Sensations become all-dominant, and not experiencing. The longing to repeat an experience is the demand for sensation; and while sensations can be repeated, experiencing cannot.

It is the desire for sensation that makes us cling to music, possess beauty. Dependence on outward line and form only indicates the emptiness of our own being, which we fill with music, with art, with deliberate silence. It is because this unvarying emptiness is filled or covered over with sensations that there is the everlasting fear of what *is*, of what we are. Sensations have a beginning and an end, they can be repeated and expanded; but experiencing is not within the limits of time. What is essential is experiencing, which is denied in the pursuit of sensation. Sensations are limited, personal, they cause conflict and misery; but experiencing, which is wholly different from the repetition of an experience, is without continuity. Only in experiencing is there renewal, transformation.

AUTHORITY

THE SHADOWS WERE dancing on the green lawn; and though the sun was hot, the sky was very blue and soft. From across the fence a cow was looking at the green lawn and at the people. The gathering of people was strange to her, but the green grass was familiar, though the rains were long gone and the earth was burnt brown. A lizard was picking off flies and other insects on the trunk of an oak. The distant mountains were hazy and inviting.

She said, under the trees after the talk, that she had come to listen in case the teacher of teachers spoke. She had been very earnest, but now that earnestness had become obstinacy. This obstinacy was covered over by smiles and by reasonable tolerance, a tolerance that had been very carefully thought out and cultivated; it was a thing of the mind and so could be inflamed into violent, angry intolerance. She was big and soft-spoken; but there lurked condemnation, nourished by her convictions and beliefs. She was suppressed and hard, but had given herself over to brotherhood and to its good cause. She added, after a pause, that she would know when the teacher spoke, for she and her group had some mysterious way of knowing it, which was not given to others. The pleasure of exclusive knowledge was so obvious in the way she said it, in the gesture and the tilt of the head.

Exclusive, private knowledge offers deeply satisfying pleasure. To know something that others do not know is a constant source of satisfaction; it gives one the feeling of being in touch with deeper things which afford prestige and authority. You are directly in contact, you have something which others have not, and so you are important, not only to yourself, but to others. The others look up to you, a little apprehensively, because they want to share what you have; but you give, always knowing more. You are the leader, the authority; and this position comes easily, for people want to be told, to be led. The more we are aware that we are lost and confused, the more eager we are to be guided and told; so authority is built up in the name of the State, in the name of religion, in the name of a Master or a party leader.

The worship of authority, whether in big or little things, is evil, the more so in religious matters. There is no intermediary between you and reality; and if there is one, he is a perverter, a mischief-maker, it does not matter *who* he is, whether the highest saviour or your latest *guru* or teacher. The one who knows does not know; he can know only his own prejudices, his self-projected beliefs and sensory demands. He cannot know truth, the immeasurable. Position and authority can be built up, cunningly cultivated, but not humility. Virtue gives freedom; but cultivated humility is not virtue, it is mere sensation and therefore harmful and destructive; it is a bondage, to be broken again and again.

It is important to find out, not who is the Master, the saint, the leader, but why you follow. You only follow to become something, to gain, to be clear. Clarity cannot be given by another. Confusion is in *us*; we have brought it about, and we have to clear it away. We may achieve a gratifying position, an inward security, a place in the hierarchy of organized belief; but all this is self-enclosing activity leading to conflict and misery. You may feel momentarily happy in your achievement, you may persuade yourself that your position is inevitable, that it is your lot; but as long as you want to become something, at whatever level, there is bound to be misery and confusion. Being as nothing is not negation. The positive or negative action of will, which is desire sharpened and heightened, always leads to strife and conflict; it is not the means of understanding. The setting up of authority and the following of it is the denial of understanding. When there is understanding there is freedom, which cannot be bought, or given by another. What is bought can be lost, and what is given can be taken away; and so authority and its fear are bred. Fear is not to be put away by appeasements and candles; it ends with the cessation of the desire to become.

MEDITATION

HE HAD PRACTISED for a number of years what he called meditation; he had followed certain disciplines after reading many books on the subject, and had been to a monastery of some kind where they meditated several hours a day. He was not sentimental about it, nor was he blurred by the tears of self-sacrifice. He said that, though after these many years his mind was under control, it still sometimes got out of control; that there was no joy in his meditation; and that the self-imposed disciplines were making him rather hard and arid. Somehow he was very dissatisfied with the whole thing. He had belonged to several so-called religious societies, but now he had finished with them all and was seeking independently the God they all promised. He was getting on in years and was beginning to feel rather weary.

Right meditation is essential for the purgation of the mind, for without the emptying of the mind there can be no renewal. Mere continuity is decay. The mind withers away by constant repetition, by the friction of wrong usage, by sensations which make it dull and weary. The control of the mind is not important; what is important is to find out the interests of the mind. The mind is a bundle of conflicting interests, and merely to strengthen one interest against another is what we call concentration, the process of discipline. Discipline is the cultivation of resistance, and where there is resistance there is no understanding. A well-disciplined mind is not a free mind, and it is only in freedom that any discovery can be made. There must be spontaneity to uncover the movements of the self, at whatever level it may be placed. Though there may be unpleasant discoveries, the movements of the self must be exposed and understood; but disciplines destroy the spontaneity in which discoveries are made. Disciplines, however exacting, fix the mind in a pattern. The mind will adjust itself to that for which it has been trained; but that to which it adjusts itself is not the real. Disciplines are mere impositions and so can never be the means of denudation. Through self-discipline the mind can strengthen itself in its purpose; but this purpose is self-projected and so it is not the real. The mind creates reality in its own image, and disciplines merely give vitality to that image.

Only in discovery can there be joy—the discovery from moment to moment of the ways of the self. The self, at whatever level it is placed, is still of the mind. Whatever the mind can think about is of the mind. The mind cannot think about something which is not of itself; it cannot think of the unknown. The self at any level is the known; and though there may be layers of the self of which the superficial mind is not aware, they are still within the field of the known. The movements of the self are revealed in the action of relationship; and when relationship is not confined within a pattern, it gives an opportunity for self-revelation. Relationship is the action of the self, and to understand this action there must be awareness without choice; for to choose is to emphasize one interest against another. This awareness is the experiencing of the action of the self, and in this experiencing there is neither the experiencer nor the experienced. Thus the mind is emptied of its accumulations; there is no longer the "me," the gatherer. The accumulations, the stored-up memories are the "me"; the "me" is not an entity apart from the accumulations. The "me" separates itself from its characteristics as the observer, the watcher, the controller, in order to safeguard itself, to give itself continuity amidst impermanency. The experiencing of the integral, unitary process frees the mind from its dualism. Thus the total process of the mind, the open as well as the hidden, is experienced and understood—not piece by piece, activity by activity, but in its entirety. Then dreams and everyday activities are ever an emptying process. The mind must be utterly empty to receive; but the craving to be empty in order to receive is a deep-seated impediment, and this also must be understood completely, not at any particular level. The craving to experience must wholly cease, which happens only when the experiencer is not nourishing himself on experiences and their memories.

The purgation of the mind must take place not only on its upper levels, but also in its hidden depths; and this can happen only when the naming or terming process comes to an end. Naming only strengthens and gives continuity to the experiencer, to the desire for permanency, to the characteristic of particularizing memory. There must be silent awareness of naming, and so the understanding of it. We name not only to communicate, but also to give continuity and substance to an experience, to revive it and to repeat its sensations. This naming process must cease, not only on the superficial levels of the mind, but throughout its entire structure. This is an arduous task, not to be easily understood or lightly experienced; for our whole consciousness is a process of naming or terming experience, and then storing or recording it. It is this process that gives nourishment and strength to the illusory entity, the experiencer as distinct and separate from the experience. Without thoughts there is no thinker. Thoughts create the thinker, who isolates himself to give himself permanency; for thoughts are always impermanent.

There is freedom when the entire being, the superficial as well as the hidden, is purged of the past. Will is desire; and if there is any action of the will, any effort to be free, to denude oneself, then there can never be freedom, the total purgation of the whole being. When all the many layers of consciousness are quiet, utterly still, only then is there the immeasurable, the bliss that is not of time, the renewal of creation.

ANGER

EVEN AT THAT altitude the heat was penetrating. The window-panes felt warm to the touch. The steady hum of the plane's motors was soothing, and many of the passengers were dozing. The earth was far below us, shimmering in the heat, an unending brown with an occasional patch of green. Presently we landed, and the heat became all but unbearable; it was literally painful, and even in the shade of a building the top of one's head felt as if it would burst. The summer was well along and the country was almost a desert. We took off again and the plane climbed, seeking the cool winds. Two new passengers sat in the opposite seats and they were talking loudly; it was impossible not to overhear them. They began quietly enough; but soon anger crept into their voices, the anger of familiarity and resentment. In their violence they seemed to have forgotten the rest of the passengers; they were so upset with each other that they alone existed, and none else.

Anger has that peculiar quality of isolation; like sorrow, it cuts one off, and for the time being, at least, all relationship comes to an end. Anger has the temporary strength and vitality of the isolated. There is a strange despair in anger; for isolation is despair. The anger of disappointment, of jealousy, of the urge to wound, gives a violent release whose pleasure is self-justification. We condemn others, and that very condemnation is a justification of ourselves. Without some kind of attitude, whether of self-righteousness or self-abasement, what are we? We use every means to bolster ourselves up; and anger, like hate, is one of the easiest ways. Simple anger, a sudden flare-up which is quickly forgotten, is one thing; but the anger that is deliberately built up, that has been brewed and that seeks to hurt and destroy, is quite another matter. Simple anger may have some physiological cause which can be seen and remedied; but the anger that is the outcome of a psychological cause is much more subtle and difficult to deal with. Most of us do not mind being angry, we find an excuse for it. Why should we not be angry when there is ill-treatment of another or of ourselves? So we become righteously angry. We never just say we are angry, and stop there; we go into elaborate explanations of its cause. We never just say that we are jealous or bitter, but justify or explain it. We ask how there can be love without jealousy, or say that someone else's actions have made us bitter, and so on.

It is the explanation, the verbalization, whether silent or spoken, that sustains anger, that gives it scope and depth. The explanation, silent or spoken, acts as a shield against the discovery of ourselves as we are. We want to be praised or flattered, we expect something; and when these things do not take place, we are disappointed, we become bitter or jealous. Then, violently or softly, we blame someone else; we say the other is responsible for our bitterness. You are of great significance because I depend upon you for my happiness, for my position or prestige. Through you, I fulfil, so you are important to me; I must guard you, I must possess you. Through you, I escape from myself; and when I am thrown back upon myself, being fearful of my own state, I become angry. Anger takes many forms : disappointment, resentment, bitterness, jealousy, and so on.

The storing up of anger, which is resentment, requires the antidote of forgiveness; but the storing up of anger is far more significant than forgiveness. Forgiveness is unnecessary when there is no accumulation of anger. Forgiveness is essential if there is resentment; but to be free from flattery and from the sense of injury, without the hardness of indifference, makes for mercy, charity. Anger cannot be got rid of by the action of will, for will is part of violence. Will is the outcome of desire, the craving to be; and desire in its very nature is aggressive, dominant. To suppress anger by the exertion of will is to transfer anger to a different level, giving it a different name; but it is still part of violence. To be free from violence, which is not the cultivation of non-violence, there must be the understanding of desire. There is no spiritual substitute for desire; it cannot be suppressed or sublimated. There must be a silent and choiceless awareness of desire; and this passive awareness is the direct experiencing of desire without an experiencer giving it a name.

71

HE SAID HE had gone into the question very thoroughly, had read as much as he could of what had been written on the subject, and he was convinced that there were Masters in different parts of the world. They did not show themselves physically except to their special disciples, but they were in communication with others through other means. They exerted a beneficent influence and guided the leaders of the world's thought and action, though the leaders themselves were unaware of it; and they brought about revolution and peace. He was convinced, he said, that each continent had a group of Masters, shaping its destiny and giving it their blessing. He had known several pupils of the Masters—at least they had told him they were, he added guardedly. He was entirely earnest and desired more knowledge about the Masters. Was it possible to have direct experience, direct contact with them?

How still the river was! Two brilliant little kingfishers were flying up and down close to the bank and just above the surface; there were some bees gathering water for their hives, and a fisherman's boat lay in the middle of the stream. The trees along the river were thick with leaves, and their shadows were heavy and dark. In the fields the newly planted rice was a vivid green, and there were white rice-birds calling. It was a very peaceful scene, and it seemed a pity to talk over our petty little problems. The sky was the tender blue of evening. The noisy towns were far away; there was a village across the river, and a winding path went meandering along the bank. A boy was singing in a clear, high voice which did not disturb the tranquillity of the place.

We are an odd people; we wander in search of something in far-off places when it is so close to us. Beauty is ever there, never here; truth is never in our homes but in some distant place. We go to the other side of the world to find the Master, and we are not aware of the servant; we do not understand the common things of life, the everyday struggles and joys, and yet we attempt to grasp the mysterious and the hidden. We do not know ourselves, but we are willing to serve or follow him who promises a reward, a hope, a Utopia. As long as we are confused, what we choose must also be confused. We cannot perceive clearly when we are half-blind; and what we then see is only partial and so not real. We know all this, and yet our desires, our cravings are so strong that they drive us into illusions and endless miseries.

Belief in the Master creates the Master, and experience is shaped by belief. Belief in a particular pattern of action, or in an ideology, does produce what is longed for; but at what cost and at what suffering! If an individual has capacity, then belief becomes a potent thing in his hands, a weapon more dangerous than a gun. For most of us, belief has greater meaning than actuality. The understanding of what *is* does not require belief; on the contrary, belief, idea, prejudice, is a definite hindrance to understanding. But we prefer our beliefs, our dogmas; they warm us, they promise, they encourage. If we understood the way of our beliefs and why we cling to them, one of the major causes of antagonism would disappear.

The desire to gain, individually or for a group, leads to ignorance and illusion, to destruction and misery. This desire is not only for more and more physical comforts, but also for power : the power of money, of knowledge, of identification. The craving for more is the beginning of conflict and misery. We try to escape from this misery through every form of self-deception, through suppression, substitution and sublimation; but craving continues, perhaps at a different level. Craving at any level is still conflict and pain. One of the easiest of escapes is the *guru*, the Master. Some escape through a political ideology with its activities, others through the sensations of ritual and discipline, and still others through the Master. Then the means of escape become all-important, and fear and obstinacy guard the means. Then it does not matter what *you* are; it is the Master who is important. You are important only as a server, whatever that may mean, or as a disciple. To become one of these, you have to do certain things, conform to certain patterns, undergo certain hardships. You are willing to do all this and more, for identification gives pleasure and power. In the name of the Master, pleasure and power have become respectable. You are no longer lonely, confused, lost; you belong to him, to the party, to the idea. You are safe.

After all, that is what most of us want : to be safe, to be secure. To be lost with the many is a form of psychological security; to be identified with a group or with an idea, secular or spiritual, is to feel safe. That is why most of us cling to nationalism, even though it brings increasing destruction and misery; that is why organized religion has such a strong hold on people, even though it divides and breeds antagonism. The craving for individual or group security brings on destruction, and to be safe psychologically engenders illusion. Our life is illusion and misery, with rare moments of clarity and joy, so anything that promises a haven we eagerly accept. Some see the futility of political Utopias and so turn religious, which is to find security and hope in Masters, in dogmas, in ideas. As belief shapes experience, the Masters become an inescapable reality. Once it has experienced the pleasure which identification brings, the mind is firmly entrenched and nothing can shake it; for its criterion is experience.

But experience is not reality. Reality cannot be experienced. It is. If the experiencer thinks he experiences reality, then he knows only illusion. All knowledge of reality is illusion. Knowledge or experience must cease for the being of reality. Experience cannot meet reality. Experience shapes knowledge, and knowledge bends experience; they must both cease for reality to be.

SEPARATENESS

HE WAS A small and aggressive man, a professor at one of the universities. He had read so much that it was difficult for him to know where his own thoughts began and the thoughts of others ended. He said he had been an ardent nationalist and in a way had suffered for it. He had also been a practising religionist; but now he had thrown away all that rubbish, thank

God, and was free of superstition. He asserted vehemently that all this psychological talk and discussion was misleading the people, and that what was of the greatest importance was the economic reorganization of man; for man lived by bread first, and after that everything else came to him. There must be a violent revolution and a new classless society established. The means did not matter if the end were achieved. If necessary they would foment chaos, and then take over and establish order of the right kind. Collectivism was essential, and all individual exploitation must be stamped out. He was very explicit about the future; and as man was the product of environment, they would shape man for the future; they would sacrifice everything for the future, for the world that is to be. The liquidation of present man was of little importance, for they knew the future.

We may study history and translate historical facts according to our prejudices; but to be certain of the future is to be in illusion. Man is not the result of one influence only, he is vastly complex; and to emphasize one influence while minimizing others is to breed an imbalance which will lead to yet greater chaos and misery. Man is a total process. The totality must be understood and not merely a part, however temporarily important the part may be. The sacrificing of the present for the future is the insanity of those who are power-mad; and power is evil. These take to themselves the rights of human direction; they are the new priests. Means and end are not separate, they are a joint phenomenon; the means create the end. Through violence there can never be peace; a police State cannot produce a peaceful citizen; through compulsion, freedom cannot be achieved. A classless society cannot be established if the party is all-powerful, it can never be the outcome of dictatorship. All this is obvious.

The separateness of the individual is not destroyed through his identification with the collective or with an ideology. Substitution does not do away with the problem of separateness, nor can it be suppressed. Substitution and suppression may work for the time being, but separateness will erupt again more violently. Fear may temporarily push it into the background, but the problem is still there. The problem is not how to get rid of separateness, but why each one of us gives so much importance to it. The very people who desire to establish a classless society are by their acts of power and authority breeding division. You are separate from me, and I from another, and that is a fact; but why do we give importance to this feeling of separateness, with all its mischievous results? Though there is a great similarity between us all, yet we are dissimilar; and this dissimilarity gives each one the sense of importance in being separate : the separate family, name, property, and the feeling of being a separate entity. This separateness, this sense of individuality has caused enormous harm, and hence the desire for collective work and action, the sacrificing of the individual to the whole, and so on. Organized religions have tried to submit the will of the particular to that of the whole; and now the party, which assumes the role of the State, is doing its best to submerge the individual.

Why is it that we cling to the feeling of separateness? Our sensations are separate and we live by sensations; we *are* sensations. Deprive us of sensations, pleasurable or painful, and we are not. Sensations are important to us, and they are identified with separateness. Private life and life as the citizen have different sensations at different levels, and when they clash there is conflict. But sensations are always at war with each other, whether in private life or in that of the citizen. Conflict is inherent in sensation. As long as I want to be powerful or humble, there must be the conflicts of sensation, which bring about private and social misery. The constant desire to be more or to be less gives rise to the feeling of individuality and its separateness. If we can remain with this fact without condemning or justifying it, we will discover that sensations do not make up our whole life. Then the mind as memory, which is sensation, becomes calm, no longer torn by its own conflicts; and only then, when the mind is silent and tranquil, is there a possibility of loving without the "me" and the "mine." Without this love, collective action is merely compulsion, breeding antagonism and fear, from which arise private and social conflicts.

POWER

HE WAS A very poor man, but capable and clever; he was content, or at least appeared so, with what little he possessed, and he had no family burdens. He often came to talk things over, and he had great dreams for the future; he was eager and enthusiastic, simple in his pleasures, and delighted in doing little things for others. He was not, he said, greatly attracted to money or to physical comfort; but he liked to describe what he would do if he *had* money, how he would support this or that, how he would start the perfect school, and so on. He was rather dreamy and easily carried away by his own enthusiasm and by that of others.

Several years passed, and then one day he came again. There was a strange transformation in him. The dreamy look had gone; he was matter-of-fact, definite, almost brutal in his opinions, and rather harsh in his judgments. He had travelled, and his manner was highly polished and sophisticated; he turned his charm on and off. He had been left a lot of money and was successful in increasing it many times, and he had become an altogether changed man. He hardly ever comes now; and when on rare occasions we do meet, he is distant and self-enclosed.

Both poverty and riches are a bondage. The consciously poor and the consciously rich are the playthings of circumstances. Both are corruptible, for both seek that which is corrupting : power. Power is greater than possessions; power is greater than wealth and ideas. These do give power; but they can be put away, and yet the sense of power remains. One may beget power through simplicity of life, through virtue, through the party, through renunciation; but such means are a mere substitution and they should not deceive one. The desire for position, prestige and power—the power that is gained through aggression and humility, through asceticism and knowledge, through exploitation and self-denial—is subtly persuasive and almost instinctive. Success in any form is power, and failure is merely the denial of success. To be powerful, to be successful is to be slavish, which is the denial of virtue. Virtue gives freedom, but it is not a thing to be gained. Any achievement, whether of the individual or of the collective, becomes a means to power. Success in this world, and the power that self-control and self-denial bring, are to be avoided; for both distort understanding. It is the desire for success that prevents humility; and without humility how can there be understanding? The man of success is hardened, self-enclosed; he is burdened with his own importance, with his responsibilities, achievements and memories. There must be freedom from self-assumed responsibilities and from the burden of achievement; for that which is weighed down cannot be swift, and to understand requires a swift and pliable mind. Mercy is denied to the successful, for they are incapable of knowing the very beauty of life which is love.

The desire for success is the desire for domination. To dominate is to possess, and possession is the way of isolation. This self-isolation is what most of us seek, through name, through relationship, through work, through ideation. In isolation there is power, but power breeds antagonism and pain; for isolation is the outcome of fear, and fear puts an end to all communion. Communion is relationship; and however pleasurable or painful relationship may be, in it there is the possibility of self-forgetfulness. Isolation is the way of the self, and all activity of the self brings conflict and sorrow.

SINCERITY

THERE WAS A little patch of green lawn, with brilliant flowers along its borders. It was beautifully kept and a great deal of care was given to it, for the sun did its best to burn the lawn and wither the flowers. Beyond this delicious garden, past many houses, was the blue sea, sparkling in the sun, and on it was a white sail. The room overlooked the garden, the houses and the tree tops, and from its window, in the early morning and early evening, the sea was pleasant to look upon. During the day its waters became bright and hard; but there was always a sail, even at high noon. The sun would go down into the sea, making a bright red path; there would be no twilight. The evening star would hover over the horizon, and disappear. The slip of the young moon would capture the evening, but she too would disappear into the restless sea, and darkness would be upon the waters.

He spoke at length of God, of his morning and evening prayers, of his fasts, his vows, his burning desires. He expressed himself very clearly and definitely, there was no hesitation for the right word; his mind was well trained, for his profession demanded it. He was a bright-eyed and alert man, though there was a certain rigidity about him. Obstinacy of purpose and absence of pliability were shown in the way he held his body. He was obviously driven by an extraordinarily powerful will, and though he smiled easily his will was ever on the alert, watchful and dominant. He was very regular in his daily life, and he broke his established habits only by sanction of the will. Without will, he said, there could be no virtue; will was essential to break down evil. The battle between good and evil was everlasting, and will alone held evil at bay. He had a gentle side too, for he would look at the lawn and the gay flowers, and smile; but he never let his mind wander beyond the pattern of will and its action. Though he sedulously avoided harsh words, anger and any show of impatience, his will made him strangely violent. If beauty fitted into the pattern of his purpose, he would accept it; but there always lurked the fear of sensuality, whose ache he tried to contain. He was well read and urbane, and his will went with him like his shadow.

Sincerity can never be simple; sincerity is the breeding-ground of the will, and will cannot uncover the ways of the self. Self-knowledge is not the product of will; self-knowledge comes into being through awareness of the moment-by-moment responses to the movement of life. Will shuts off these spontaneous responses, which alone reveal the structure of the self. Will is the very essence of desire; and to the understanding of desire, will becomes a hindrance. Will in any form, whether of the upper mind or of the deep-rooted desires, can never be passive; and it is only in passivity, in alert silence, that truth can be. Conflict is always between desires, at whatever level the desires may be placed. The strengthening of one desire in opposition to the others only breeds further resistance, and this resistance is will. Understanding can never come through resistance. What is important is to understand desire, and not to overcome one desire by another.

The desire to achieve, to gain is the basis of sincerity; and this urge, however superficial or deep, makes for conformity, which is the beginning of fear. Fear limits self-knowledge to the experienced, and so there is no possibility of transcending the experienced. Thus limited, self-knowledge only cultivates wider and deeper self-consciousness, the "me" becoming more and more at different levels and at different periods; so conflict and pain continue. You may deliberately forget or lose yourself in some activity, in cultivating a garden or an ideology, in whipping up in a whole people the raging fervour for war; but you are now the country, the idea, the activity, the god. The greater the identification, the more your conflict and pain are covered over, and so the everlasting struggle to be identified with something. This desire to be one with a chosen object brings the conflict of sincerity, which utterly denies simplicity. You may put ashes on your head, or wear a simple cloth, or wander as a beggar; but this is not simplicity.

Simplicity and sincerity can never be companions. He who is identified with something, at whatever level, may be sincere, but he is not simple. The will to be is the very antithesis of simplicity. Simplicity comes into being with freedom from the acquisitive drive of the desire to achieve. Achievement is identification, and identification is will. Simplicity is the alert, passive awareness in which the experiencer is not recording the experience. Self-analysis prevents this negative awareness; in analysis there is always a motive—to be free, to understand, to gain—and this desire only emphasizes self-consciousness. Likewise, introspective conclusions arrest self-knowledge.

FULFILMENT

SHE WAS MARRIED, but had no children. In the worldly way, she said, she was happy; money was no problem, and there were cars, good hotels and wide travel. Her husband was a successful business man whose chief interest was to adorn his wife, to see that she was comfortable and had everything she desired. They were both quite young and friendly. She was interested in science and art, and had dabbled in religion; but now, she said, the things of the spirit were pushing everything else aside. She was familiar with the teachings of the various religions; but being dissatisfied with their organized efficiency, their rituals and dogmas, she wanted seriously to go in search of real things. She was intensely discontented, and had been to teachers in different parts of the world; but nothing had given her lasting satisfaction. Her discontent, she said, did not arise from her having had no children; she had gone into all that pretty thoroughly. Nor was the discontent caused by any social frustrations. She had spent some time with one of the prominent analysts, but there was still this inward ache and emptiness.

To seek fulfilment is to invite frustration. There is no fulfilment of the self, but only the strengthening of the self through possessing what it craves for. Possession, at whatever level, makes the self feel potent, rich, active, and this sensation is called fulfilment; but as with all sensations, it soon fades, to be replaced by yet another gratification. We are all familiar with this process of replacement or substitution, and it is a game with which most of us are content. There are some, however, who desire a more enduring gratification, one that will last for the whole of one's life; and having found it, they hope never to be disturbed again. But there is a constant, unconscious fear of disturbance, and subtle forms of resistance are cultivated behind which the mind takes shelter; and so the fear of death is inevitable. Fulfilment and the fear of death are the two sides of one process: the strengthening of the self. After all, fulfilment is complete identification with something—with children, with property, with ideas. Children and property are rather risky, but ideas offer greater safety and security. Words, which are ideas and memories, with their sensations, become important; and fulfilment or completeness then becomes the word.

There is no self-fulfilment, but only self-perpetuation, with its ever-increasing conflicts, antagonisms and miseries. To seek lasting gratification at any level of our being is to bring about confusion and sorrow; for gratification can never be permanent. You may remember an experience which was satisfying, but the experience is dead, and only the memory of it remains. This memory has no life in itself; but life is given to it through your inadequate response to the present. You are living on the dead, as most of us do. Ignorance of the ways of the self leads to illusion; and once caught in the net of illusion, it is extremely hard to break through it. It is difficult to recognize an illusion, for, having created it, the mind cannot be aware of it. It must be approached negatively, indirectly. Unless the ways of desire are understood, illusion is inevitable. Understanding comes, not through the exertion of will, but only when the mind is still. The mind cannot be *made* still, for the maker himself is a product of the mind, of desire. There must be an awareness of this total process, a choiceless awareness; then only is there a possibility of not breeding illusion. Illusion is very gratifying, and hence our attachment to it. Illusion may bring pain, but this very pain exposes our incompleteness and drives us to be wholly identified with the illusion. Thus illusion has great significance in our lives; it helps to cover up what *is*, not externally but inwardly. This disregard of the inward what *is* leads to wrong interpretation of what *is* outwardly, which brings about destruction and misery. The covering up of what *is* is prompted by fear. Fear can never be overcome by an act of will, for will is the outcome of resistance. Only through passive yet alert awareness is there freedom from fear.

WORDS

HE HAD READ extensively; and though he was poor, he considered himself rich in knowledge, which gave him a certain happiness. He spent many hours with his books and a great deal of time by himself. His wife was dead, and his two children were with some relatives; and he was rather glad to be out of the mess of all relationship, he added. He was oddly self-contained, independent and quietly assertive. He had come a long way, he said, to go into the question of meditation, and especially to consider the use of certain chants and phrases, whose constant repetition was highly conducive to the pacification of the mind. Also, in the words themselves there was a certain magic; the words must be pronounced rightly and chanted correctly. These words were handed down from ancient times; and the very beauty of the words, with their rhythmic cadence, brought about an atmosphere that was helpful to concentration. And forthwith he began to chant. He had a pleasant voice, and there was a mellowness born of the love of the words and their meaning; he chanted with the ease of long practice and devotion. The moment he began to chant, he was lost to everything.

From across the field came the sound of a flute; it was haltingly played, but the tone was clear and pure. The player was sitting in the rich shadow of a large tree, and beyond him in the distance were the mountains. The silent mountains, the chant, and the sound of the flute seemed to meet and disappear, to begin again. The noisy parrots flashed by; and once again there were the notes of the flute, and the deep, powerful chant. It was early in the morning, and the sun was coming over the trees. People were going from their villages to the town, chatting and laughing. The flute and the chant were insistent, and a few passers-by stopped to listen; they sat down on the path and were caught up in the beauty of the chant and the glory of the morning, which were not in any way disturbed by the whistle of a distant train; on the contrary, all sounds seemed to mingle and fill the earth. Even the loud calling of a crow was not jarring.

How strangely we are caught in the sound of words, and how important the words themselves have become to us: country, God, priest, democracy, revolution. We live on words and delight in the sensations they produce; and it is these sensations that have become so important. Words are satisfying because their sounds reawaken forgotten sensations; and their satisfaction is greater when words are substituted for the actual, for what *is*. We try to fill our inward emptiness with words, with sound, with noise, with activity; music and the chant are a happy escape from ourselves, from our pettiness and boredom. Words fill our libraries; and how incessantly we talk! We hardly dare to be without a book, to be unoccupied, to be alone. When we are alone, the mind is restless, wandering all over the place, worrying, remembering, struggling; so there is never an aloneness, the mind is never still.

Obviously, the mind can be made still by the repetition of a word, of a chant, of a prayer. The mind can be drugged, put to sleep; it can be put to sleep pleasantly or violently, and during this sleep there may be dreams. But a mind that is made quiet by discipline, by ritual, by repetition, can never be alert, sensitive and free. This bludgeoning of the mind, subtly or crudely, is not meditation. It is pleasant to chant and to listen to one who can do it well; but sensation lives only on further sensation, and sensation leads to illusion. Most of us like to live on illusions, there is pleasure in finding deeper and wider illusions; but it is fear of losing our illusions that makes us deny or cover up the real, the actual. It is not that we are incapable of understanding the actual; what makes us fearful is that we reject the actual and cling to the illusion. Getting caught deeper and deeper in illusion is not meditation, nor is decorating the cage which holds us. Awareness, without any choice, of the ways of the mind, which is the breeder of illusion, is the beginning of meditation.

It is odd how easily we find substitutes for the real thing, and how contented we are with them. The symbol, the word, the image, becomes all-important, and around this symbol we build the structure of self-deception, using knowledge to strengthen it; and so experience becomes a hindrance to the understanding of the real. We name, not only to communicate, but to strengthen experience; this strengthening of experience is self-consciousness, and once caught in its process, it is extremely difficult to let go, that is, to go beyond self-consciousness. It is essential to die to the experience of yesterday and to the sensations of today, otherwise there is repetition; and the repetition of an act, of a ritual, of a word, is vain. In repetition there can be no renewal. The death of experience is creation.

IDEA AND FACT

SHE HAD BEEN married for a number of years, but had had no children; she was unable to have them, and was gravely disturbed by this fact. Her sisters had children, and why was she cursed? She had been married quite young, as was the custom, and had seen a lot of suffering; but she had known quiet joy too. Her husband was some kind of bureaucrat in a big corporation or Government department. He too was concerned about their not having children, but it appeared that he was becoming reconciled to this fact; and besides, she added, he was a very busy man. One could see that she dominated him, though not too heavily. She leaned on him, and so she could not help dominating him. Since she had no children, she was trying to fulfil herself in him; but in this she was disappointed, for he was weak and she had to take charge of things. In the office, she said smilingly, he was considered a stickler, a tyrant who threw his weight around; but at home he was mild and easy going. She wanted him to fit into a certain pattern, and she was forcing him, of course very gently, into her mould; but he was not coming up to scratch. She had nobody to lean on and give her love to.

The idea is more important to us than the fact; the concept of what one *should* be has more significance than what one *is*. The future is always more alluring than the present. The image, the symbol, is of greater worth than the actual; and on the actual we try to superimpose the idea, the pattern. So we create a contradiction between what *is* and what *should* be. What *should* be is the idea, the fiction, and so there is a conflict between the actual and the illusion—not in themselves, but in us. We like the illusion better than the actual; the idea is more appealing, more satisfying, and so we cling to it. Thus the illusion becomes the real and the actual becomes the false, and in this conflict between the so-called real and the so-called false we are caught.

Why do we cling to the idea, deliberately or unconsciously, and put aside the actual? The idea, the pattern, is self-projected; it is a form of self-worship, of self-perpetuation, and hence gratifying. The idea gives power to dominate, to be assertive, to guide, to shape; and in the idea, which is self-projected, there is never the denial of the self, the disintegration of the self. So the pattern or idea enriches the self; and this is also considered to be love. I love my son or my husband and I want him to be this or that, I want him to be something other than he is.

If we are to understand what *is,* the pattern or idea must be put aside. To set aside the idea becomes difficult only when there is no urgency in the understanding of what *is.* Conflict exists in us between the idea and what *is* because the self-projected idea offers greater satisfaction than what *is.* It is only when what *is,* the actual, *has* to be faced that the pattern is broken; so it is not a matter of how to be free from the idea, but of how to face the actual. It is possible to face the actual only when there is an understanding of the process of gratification, the way of the self.

We all seek self-fulfilment, though in many different ways : through money or power, through children or husband, through country or idea, through service or sacrifice, through domination or submission. But *is* there self-fulfilment? The object of fulfilment is ever self-projected, self-chosen, so this craving to fulfil is a form of self-perpetuation. Whether consciously or unconsciously, the way of self-fulfilment is self-chosen, it is based on the desire for gratification, which must be permanent; so the search for self-fulfilment is the search for the permanency of desire. Desire is ever transient, it has no fixed abode; it may perpetuate for a time the object to which it clings, but desire in itself has no permanency. We are instinctively aware of this, and so we try to make permanent the idea, the belief, the thing, the relationship; but as this also is impossible, there is the creation of the experiencer as a permanent essence, the "I" separate and different from desire, the thinker separate and different from his thoughts. This separation is obviously false, leading to illusion.

The search for permanency is the everlasting cry of self-fulfilment; but the self can never fulfil, the self is impermanent, and that in which it fulfils must also be impermanent. Self-continuity is decay; in it there is no transforming element nor the breath of the new. The self must end for the new to be. The self is the idea, the pattern, the bundle of memories; and each fulfilment is the further continuity of idea, of experience. Experience is always conditioning; the experiencer is ever separating and differentiating himself from experience. So there must be freedom from experience, from the desire to experience. Fulfilment is the way of covering up inward poverty, emptiness, and in fulfilment there is sorrow and pain.

CONTINUITY

THE MAN IN the opposite seat began by introducing himself, as he wanted to ask several questions. He said that he had read practically every serious book on death and the hereafter, books from ancient times as well as the modern ones. He had been a member of the Psychical Research Society, had attended many seances with excellent and reputable mediums, and had seen many manifestations which were in no way faked. Because he had gone into this question so seriously, on several occasions he himself had seen things of a super-physical nature; but of course, he added, they might have been born of his imagination, though he considered that they were not. However, in spite of the fact that he had read extensively, had talked to many people who were well informed, and had seen undeniable physical manifestations of those who were dead, he was still not satisfied that he had understood the truth of the matter. He had seriously debated the problem of belief and non-belief; he had friends among those who firmly believed in one's continuity after death, and also among those who denied the whole thing and held that life ended with the death of the physical body. Though he had acquired considerable knowledge and experience in psychic matters, there remained in his mind an element of doubt; and as he was getting on in years he wanted to know the truth. He was not afraid of death, but the truth about it must be known.

The train had come to a stop, and just then a two-wheeled carriage was passing, drawn by a horse. On the carriage was a human corpse, wrapped in an unbleached cloth and tied to two long green bamboo poles, freshly cut. From some village it was being taken to the river to be burnt. As the carriage moved over the rough road, the body was being brutally shaken, and under its cloth the head was obviously getting the worst of it. There was only one passenger in the carriage besides the driver; he must have been a near relative, for his eyes were red with much crying. The sky was the delicate blue of early spring, and children were playing and shouting in the dirt of the road. Death must have been a common sight, for everyone went on with what they were doing. Even the inquirer into death did not see the carriage and its burden.

Belief conditions experience, and experience then strengthens belief. What you believe, you experience. The mind dictates and interprets experience, invites or rejects it. The mind itself is the result of experience, and it can recognize or experience only that with which it is familiar, which it knows, at whatever level. The mind cannot experience what is not already known. The mind and its response are of greater significance than the experience; and to rely on experience as a means of understanding truth is to be caught in ignorance and illusion. To desire to experience truth is to deny truth; for desire conditions, and belief is another cloak of desire. Knowledge, belief, conviction, conclusion and experience are hindrances to truth; they are the very structure of the self. The self cannot be if there is no cumulative effect of experience; and the fear of death is the fear of not being, of not experiencing. If there were the assurance, the certainty of experiencing, there would be no fear. Fear exists only in the relationship between the known and the unknown. The known is ever trying to capture the unknown; but it can capture only that which is already known. The unknown can never be experienced by the known; the known, the experienced must cease for the unknown to be.

The desire to experience truth must be searched out and understood; but if there is motive in the search, then truth does not come into being. Can there be search without a motive, conscious or unconscious? *With* a motive, is there search? If you already know what you want, if you have formulated an end, then search is a means to achieve that end, which is self-projected. Then search is for gratification, not for truth; and the means will be chosen according to the gratification. The understanding of what *is* needs no motive; the motive and the means prevent understanding. Search, which is choiceless awareness, is not *for* something; it is to be aware of the craving for an end and of the means to it. This choiceless awareness brings an understanding of what *is*.

It is odd how we crave for permanency, for continuity. This desire takes many forms, from the crudest to the most subtle. With the obvious forms we are well acquainted : name, shape, character, and so on. But the subtler craving is much more difficult to uncover and understand. Identity as idea, as being, as knowledge, as becoming, at whatever level, is difficult to perceive and bring to light. We only know continuity, and never non-continuity. We know the continuity of experience, of memory, of incidents, but we do not know that state in which this continuity is not. We call it death, the unknown, the mysterious, and so on, and through naming it we hope somehow to capture it—which again is the desire for continuity.

Self-consciousness is experience, the naming of experience, and so the recording of it; and this process is going on at various depths of the mind. We cling to this process of self-consciousness in spite of its passing joys, its unending conflict, confusion and misery. This is what we know; this is our existence, the continuity of our very being, the idea, the memory, the word. The idea continues, all or part of it, the idea that makes up the "me"; but does this continuity bring about freedom, in which alone there is discovery and renewal?

What has continuity can never be other than that which it is, with certain modifications; but these modifications do not give it a newness. It may take on a different cloak, a different colour; but it is still the idea, the memory, the word. This centre of continuity is not a spiritual essence, for it is still within the field of thought, of memory, and so of time. It can experience only its own projection, and through its self-projected experience it gives itself further continuity. Thus, as long as it exists, it can never experience beyond itself. It must die; it must cease to give itself continuity through idea, through memory, through word. Continuity is decay, and there is life only in death. There is renewal only with the cessation of the centre; then rebirth is not continuity; then death is as life, a renewal from moment to moment. This renewal is creation.

Self-Defence

HE WAS A well-known man, and was in a position to harm others, which he did not hesitate to do. He was cunningly shallow, devoid of generosity, and worked to his own advantage. He said he was not too keen to talk things over, but circumstances had forced him to come, and here he was. From everything he said and did not say, it was fairly clear that he was very ambitious and shaped the people about him; he was ruthless when it paid, and gentle when he wanted something. He had consideration for those above him, treated his equals with condescending tolerance, and of those below him he was utterly unaware. He never so much as glanced at the chauffeur who brought him. His money made him suspicious, and he had few friends. He talked of his children as though they were toys to amuse him, and he could not bear to be alone, he said. Some-one had hurt him, and he could not retaliate because that person was beyond his reach; so he was taking it out of those he *could* reach. He was unable to understand why he was being unneces-sarily brutal, why he wanted to hurt those whom he said he loved. As he talked, he slowly began to thaw and became almost friendly. It was the friendliness of the moment whose warmth would be shut off instantly if it were thwarted or if anything were asked of it. As nothing was being asked of him, he was free and temporarily affectionate.

The desire to do harm, to hurt another, whether by a word, by a gesture, or more deeply, is strong in most of us; it is common and frighteningly pleasant. The very desire not to *be* hurt makes for the hurting of others; to harm others is a way of defending oneself. This self-defence takes peculiar forms, depending on circumstances and tendencies. How easy it is to hurt another, and what gentleness is needed not to hurt! We hurt others because we ourselves are hurt, we are so bruised by our own conflicts and sorrows. The more we are inwardly tortured, the greater the urge to be outwardly violent. Inward turmoil drives us to seek outward protection; and the more one defends oneself, the greater the attack on others.

What is it that we defend, that we so carefully guard? Surely, it is the idea of ourselves, at whatever level. If we did not guard the idea, the centre of accumulation, there would be no "me" and "mine." We would then be utterly sensitive, vulnerable to the ways of our own being, the conscious as well as the hidden; but as most of us do not desire to discover the process of the "me," we resist any encroachment upon the idea of ourselves. The idea of ourselves is wholly superficial; but as most of us live on the surface, we are content with illusions.

The desire to do harm to another is a deep instinct. We accumulate resentment, which gives a peculiar vitality, a feeling of action and life; and what is accumulated must be expended through anger, insult, depreciation, obstinacy, and through their opposites. It is this accumulation of resentment that necessitates forgiveness—which becomes unnecessary if there is no storing up of the hurt.

Why do we store up flattery and insult, hurt and affection? Without this accumulation of experiences and their responses, we are not; we are nothing if we have no name, no attachment, no belief. It is the fear of being nothing that compels us to accumulate; and it is this very fear, whether conscious or unconscious, that, in spite of our accumulative activities, brings about our disintegration and destruction. If we can be aware of the truth of this fear, then it is the truth that liberates us from it, and not our purposeful determination to be free.

You are nothing. You may have your name and title, your property and bank account, you may have power and be famous; but in spite of all these safeguards, you are as nothing. You may be totally unaware of this emptiness, this nothingness, or you may simply not want to be aware of it; but it is there, do what you will to avoid it. You may try to escape from it in devious ways, through personal or collective violence, through individual or collective worship, through knowledge or amusement; but whether you are asleep or awake, it is always there. You can come upon your relationship to this nothingness and its fear only by being choicelessly aware of the escapes. You are not related to it as a separate, individual entity; you are not the observer watching it; without you, the thinker, the observer, it is not. You and nothingness are one; you and nothingness are a joint phenomenon, not two separate processes. If you, the thinker, are afraid of it and approach it as something contrary and opposed to you, then any action you may take towards it must inevitably lead to illusion and so to further conflict and misery. When there is the discovery, the experiencing of that nothingness as you, then fear—which exists only when the thinker is separate from his thoughts and so tries to establish a relationship with them—completely drops away. Only then is it possible for the mind to be still; and in this tranquillity, truth comes into being.

"MY PATH AND YOUR PATH"

HE WAS A scholar, spoke many languages, and was addicted to knowledge as another is to drink. He was everlastingly quoting the sayings of others to bolster up his own opinions. He dabbled in science and art, and when he gave his opinion it was with a shake of the head and a smile that conveyed in a subtle way that it was not merely his opinion, but the final truth. He said he had his own experiences which were authoritative and conclusive to him. "You have your experiences too, but you cannot convince me," he said. "You go your way, and I mine. There are different paths to truth, and we shall all meet there some day." He was friendly in a distant way, but firm. To him, the Masters, though not actual, visible *gurus*, were a reality, and to become their disciple was essential. He, with several others, conferred disciple-ship on those who were willing to accept this path and their authority; but he and his group did not belong to those who, through spiritualism, found guides among the dead. To find the Masters you had to serve, work, sacrifice, obey and practise certain virtues; and of course belief was necessary.

To rely on experience as a means to the discovery of what *is*, is to be caught in illusion. Desire, craving, conditions experience; and to depend on experience as a means to the understanding of truth is to pursue the way of self-aggrandizement. Experience can never bring freedom from sorrow; experience is not an adequate response to the challenge of life. The challenge must be met newly, freshly, for the challenge is always new. To meet the challenge adequately, the conditioning memory of experience must be set aside, the responses of pleasure and pain must be deeply understood. Experience is an impediment to truth, for experience is of time, it is the outcome of the past; and how can a mind which is the result of experience, of time, understand the timeless? The truth of experience does not depend on personal idiosyncrasies and fancies; the truth of it is perceived only when there is awareness without condemnation, justification, or any form of identification. Experience is not an approach to truth; there is no "your experience" or "my experience," but only the intelligent understanding of the problem.

Without self-knowledge, experience breeds illusion; with self-knowledge, experience, which is the response to challenge, does not leave a cumulative residue as memory. Self-knowledge is the discovery from moment to moment of the ways of the self, its intentions and pursuits, its thoughts and appetites. There can never be "your experience" and "my experience"; the very term "my experience" indicates ignorance and the acceptance of illusion. But many of us like to live in illusion, because there is great satisfaction in it; it is a private heaven which stimulates us and gives a feeling of superiority. If I have capacity, gift or cunning, I become a leader, an intermediary, a representative of that illusion; and as most people love the avoidance of what *is*, there is built up an organization with properties and rituals, with vows and secret gatherings. Illusion is clothed according to tradition, keeping it within the field of respectability; and as most of us seek power in one form or another, the hierarchical principle is established, the novice and the initiate, the pupil and the Master, and even among the Masters there are degrees of spiritual growth. Most of us love to exploit and be exploited, and this system offers the means, whether hidden or open.

To exploit is to be exploited. The desire to use others for your psychological necessities makes for dependence, and when you depend you must hold, possess; and what you possess, possesses you. Without dependence, subtle or gross, without possessing things, people and ideas, you are empty, a thing of no importance. You want to be something, and to avoid the gnawing fear of being nothing you belong to this or that organization, to this or that ideology, to this church or that temple; so you are exploited, and you in your turn exploit. This hierarchical structure offers an excellent opportunity for self-expansion. You may want brotherhood, but how can there be brotherhood if you are pursuing spiritual distinctions? You may smile at worldly titles; but when you admit the Master, the saviour, the *guru* in the realm of the spirit, are you not carrying over the worldly attitude? Can there be hierarchical divisions or degrees in spiritual growth, in the understanding of truth, in the realization of God? Love admits no division. Either you love, or do not love; but do not make the lack of love into a long-drawn-out process whose end is love. When you *know* you do not love, when you are choicelessly aware of that fact, then there is a possibility of transformation; but to sedulously cultivate this distinction between the Master and the pupil, between those who have attained and those who have not, between the saviour and the sinner, is to deny love. The exploiter, who is in turn exploited, finds a happy hunting-ground in this darkness and illusion.

Separation between God or reality and yourself is brought about by you, by the mind that clings to the known, to certainty, to security. This separation cannot be bridged over; there is no ritual, no discipline, no sacrifice that can carry you across it; there is no saviour, no Master, no *guru* who can lead you to the real or destroy this separation. The division is not between the real and yourself; it is *in* yourself, it is the conflict of opposing desires. Desire creates its own opposite; and transformation is not a matter of being centred in one desire, but of being free from the conflict which craving brings. Craving at any level of one's being breeds further conflict, and from this we try to escape in every possible manner, which only increases the conflict both within and without. This conflict cannot be dissolved by someone else, however great, nor through any magic or ritual. These may put you pleasantly to sleep, but on waking the problem is still there. But most of us do not want to wake up, and so we live in illusion. With the dissolution of conflict, there is tranquillity, and then only can reality come into being. Masters, saviours and *gurus* are unimportant, but what is essential is to understand the increasing conflict of desire; and this understanding comes only through self-knowledge and constant awareness of the movements of the self.

Self-awareness is arduous, and since most of us prefer an easy, illusory way, we bring into being the authority that gives shape and pattern to our life. This authority may be the collective, the

State; or it may be the personal, the Master, the saviour, the *guru*. Authority of any kind is blinding, it breeds thoughtlessness; and as most of us find that to be thoughtful is to have pain, we give ourselves over to authority.

Authority engenders power, and power always becomes centralized and therefore utterly corrupting; it corrupts not only the wielder of power, but also him who follows it. The authority of knowledge and experience is perverting, whether it be vested in the Master, his representative or the priest. It is your own life, this seemingly endless conflict, that is significant, and not the pattern or the leader. The authority of the Master and the priest takes you away from the central issue, which is the conflict within yourself. Suffering can never be understood and dissolved through the search for a way of life. Such a search is mere avoidance of suffering, the imposition of a pattern, which is escape; and what is avoided only festers, bringing more calamity and pain. The understanding of yourself, however painful or passingly pleasurable, is the beginning of wisdom.

There is no path to wisdom. If there is a path, then wisdom is the formulated, it is already imagined, known. Can wisdom be known or cultivated? Is it a thing to be learnt, to be accumulated? If it is, then it becomes mere knowledge, a thing of experience and of the books. Experience and knowledge are the continuous chain of responses and so can never comprehend the new, the fresh, the uncreated. Experience and knowledge, being continuous, make a path to their own self-projections, and hence they are constantly binding. Wisdom is the understanding of what *is* from moment to moment, without the accumulation of experience and knowledge. What is accumulated does not give freedom to understand, and without freedom there is no discovery; and it is this endless discovery that makes for wisdom. Wisdom is ever new, ever fresh, and there is no means of gathering it. The means destroys the freshness, the newness, the spontaneous discovery.

The many paths to one reality are the invention of an intolerant mind; they are the outcome of a mind that cultivates tolerance. "I follow my path, and you follow yours, but let us be friends, and we shall eventually meet." Will you and I meet if you are going north and I south? Can we be friendly if you have one set of beliefs and I another, if I am a collective murderer and you are peaceful? To be friendly implies relationship in work, in thought; but is there any relationship between the man who hates and the man who loves? Is there any relationship between the man in illusion and the one who is free? The free man may try to establish some kind of relationship with the one in bondage; but he who is in illusion can have no relationship with the man who is free.

The separate, clinging to their separateness, try to establish a relationship with others who are also self-enclosed; but such attempts invariably breed conflict and pain. To avoid this pain, the clever ones invent tolerance, each looking over his self-enclosing barrier and attempting to be kind and generous. Tolerance is of the mind, not of the heart. Do you talk of tolerance when you love? But when the heart is empty, then the mind fills it with its cunning devices and fears. There is no communion where there is tolerance.

There is no path to truth. Truth must be discovered, but there is no formula for its discovery. What is formulated is not true. You must set out on the uncharted sea, and the uncharted sea is yourself. You must set out to discover yourself, but not according to any plan or pattern, for then there is no discovery. Discovery brings joy—not the remembered, comparative joy, but joy that is ever new. Self-knowledge is the beginning of wisdom in whose tranquillity and silence there is the immeasurable.

AWARENESS

THERE WERE IMMENSE clouds, like billowy white waves, and the sky was serene and blue. Many hundreds of feet below where we stood was the blue curving bay, and far off was the mainland. It was a lovely evening, calm and free, and on the horizon was the smoke of a steamer. The orange groves stretched to the foot of the mountain, and their fragrance filled the air. The evening was turning blue, as it always did; the air itself became blue, and the white houses lost their brilliance in that delicate colour. The blue of the sea seemed to spill over and cover the land, and the mountains above were also a transparent blue. It was an enchanted scene, and there was immense silence. Though there were a few noises of the evening, they were within this silence, they were part of the silence, as we were too. This silence was making everything new, washing away the centuries of squalor and pain from the heart of things; one's eyes were cleansed, and the mind was of that silence. A donkey brayed; the echoes filled the valley, and the silence accepted them. The end of the day was the death of all yesterdays, and in this death there was a rebirth, without the sadness of the past. Life was new in the immensity of silence.

In the room a man was waiting, anxious to talk things over. He was peculiarly intense, but sat quietly. He was obviously a city-dweller, and his smart clothes made him seem rather out of place in that small village and in that room. He talked of his activities, the difficulties of his profession, the trivialities of family life, and the urgency of his desires. All these problems he could grapple with as intelligently as another; but what really bothered him were his sexual appetites. He was married and had children, but there was more to it. His sexual activities had become a very serious problem to him and were driving him almost crazy. He had talked to certain doctors and analysts, but the problem still existed and he must somehow get to the bottom of it.

How eager we are to solve our problems! How insistently we search for an answer, a way out, a remedy! We never consider the problem itself, but with agitation and anxiety grope for an answer which is invariably self-projected. Though the problem is self-created, we try to find an answer away from it. To look for an answer is to avoid the problem—which is just what most of us want to do. Then the answer becomes all-significant, and not the problem. The solution is not separate from the problem; the answer is *in* the problem, not away from it. If the answer is separate from the main issue, then we create other problems: the problem of how to realize the answer, how to carry it out, how to put it into practice, and so on. As the search for an answer is the avoidance of the problem, we get lost in ideals, convictions, experiences, which are self-projections; we worship these home-made idols and so get more and more confused and weary. To come to a conclusion is comparatively easy; but to understand a problem is arduous, it demands quite a different approach, an approach in which there is no lurking desire for an answer.

Freedom from the desire for an answer is essential to the understanding of a problem. This freedom gives the ease of full attention; the mind is not distracted by any secondary issues. As long as there is conflict with or opposition to the problem, there can be no understanding of it; for this conflict is a distraction. There is understanding only when there is communion, and communion is impossible as long as there is resistance or contention, fear or acceptance. One must establish right relationship with the problem, which is the beginning of understanding; but how can there be right relationship with a problem when you are only concerned with getting rid of it, which is to find a solution for it? Right relationship means communion, and communion cannot exist if there is positive or negative resistance. The approach to the problem is more important than the problem itself; the approach shapes the problem, the end. The means and the end are not different from the approach. The approach decides the fate of the problem. How you regard the problem is of the greatest importance, because your attitude and prejudices, your fears and hopes will colour it. Choiceless awareness of the manner of your approach will bring right relationship with the problem. The problem is self-created, so there must be self-knowledge. You and the problem are one, not two separate processes. You *are* the problem.

The activities of the self are frighteningly monotonous. The self is a bore; it is intrinsically enervating, pointless, futile. Its opposing and conflicting desires, its hopes and frustrations, its realities and illusions are enthralling, and yet empty; its activities lead to its own weariness. The self is ever climbing and ever falling down, ever pursuing and ever being frustrated, ever gaining and ever losing; and from this weary round of futility it is ever trying to escape. It escapes through outward activity or through gratifying illusions, through drink, sex, radio, books, knowledge, amusements, and so on. Its power to breed illusion is complex and vast. These illusions are home-made, self-projected; they are the ideal, the idolatrous conception of Masters and saviours, the future as a means of self-aggrandizement, and so on. In trying to escape from its own monotony, the self pursues inward and outward sensations and excitements. These are the substitutes for self-abnegation, and in the substitutes it hopefully tries to get lost. It often succeeds, but the success only increases its own weariness. It pursues one substitute after another, each creating its own problem, its own conflict and pain.

Self-forgetfulness is sought within and without; some turn to religion, and others to work and activity. But there is no means of forgetting the self. The inner or outward noise can suppress the self, but it soon comes up again in a different form, under a different guise; for what is suppressed must find a release. Self-forgetfulness through drink or sex, through worship or knowledge, makes for dependence, and that on which you depend creates a problem. If you depend for release, for self-forgetfulness, for happiness, on drink or on a Master, then they become your problem. Dependence breeds possessiveness, envy, fear; and then fear and the overcoming of it become your anxious problem. In the search for happiness we create problems, and in them we get caught. We find a certain happiness in the self-forgetfulness of sex, and so we use it as a means to achieve what we desire. Happiness *through* something must invariably beget conflict, for then the means is vastly more significant and important than happiness itself. If I get happiness through the beauty of that chair, then the chair becomes all-important to me and I must guard it against others. In this struggle, the happiness which I once felt in the beauty of the chair is utterly forgotten, lost, and I am left with the chair. In itself, the chair has little value; but I have given it an extraordinary value, for it is the means of my happiness. So the means becomes a substitute for happiness.

When the means of my happiness is a living person, then the conflict and confusion, the antagonism and pain are far greater. If relationship is based on mere usage, is there any relationship, except the most superficial, between the user and the used? If I use you for my happiness, am I really related to you? Relationship implies communion with another on different levels; and is there communion with another when he is only a tool, a means of my happiness? In thus using another, am I not really seeking self-isolation, in which I think I shall be happy? This self-isolation I call relationship; but actually there is no communion in this process. Communion can exist only where there is no fear; and there is gnawing fear and pain where there is usage and so dependence. As nothing can live in isolation, the attempts of the mind to isolate itself lead to its own frustration and misery. To escape from this sense of incompleteness, we seek completeness in ideas, in people, in things; and so we are back again where we started, in the search for substitutes.

Problems will always exist where the activities of the self are dominant. To be aware which are and which are not the activities of the self needs constant vigilance. This vigilance is not disciplined attention, but an extensive awareness which is choiceless. Disciplined attention gives strength to the self; it becomes a substitute and a dependence. Awareness, on the other hand, is not self-induced, nor is it the outcome of practice; it is understanding the whole content of the problem, the hidden as well as the superficial. The surface must be understood for the hidden to show itself; the hidden cannot be exposed if the surface mind is not quiet. This whole process is not verbal, nor is it a matter of mere experience. Verbalization indicates dullness of mind; and experience, being cumulative, makes for repetitiousness. Awareness is not a matter of determination, for purposive direction is resistance, which tends towards exclusiveness. Awareness is the silent and choiceless observation of what *is*; in this awareness the problem unrolls itself, and thus it is fully and completely understood.

A problem is never solved on its own level; being complex, it must be understood in its total process. To try to solve a problem on only one level, physical or psychological, leads to further conflict and confusion. For the resolution of a problem, there must be this awareness, this passive alertness which reveals its total process.

Love is not sensation. Sensations give birth to thought through words and symbols. Sensations and thought replace love; they become the substitute for love. Sensations are of the mind, as sexual appetites are. The mind breeds the appetite, the passion, through remembrance, from which it derives gratifying sensations. The mind is composed of different and conflicting interests or desires, with their exclusive sensations; and they clash when one or other begins to predominate, thus creating a problem. Sensations are both pleasant and unpleasant, and the mind holds to the pleasant, thus becoming a slave to them. This bondage becomes a problem because the mind is the repository of contradictory sensations. The avoidance of the painful is also a bondage, with its own illusions and problems. The mind is the maker of problems, and so cannot resolve them. Love is not of the mind; but when the mind takes over there is sensation, which it then calls love. It is this love of the mind that can be thought about, that can be clothed and identified. The mind can recall or anticipate pleasurable sensations, and this process is appetite, no matter at what level it is placed. Within the field of the mind, love cannot be. Mind is the area of fear and calculation, envy and domination, comparison and denial, and so love is not. Jealousy, like pride, is of the mind; but it is not love. Love and the processes of the mind cannot be bridged over, cannot be made one. When sensations predominate, there is no space for love; so the things of the mind fill the heart. Thus love becomes the unknown, to be pursued and worshipped; it is made into an ideal, to be used and believed in, and ideals are always self-projected. So the mind takes over completely, and love becomes a word, a sensation. Then love is made comparative, "I love more and you love less." But love is neither personal nor impersonal; love is a state of being in which sensation as thought is wholly absent.

HER SON HAD recently died, and she said she did not know what to do now. She had so much time on her hands, she was so bored and weary and sorrowful that she was ready to die. She had brought him up with loving care and intelligence, and he had gone to one of the best schools and to college. She had not spoiled him, though he had had everything that was necessary. She had put her faith and hope in him, and had given him all her love; for there was no one else to share it with, she and her husband having separated long ago. Her son had died through some wrong diagnosis and operation—though, she added smilingly, the doctors said that the operation was "successful." Now she was left alone, and life seemed so vain and pointless. She had wept when he died, until there were no more tears, but only a dull and weary emptiness. She had had such plans for both of them, but now she was utterly lost.

The breeze was blowing from the sea, cool and fresh, and under the tree it was quiet. The colours on the mountains were vivid, and the blue jays were very talkative. A cow wandered by, followed by her calf, and a squirrel dashed up a tree, wildly chattering. It sat on a branch and began to scold, and the scolding went on for a long time, its tail bobbing up and down. It had such sparkling bright eyes and sharp claws. A lizard came out to warm itself, and caught a fly. The tree tops were gently swaying, and a dead tree against the sky was straight and splendid. It was being bleached by the sun. There was another dead tree beside it, dark and curving, more recent in its decay. A few clouds rested on the distant mountains.

What a strange thing is loneliness, and how frightening it is! We never allow ourselves to get too close to it; and if by chance we do, we quickly run away from it. We will do anything to escape from loneliness, to cover it up. Our conscious and unconscious preoccupation seems to be to avoid it or to overcome it. Avoiding and overcoming loneliness are equally futile; though suppressed or neglected, the pain, the problem, is still there. You may lose yourself in a crowd, and yet be utterly lonely; you may be intensely active, but loneliness silently creeps upon you; put the book down, and it is there. Amusements and drinks cannot drown loneliness; you may temporarily evade it, but when the laughter and the effects of alcohol are over, the fear of loneliness returns. You may be ambitious and successful, you may have vast power over others, you may be rich in knowledge, you may worship and forget yourself in the rigmarole of rituals; but do what you will, the ache of loneliness continues. You may exist only for your son, for the Master, for the expression of your talent; but like the darkness, loneliness covers you. You may love or hate, escape from it according to your temperament and psychological demands; but loneliness is there, waiting and watching, withdrawing only to approach again.

Loneliness is the awareness of complete isolation; and are not our activities self-enclosing? Though our thoughts and emotions are expansive, are they not exclusive and dividing? Are we not seeking dominance in our relationships, in our rights and possessions, thereby creating resistance? Do we not regard work as "yours" and "mine"? Are we not identified with the collective, with the country, or with the few? Is not our whole tendency to isolate ourselves, to divide and separate? The very activity of the self, at whatever level, is the way of isolation; and loneliness is the consciousness of the self without activity. Activity, whether physical or psychological, becomes a means of self-expansion; and when there is no activity of any kind, there is an awareness of the emptiness of the self. It is this emptiness that we seek to fill, and in filling it we spend our life, whether at a noble or ignoble level. There may seem to be no sociological harm in filling this emptiness at a noble level; but illusion breeds untold misery and destruction, which may not be immediate. The craving to fill this emptiness—or to run away from it, which is the same thing— cannot be sublimated or suppressed; for who is the entity that is to suppress or sublimate? Is not that very entity another form of craving? The objects of craving may vary, but is not all craving similar? You may change the object of your craving from drink to ideation; but without understanding the process of craving, illusion is inevitable.

There is no entity separate from craving; there is only craving, there is no one who craves. Craving takes on different masks at different times, depending on its interests. The memory of these varying interests meets the new, which brings about conflict, and so the chooser is born, establishing himself as an entity separate and distinct from craving. But the entity is not different from its qualities. The entity who tries to fill or run away from emptiness, incompleteness, loneliness, is not different from that which he is avoiding; he *is* it. He cannot run away from himself; all that he can do is to understand himself. He *is* his loneliness, his emptiness; and as long as he regards it as something separate from himself, he will be in illusion and endless conflict. When he directly experiences that he is his own loneliness, then only can there be freedom from fear. Fear exists only in relationship to an idea, and idea is the response of memory as thought. Thought is the result of experience; and though it can ponder over emptiness, have sensations with regard to it, it cannot know emptiness directly. The word "loneliness," with its memories of pain and fear, prevents the experiencing of it afresh. The word is memory, and when the word is no longer significant, then the relationship between the experiencer and the experienced is wholly different; then that relationship is direct and not through a word, through memory; then the experiencer *is* the experience, which alone brings freedom from fear.

Love and emptiness cannot abide together; when there is the feeling of loneliness, love is not. You may hide emptiness under the word "love," but when the object of your love is no longer there or does not respond, then you are aware of emptiness, you are frustrated. We use the word "love" as a means of escaping from ourselves, from our own insufficiency. We cling to the one we love, we are jealous, we miss him when he is not there and are utterly lost when he dies; and then we seek comfort in some other form, in some belief, in some substitute. Is all this love? Love is not an idea, the result of association; love is not something to be used as an escape from our own wretchedness; and when we *do* so use it, we make problems which have no solutions. Love is not an abstraction, but its reality can be experienced only when idea, mind, is no longer the supreme factor.

CONSISTENCY

HE WAS OBVIOUSLY intelligent, active, and given to reading a few select books. Though married, he was not a family man. He called himself an idealist and a social worker; he had been to prison for political reasons, and had many friends. He was not concerned with making a name either for himself or for the party, which he recognized as the same thing. He was really interested in doing social work which might lead to some human happiness. He was what you might call a religious man, but not sentimental or superstitious, nor a believer in any particular doctrine or ritual. He said he had come to talk over the problem of contradiction, not only within himself but in Nature and in the world. It seemed to him that this contradiction was inevitable : the intelligent and the stupid, the conflicting desires within oneself, the word in conflict with the act and the act with the thought. This contradiction he had found everywhere.

To be consistent is to be thoughtless. It is easier and safer to follow a pattern of conduct without deviation, to conform to an ideology or a tradition, than to risk the pain of thought. To obey authority, inner or outer, needs no questioning; it obviates thought, with its anxieties and disturbances. To follow our own conclusions, experiences, determinations, creates no contradictions within us; we are being consistent to our own purpose; we choose a particular path and follow it, unyielding and determined. Do not most of us seek a way of life which is not too disturbing, in which at least there is psychological security? And how we respect a man who lives up to his ideal! We make examples of such men, they are to be followed and worshipped. The approximation to an ideal, though it requires a certain amount of exertion and struggle, is on the whole pleasurable and gratifying; for after all, ideals are home-made, self-projected. You choose your hero, religious or worldly, and follow him. The desire to be consistent gives a peculiar strength and satisfaction, for in sincerity there is security. But sincerity is not simplicity, and without simplicity there can be no understanding. To be consistent to a well-thought-out pattern of conduct gratifies the urge for achievement, and in its success there is comfort and security. The setting up of an ideal and the constant approximation to it cultivates resistance, and adaptability is within the limits of the pattern. Consistency offers safety and certainty, and that is why we cling to it with desperation.

To be in self-contradiction is to live in conflict and sorrow. The self, in its very structure, is contradictory; it is made up of many entities with different masks, each in opposition to the others. The whole fabric of the self is the result of contradictory interests and values, of many varying desires at different levels of its being; and these desires all beget their own opposites. The self, the "me," is a network of complex desires, each desire having its own impetus and aim, often in opposition to other hopes and pursuits. These masks are taken on according to stimulating circumstances and sensations; so within the structure of the self, contradiction is inevitable. This contradiction within us breeds illusion and pain, and to escape from it we resort to all manner of self-deceptions which only increase our conflict and misery. When the inner contradiction becomes unbearable, consciously or unconsciously we try to escape through death, through insanity; or we give ourselves over to an idea, to a group, to a country, to some activity that will completely absorb our being; or we turn to organized religion, with its dogmas and rituals. So this split in ourselves leads either to further self-expansion or to self-destruction, insanity. Trying to be other than what we are cultivates contradiction; the fear of what *is* breeds the illusion of its opposite, and in the pursuit of the opposite we hope to escape from fear. Synthesis is not the cultivation of the opposite; synthesis does not come about through opposition, for all opposites contain the elements of their own opposites. The contradiction in ourselves leads to every kind of physical and psychological response, whether gentle or violent, respectable or dangerous; and consistency only further confuses and obscures the contradiction. The one-pointed pursuit of a single desire, of a particular interest, leads to self-enclosing opposition. Contradiction within brings conflict without, and conflict indicates contradiction. Only through understanding the ways of desire is there freedom from self-contradiction.

Integration can never be limited to the upper layers of the mind; it is not something to be learnt in a school; it does not come into being with knowledge or with self-immolation. Integration alone brings freedom from consistency and contradiction; but integration is not a matter of fusing into one all desires and multiple interests. Integration is not conformity to a pattern, however noble and cunning; it must be approached, not directly, positively, but obliquely, negatively. To have a conception of integration is to conform to a pattern, which only cultivates stupidity and destruction. To pursue integration is to make of it an ideal, a self-projected goal. Since all ideals are self-projected, they inevitably cause conflict and enmity. What the self projects must be of its own nature, and therefore contradictory and confusing. Integration is not an idea, a mere response of memory, and so it cannot be cultivated. The desire for integration comes into being because of conflict; but through cultivating integration, conflict is not transcended. You may cover up, deny contradiction, or be unconscious of it; but it is there, waiting to break out.

Conflict is our concern, and not integration. Integration, like peace, is a by-product, not an end in itself; it is merely a result, and so of secondary importance. In understanding conflict there will not only be integration and peace, but something infinitely greater. Conflict cannot be suppressed or sublimated, nor is there a substitute for it. Conflict comes with craving, with the desire to continue, to become more—which does not mean that there must be stagnating contentment. "More" is the constant cry of the self; it is the craving for sensation, whether of the past or of the future. Sensation is of the mind, and so the mind is not the instrument for the understanding of conflict. Understanding is not verbal, it is not a mental process, and therefore not a matter of experience. Experience is memory, and without word, symbol, image, there is no memory. You may read volumes about conflict, but it can have nothing to do with the understanding of conflict. To understand conflict, thought must not interfere; there must be an awareness of conflict without the thinker. The thinker is the chooser who invariably takes sides with the pleasant, the gratifying, and thereby sustains conflict; he may get rid of one particular conflict, but the soil is there for further conflict. The thinker justifies or condemns, and so prevents understanding. With the thinker absent, there is the direct experiencing of conflict, but not as an experience which an experiencer is undergoing. In the state of experiencing there is neither the experiencer nor the experienced. Experiencing is direct; then relationship is direct, and not through memory. It is this direct relationship that brings understanding. Understanding brings freedom from conflict; and with freedom from conflict there is integration.

ACTION AND IDEA

HE WAS MILD and gentle, with a ready and pleasant smile. He was dressed very simply, and his manner was quiet and unobtrusive. He said that he had practised non-violence for many years and was well aware of its power and spiritual significance. He had written several books concerning it, and had brought one of them along. He explained that he had not voluntarily killed anything for many years, and was a strict vegetarian. He went into the details of his vegetarianism, and said that his shoes and sandals were made from the hides of animals that had died naturally. He had made his life as simple as possible, had studied dietetics and ate only what was essential. He asserted that he had not been angry for several years now, though he was on occasions impatient, which was merely the response of his nerves.

His speech was controlled and gentle. The power of non-violence would transform the world, he said, and he had dedicated his life to it. He was not the kind of man who talked about himself easily, but on the subject of non-violence he was quite eloquent and words seemed to flow without effort. He had come, he added, to go more deeply into his favourite subject.

Across the way, the large pool was tranquil. Its waters had been very agitated, as there had been a strong breeze; but now it was quite still and was reflecting the large leaves of a tree. One or two lilies floated quietly on its surface, and a bud was just showing itself above the water. Birds began to come, and several frogs came out and jumped into the pool. The ripples soon died away, and once more the waters were still. On the very top of a tall tree sat a bird, preening itself and singing; it would fly in a curve and come back to its high and solitary perch; it was so delighted with the world and with itself. Nearby sat a fat man with a book, but his mind was far away; he would try to read, but his mind raced off again and again. Ultimately he gave up the struggle and let the mind have its way. A lorry was coming up the hill slowly and wearily, and again the gears had to be changed.

We are so concerned with the reconciliation of effects, with the outward gesture and appearance. We seek first to bring about outward order; outwardly we regulate our life according to our resolutions, the inner principles that we have established. Why do we force the outer to conform to the inner? Why do we act according to an idea? Is idea stronger, more powerful than action?

The idea is first established, reasoned out or intuitively felt, and then we try to approximate action to the idea; we try to live up to it, put it into practice, discipline ourselves in the light of it—the everlasting struggle to bring action within the limits of idea. Why is there this incessant and painful struggle to shape action according to idea? What is the urge to make the outer conform to the inner? Is it to strengthen the inner, or to gain assurance from the outer when the inner is uncertain? In deriving comfort from the outer, does not the outer assume greater significance and importance? The outer reality has significance; but when it is looked upon as a gesture of sincerity, does it not indicate more than ever that idea is dominant? Why has idea become all-powerful? To make us act? Does idea help us to act, or does it hinder action?

Surely, idea limits action; it is the fear of action that brings forth idea. In idea there is safety, in action there is danger. To control action, which is limitless, idea is cultivated; to put a brake on action, idea comes into being. Think what would happen if you were really generous in action! So you have the generosity of the heart opposed by the generosity of the mind; you go so far only, for you do not know what will happen to you tomorrow. Idea governs action. Action is full, open, extensive; and fear, as idea, steps in and takes charge. So idea becomes all-important, and not action.

We try to make action conform to idea. The idea or ideal is non-violence, and our actions, gestures, thoughts are moulded according to that pattern of the mind; what we eat, what we wear, what we say, becomes very significant, for by it we judge our sincerity. Sincerity becomes important, and not being non-violent; your sandals and what you eat become consumingly interesting, and being non-violent is forgotten. Idea is always secondary, and the secondary issues dominate the primary. You can write, lecture, gossip about idea; there is great scope in idea for self-expansion, but there is no self-expansive gratification in being non-violent. Idea, being self-projected, is stimulating and gratifying, positively or negatively; but being non-violent has no glamour. Non-violence is a result, a by-product, and not an end in itself. It is an end in itself only when idea predominates. Idea is always a conclusion, an end, a self-projected goal. Idea is movement within the known; but thought cannot formulate what it is to be non-violent. Thought can ponder over non-violence, but it cannot be non-violent. Non-violence is not an idea; it cannot be made into a pattern of action.

IT WAS A well-proportioned room, quiet and restful. The furniture was elegant and in very good taste; the carpet was thick and soft. There was a marble fireplace, with a fire in it. There were old vases from different parts of the world, and on the walls were modern paintings as well as some by the old masters. Considerable thought and care had been spent on the beauty and comfort of the room, which reflected wealth and taste. The room overlooked a small garden, with a lawn that must have been mowed and rolled for many, many years.

Life in a city is strangely cut off from the universe; man-made buildings have taken the place of valleys and mountains, and the roar of traffic has been substituted for that of boisterous streams. At night one hardly ever sees the stars, even if one wishes to, for the city lights are too bright; and during the day the sky is limited and held. Something definitely happens to the city-dwellers; they are brittle and polished, they have churches and museums, drinks and theatres, beautiful clothes and endless shops. There are people everywhere, on the streets, in the buildings, in the rooms. A cloud passes across the sky, and so few look up. There is rush and turmoil.

But in this room there was quiet and sustained dignity. It had that atmosphere peculiar to the rich, the feeling of aloof security and assurance, and the long freedom from want. He was saying that he was interested in philosophy, both of the East and of the West, and how absurd it was to begin with the Greeks, as though nothing existed before them; and presently he began to talk of his problem : how to give, and to whom to give. The problem of having money, with its many responsibilities, was somewhat disturbing him. Why was he making a problem of it? Did it matter to whom he gave, and with what spirit? Why had it become a problem?

His wife came in, smart, bright and curious. Both of them seemed well read, sophisticated and worldly wise; they were clever and interested in many things. They were the product of both town and country, but mostly their hearts were in the town. That one thing, compassion, seemed so far away. The qualities of the mind were deeply cultivated; there was a sharpness, a brutal approach, but it did not go very far. She wrote a little, and he was some kind of politician; and how easily and confidently they spoke. Hesitancy is so essential to discovery, to further understanding; but how can there be hesitancy when you know so much, when the self-protective armour is so highly polished and all the cracks are sealed from within? Line and form become extraordinarily important to those who are in bondage to the sensate; then beauty is sensation, goodness a feeling, and truth a matter of intellection. When sensations dominate, comfort becomes essential, not only to the body, but also to the psyche; and comfort, especially that of the mind, is corroding, leading to illusion.

We *are* the things we possess, we *are* that to which we are attached. Attachment has no nobility. Attachment to knowledge is not different from any other gratifying addiction. Attachment is self-absorption, whether at the lowest or at the highest level. Attachment is self-deception, it is an escape from the hollowness of the self. The things to which we are attached—property, people, ideas—become all-important, for without the many things which fill its emptiness, the self is not. The fear of not being makes for possession; and fear breeds illusion, the bondage to conclusions. Conclusions, material or ideational, prevent the fruition of intelligence, the freedom in which alone reality can come into being; and without this freedom, cunning is taken for intelligence. The ways of cunning are always complex and destructive. It is this self-protective cunning that makes for attachment; and when attachment causes pain, it is this same cunning that seeks detachment and finds pleasure in the pride and vanity of renunciation. The understanding of the ways of cunning, the ways of the self, is the beginning of intelligence.

Obsession

He said he was obsessed by stupid little things, and that these obsessions constantly changed. He would worry over some imaginary physical defect, and within a few hours his worry would have fixed itself upon another incident or thought. He seemed to live from one anxious obsession to another. To overcome these obsessions, he continued, he would consult books, or talk over his problem with a friend, and he had also been to a psychologist; but somehow he had found no relief. Even after a serious and absorbing meeting, these obsessions would immediately come on. If he found the cause, would it put an end to them?

Does discovery of a cause bring freedom from the effect? Will knowledge of the cause destroy the result? We know the causes, both economic and psychological, of war, yet we encourage barbarity and self-destruction. After all, our motive in searching for the cause is the desire to be rid of the effect. This desire is another form of resistance or condemnation; and when there is condemnation, there is no understanding.

"Then what is one to do?" he asked.

Why is the mind dominated by these trivial and stupid obsessions? To ask "why" is not to search for the cause as something apart from yourself which you have to find; it is merely to uncover the ways of your own thinking. So, why is the mind occupied in this manner? Is it not because it is superficial, shallow, petty, and therefore concerned with its own attractions?

"Yes," he replied, "that appears to be true; but not entirely, for I am a serious person."

Apart from these obsessions, what is your thought occupied with?

"With my profession," he said. "I have a responsible position. The whole day and sometimes far into the night, my thoughts are taken up with my business. I read occasionally, but most of my time is spent with my profession."

Do you like what you are doing?

"Yes, but it is not completely satisfactory. All my life I have been dissatisfied with what I am doing, but I cannot give up my present position, for I have certain obligations—and besides, I am getting on in years. What bothers me are these obsessions, and my increasing resentment towards' my work as well as towards people. I have not been kind; I feel increasing anxiety about the future, and I never seem to have any peace. I do my work well, but . . ."

Why are you struggling against what *is*? The house in which I live may be noisy, dirty, the furniture may be hideous, and there may be an utter lack of beauty about the whole thing; but for various reasons I may have to live there, I cannot go away to another house. It is then not a question of acceptance, but of seeing the obvious fact. If I do not see what *is*, I shall worry myself sick about that vase, about that chair or that picture; they will become my obsessions, and there will be resentment against people, against my work, and so on. If I could leave the whole thing and start over again, it would be a different matter; but I cannot. It is no good my rebelling against what *is*, the actual. The recognition of what *is* does not lead to smug contentment and ease. When I yield to what *is*, there is not only the understanding of it, but there also comes a certain quietness to the surface mind. If the surface mind is not quiet, it indulges in obsessions, actual or imaginary; it gets caught up in some social reform or religious conclusion : the Master, the saviour, the ritual, and so on. It is only when the surface mind is quiet that the hidden can reveal itself. The hidden must be exposed; but this is not possible if the surface mind is burdened with obsessions, worries. Since the surface mind is constantly in some kind of agitation, conflict is inevitable between the upper and the deeper levels of the mind; and as long as this conflict is not resolved, obsessions increase. After all, obsessions are a means of escape from our conflict. All escapes are similar, though it is obvious that some are socially more harmful.

When one is aware of the total process of obsession or of any other problem, only then is there freedom from the problem. To be extensively aware, there must be no condemnation or justification of the problem; awareness must be choiceless. To be so aware demands wide patience and sensitivity; it requires eagerness and sustained attention so that the whole process of thinking can be observed and understood.

THE SPIRITUAL LEADER

HE SAID THAT his *guru* was too great a man to be described, and that he had been a pupil of his for many years. This teacher, he went on, imparted his teachings through brutal shocks, through foul language, through insults and actions that were contradictory; and he added that many important people were among the followers. The very crudeness of the procedure forced people to think, it made them sit up and take notice, which was considered necessary because most people were asleep and needed to be shaken. This teacher said the most awful things about God, and it seemed that his pupils had to drink a great deal, as the teacher himself drank heavily at most meals. The teachings, however, were profound; they had been kept secret at one time, but now they were being made available to all.

The late autumnal sun was pouring in through the window, and one could hear the roar of the busy street. The leaves in their death were brilliant, and the air was fresh and keen. As with all cities, there was an atmosphere of depression and unnamable sorrow in contrast to the light of the evening; and the artificial gaiety was even more sorrowful. We seem to have forgotten what it is to be natural, to smile freely; our faces are so closed with worry and anxiety. But the leaves sparkled in the sun and a cloud passed by.

Even in so-called spiritual movements the social divisions are maintained. How eagerly a titled person is welcomed and given the front seat! How the followers hang around the famous! How hungry we are for distinctions and labels! This craving for distinction becomes what we call spiritual growth : those who are near and those who are far, the hierarchical division as the Master and the initiate, the pupil and the novice. This craving is obvious and somewhat understandable in the everyday world; but when the same attitude is carried over into a world where these stupid distinctions have no meaning whatever, it reveals how deeply we are conditioned by our cravings and appetites. Without understanding these cravings, it is utterly vain to seek to be free from pride.

"But," he continued, "we need guides, *gurus*, Masters. You may be beyond them, but we ordinary people need them, otherwise we shall be like lost sheep."

We choose our leaders, political or spiritual, out of our own confusion, and so they also are confused. We demand to be coaxed and comforted, to be encouraged and gratified, so we choose a teacher who will give us what we crave for. We do not search out reality, but go after gratification and sensation. It is essentially for self-glorification that we create the teacher, the Master; and we feel lost, confused and anxious when the self is denied. If you have no direct physical teacher, you fabricate one who is far away, hidden and mysterious; the former is dependent on various physical and emotional influences, and the latter is self-projected, a home-made ideal; but both are the outcome of your choice, and choice is inevitably based on bias, prejudice. You may prefer to give a more respectable and comforting name to your prejudice, but it is out of your confusion and appetites that you choose. If you are seeking gratification, you will naturally find what you desire, but do not let us call it truth. Truth comes into being when gratification, the desire for sensation, comes to an end.

"You have not convinced me that I do not need a Master," he said.

Truth is not a matter of argumentation and conviction; it is not the outcome of opinion.

"But the Master helps me to overcome my greed, my envy," he insisted.

Can another, however great, help to bring about a transformation in you? If he can, you are not transformed; you are merely dominated, influenced. This influence may last a considerable time, but you are not transformed. You have been overcome; and whether you are overcome by envy or by a so-called noble influence, you are still a slave, you are not free. We like to be slavish, to be possessed by someone, whether by a Master or by anyone else, because there is security in this possession; the Master becomes the refuge. To possess is to be possessed, but possession is not freedom from greed.

"I must resist greed," he said. "I must fight it, make every effort to destroy it, and only then will it go."

From what you say, you have been in conflict with greed for a great many years, and yet you are not free from it. Do not say that you have not tried hard enough, which is the obvious response. Can you understand anything through conflict? To conquer is not to understand. What you conquer has to be conquered again and again, but there is freedom from that which is fully understood. To understand, there must be awareness of the process of resistance. To resist is so much easier than to understand; and besides, we are educated to resist. In resistance there need be no observation, no consideration, no communication; resistance is an indication of the dullness of the mind. A mind that resists is self-enclosed and so is incapable of sensitivity, of understanding. To understand the ways of resistance is far more important than to get rid of greed. Actually, you are not listening to what is being said ; you are considering your various commitments which have grown out of your years of struggle and resistance. You are now committed, and around your commitments, which you have probably lectured and written about, you have gathered friends; you have an investment in your Master, who has helped you to resist. So your past is preventing you from listening to what is being said.

"I both agree and disagree with you," he remarked.

Which shows that you are not listening. You are weighing your commitments against what is being said, which is not to listen. You are afraid to listen and so you are in conflict, agreeing and at the same time disagreeing.

"You are probably right," he said, "but I cannot let go of all that I have gathered : my friends, my knowledge, my experience.

I know that I must let go, but I simply cannot, and there it is."

The conflict within him will now be greater than ever; for when once you are aware of what *is*, however reluctantly, and deny it because of your commitments, deep contradiction is set going. This contradiction is duality. There can be no bridging over of opposing desires; and if a bridge is created, it is resistance, which is consistency. Only in understanding what *is* is there freedom from what *is*.

It is an odd fact that followers like to be bullied and directed, whether softly or harshly. They think the harsh treatment is part of their training—training in spiritual success. The desire to be hurt, to be rudely shaken, is part of the pleasure of hurting; and this mutual degradation of the leader and the follower is the outcome of the desire for sensation. It is because you want greater sensation that you follow and so create a leader, a *guru*; and for this new gratification you will sacrifice, put up with discomfort, insults and discouragements. All this is part of mutual exploitation, it has nothing whatever to do with reality and will never lead to happiness.

STIMULATION

"The mountains have made me silent," she said. "I went to the Engadine and its beauty made me utterly silent; I was speechless at the wonder of it all. It was a tremendous experience. I wish I could hold that silence, that living, vibrant, moving silence. When you talk of silence, I suppose you mean this extraordinary experience I have had. I really would like to know if you are referring to the same quality of silence as I experienced. The effect of this silence lasted for a considerable period, and now I go back to it, I try to recapture and live in it."

You are made silent by the Engadine, another by a beautiful human form, and another by a Master, by a book, or by drink. Through outward stimulation one is reduced to a sensation which one calls silence and which is extremely pleasurable. The effect of beauty and grandeur is to drive away one's daily problems and conflicts, which is a release. Through outward stimulation, the mind is made temporarily quiet; it is perhaps a new experience, a new delight, and the mind goes back to it as a remembrance when it is no longer experiencing it. To remain in the mountains is probably not possible, as one has to be back for business; but it *is* possible to seek that state of quietness through some other form of stimulation, through drink, through a person, or through an idea, which is what most of us do. These various forms of stimulation are the means through which the mind is made still; so the means become significant, important, and we become attached to them. Because the means give us the pleasure of silence, they become dominant in our lives; they are our vested interest, a psychological necessity which we defend and for which, if necessary, we destroy each other. The means take the place of experience, which is now only a memory.

Stimulations may vary, each having a significance according to the conditioning of the person. But there is a similarity in all stimulations : the desire to escape from what *is*, from our daily routine, from a relationship that is no longer alive, and from knowledge which is always becoming stale. You choose one kind of escape, I another, and my particular brand is always assumed to be more worth while than yours; but all escape, whether in the form of an ideal, the cinema, or the church, is harmful, leading to illusion and mischief. Psychological escapes are more harmful than the obvious ones, being more subtle and complex and therefore more difficult to discover. The silence that is brought about through stimulation, the silence that is made up through disciplines, controls, resistances, positive or negative, is a result, an effect, and so not creative; it is dead.

There is a silence which is not a reaction, a result; a silence which is not the outcome of stimulation, of sensation; a silence which is not put together, not a conclusion. It comes into being when the process of thought is understood. Thought is the response of memory, of determined conclusions, conscious or unconscious; this memory dictates action according to pleasure and pain. So ideas control action, and hence there is conflict between action and idea. This conflict is always with us, and as it intensifies there is an urge to be free from it; but until this conflict is understood and resolved, any attempt to be free from it is an escape. As long as action is approximating to an idea, conflict is inevitable. Only when action is free from idea does conflict cease.

"But how can action ever be free from idea? Surely there can be no action without there being ideation first. Action follows idea, and I cannot possibly imagine any action which is not the result of idea."

Idea is the outcome of memory; idea is the verbalization of memory; idea is an inadequate reaction to challenge, to life. Adequate response to life is action, not ideation. We respond ideationally in order to safeguard ourselves against action. Ideas limit action. There is safety in the field of ideas, but not in action; so action is made subservient to idea. Idea is the self-protective pattern for action. In intense crisis there is direct action, freed from idea. It is against this spontaneous action that the mind has disciplined itself; and as with most of us the mind is dominant, ideas act as a brake on action and hence there is friction between action and ideation.

"I find my mind wandering off to that happy experience of the Engadine. Is it an escape to relive that experience in memory?"

Obviously. The actual is your life in the present : this crowded street, your business, your immediate relationships. If these were pleasing and gratifying, the Engadine would fade away; but as the actual is confusing and painful, you turn to an experience which is over and dead. You may remember that experience, but it is finished; you give it life only through memory. It is like pumping life into a dead thing. The present being dull, shallow, we turn to the past or look to a self-projected future. This escape from the present inevitably leads to illusion. To see the present as it actually is, without condemnation or justification, is to understand what *is*, and then there is action which brings about a transformation in what *is*.

Problems and Escapes

"I HAVE MANY serious problems, and I seem to make them more tortuous and painful by trying to solve them. I am at my wit's end, and I do not know what to do. Added to all this, I am deaf and have to use this beastly thing as an aid to my hearing. I have several children and a husband who has left me. I am really concerned over my children, as I want them to avoid all the miseries I have been through."

How anxious we are to find an answer to our problems! We are so eager to find an answer that we cannot study the problem; it prevents our silent observation of the problem. The problem is the important thing, and not the answer. If we look for an answer, we will find it; but the problem will persist, for the answer is irrelevant to the problem. Our search is for an escape from the problem, and the solution is a superficial remedy, so there is no understanding of the problem. All problems arise from one source, and without understanding the source, any attempt to solve the problems will only lead to further confusion and misery. One must first be very clear that one's intention to understand the problem is serious, that one sees the necessity of being free of all problems; for only then can the maker of problems be approached. Without freedom from problems, there can be no tranquillity; and tranquillity is essential for happiness, which is not an end in itself. As the pool is still when the breezes stop, so the mind is still with the cessation of problems. But the mind cannot be *made* still; if it is, it is dead, it is a stagnant pool. When this is clear, then the maker of problems can be observed. The observation must be silent and not according to any predetermined plan based on pleasure and pain.

"But you are asking the impossible! Our education trains the mind to distinguish, to compare, to judge, to choose, and it is very difficult not to condemn or justify what is observed. How can one be free of this conditioning and observe silently?"

If you see that silent observation, passive awareness is essential for understanding, then the truth of your perception liberates you from the background. It is only when you do not see the immediate necessity of passive and yet alert awareness that the "how," the search for a means to dissolve the background, arises. It is truth that liberates, not the means or the system. The truth that silent observation alone brings understanding, must be seen; then only are you free from condemnation and justification. When you see danger, you do not ask how you are to keep away from it. It is because you do not see the necessity of being passively aware that you ask "how." Why do you not see the necessity of it?

"I want to, but I have never thought along these lines before. All I can say is that I want to get rid of my problems, because they are a real torture to me. I want to be happy, like any other person."

Consciously or unconsciously we refuse to see the essentiality of being passively aware because we do not really want to let go of our problems; for what would we be without them? We would rather cling to something we know, however painful, than risk the pursuit of something that may lead who knows where. With the problems, at least, we are familiar; but the thought of pursuing the maker of them, not knowing where it may lead, creates in us fear and dullness. The mind would be lost without the worry of problems; it feeds on problems, whether they are world or kitchen problems, political or personal, religious or ideological; so our problems make us petty and narrow. A mind that is consumed with world problems is as petty as the mind that worries about the spiritual progress it is making. Problems burden the mind with fear, for problems give strength to the self, to the "me" and the "mine." Without problems, without achievements and failures, the self is not.

"But without the self, how can one exist at all? It is the source of all action."

As long as action is the outcome of desire, of memory, of fear, of pleasure and pain, it must inevitably breed conflict, confusion and antagonism. Our action is the outcome of our conditioning, at whatever level; and our response to challenge, being inadequate and incomplete, must produce conflict, which is the problem. Conflict is the very structure of the self. It is entirely possible to live without conflict, the conflict of greed, of fear, of success; but this possibility will be merely theoretical and not actual until it is discovered through direct experiencing. To exist without greed is possible only when the ways of the self are understood.

"Do you think my deafness is due to my fears and repressions? Doctors have assured me that there is nothing structurally wrong, and is there any possibility of recovering my hearing? I have been suppressed, in one way or another, all my life; I have never done anything that I really wanted to do."

Inwardly and outwardly it is easier to repress than to understand. To understand is arduous, especially for those who have been heavily conditioned from childhood. Although strenuous, repression becomes a matter of habit. Understanding can never be made into a habit, a matter of routine; it demands constant watchfulness, alertness. To understand, there must be pliability, sensitivity, a warmth that has nothing to do with sentimentality. Suppression in any form needs no quickening of awareness; it is the easiest and the stupidest way to deal with responses. Suppression is conformity to an idea, to a pattern, and it offers superficial security, respectability. Understanding is liberating, but suppression is always narrowing, self-enclosing. Fear of authority, of insecurity, of opinion, builds up an ideological refuge, with its physical counterpart, to which the mind turns. This refuge, at whatever level it may be placed, ever sustains fear; and from fear there is substitution, sublimation or discipline, which are all a form of repression. Repression must find an outlet, which may be a physical ailment or some kind of ideological illusion. The price is paid according to one's temperament and idiosyncrasies.

"I have noticed that whenever there is something unpleasant to be heard, I take refuge behind this instrument, which thereby helps me to escape into my own world. But how is one to be free from the repression of years? Will it not take a long time?"

It is not a question of time, of dredging into the past, or of careful analysis; it is a matter of seeing the truth of repression. By being passively aware, without any choice, of the whole process of repression, the truth of it is immediately seen. The truth of repression cannot be discovered if we think in terms of yesterday and tomorrow; truth is not to be comprehended through the passage of time. Truth is not a thing to be attained; it is seen or it is not seen, it cannot be perceived gradually. The will to be free from repression is a hindrance to understanding the truth of it; for will is desire, whether positive or negative, and with desire there can be no passive awareness. It is desire or craving that brought about the repression; and this same desire, though now called will, can never free itself from its own creation. Again, the truth of will must be perceived through passive yet alert awareness. The analyser, though he may separate himself from it, is part of the analysed; and as he is conditioned by the thing he analyses, he cannot free himself from it. Again, the truth of this must be seen. It is truth that liberates, not will and effort.

WHAT *IS* AND WHAT *SHOULD* BE

"I AM MARRIED and have children," she said, "but I seem to have lost all love. I am slowly drying up. Although I engage in social activities, they are a kind of pastime, and I see their futility. Nothing seems to interest me deeply and fully. I recently took a long holiday from my family routine and social activities, and I tried to paint; but my spirit was not in it. I feel utterly dead, uncreative, depressed and deeply discontented. I am still young, but the future seems to be complete blackness. I have thought of suicide, but somehow I see the utter stupidity of it. I am getting more and more confused, and my discontent seems to have no end."

What are you confused about? Is your problem that of relationship?

"No, it is not. I have been through that, and have come out of it not too bruised; but I am confused and nothing seems to satisfy me."

Have you a definite problem, or are you merely discontented generally? There must be deep down some anxiety, some fear, and probably you are not aware of it. Do you want to know what it is?

"Yes, that is why I have come to you. I really cannot go on the way I am. Nothing seems to be of any importance, and I get quite ill periodically."

Your illness may be an escape from yourself, from your circumstances.

"I am pretty sure it is. But what am I to do? I am really quite desperate. Before I leave I must find a way out of all this."

Is the conflict between two actualities, or between the actual and the fictitious? Is your discontent mere dissatisfaction, which is easily gratified, or is it a causeless misery? Dissatisfaction soon finds a particular channel through which it is gratified; dissatisfaction is quickly canalized, but discontent cannot be assuaged by thought. Does this so-called discontent arise from not finding satisfaction? If you found satisfaction, would your discontent disappear? Is it that you are really seeking some kind of permanent gratification?

"No, it is not that. I am really not seeking any kind of gratification—at least I do not think I am. All I know is that I am in confusion and conflict, and I cannot seem to find a way out of it."

When you say you are in conflict, it must be in relation to something: in relation to your husband, to your children, to your activities. If, as you say, your conflict is not with any of these, then it can only be between what you *are* and what you *want* to be, between the actual and the ideal, between what *is* and the myth of what *should* be. You have an idea of what you should be, and perhaps the conflict and confusion arise from the desire to fit into this self-projected pattern. You are struggling to be something which you are not. Is that it?

"I am beginning to see where I am confused. I think what you say is true."

The conflict is between the actual and the myth, between that which you are and that which you would like to be. The pattern of the myth has been cultivated from childhood and has progressively widened and deepened, growing in contrast to the actual, and being constantly modified by circumstances. This myth, like all ideals, goals, Utopias, is in contradiction to what *is,* the implicit, the actual; so the myth is an escape from that which you are. This escape inevitably creates the barren conflict of the opposites; and all conflict, inward or outward, is vain, futile, stupid, creating confusion and antagonism.

So, if I may say so, your confusion arises from the conflict between what you are and the myth of what you should be. The myth, the ideal, is unreal; it is a self-projected escape, it has no actuality. The actual is what you are. What you are is much more important than what you should be. You can understand what *is,* but you cannot understand what *should* be. There is no understanding of an illusion, there is only understanding of the way it comes into being. The myth, the fictitious, the ideal, has no validity; it is a result, an end, and what is important is to understand the process through which it has come into being.

To understand that which you are, whether pleasant or unpleasant, the myth, the ideal, the self-projected future state, must entirely cease. Then only can you tackle what *is.* To understand what *is,* there must be freedom from all distraction. Distraction is the condemnation or justification of what *is.* Distraction is comparison; it is resistance or discipline against the actual. Distraction is the very effort or compulsion to understand. All distractions are a hindrance to the swift pursuit of what *is.* What *is* is not static; it is in constant movement, and to follow it the mind must not be tethered to any belief, to any hope of success or fear of failure. Only in passive yet alert awareness can that which *is* unfold. This unfoldment is not of time.

CONTRADICTION

HE WAS A well-known and well-established politician, somewhat arrogant, and hence his impatience. Highly educated, he was rather ponderous and tortuous in his expositions. He could not afford to be subtle, for he was too much involved with appeasement; he was the public, the State, the power. He was a fluent speaker, and the very fluency was its own misfortune; he was incorruptible, and therein lay his hold on the public. He was oddly uncomfortable sitting in that room; the politician was far away, but the man was there, nervous and aware of himself. The bluster, the cocksureness was gone, and there was anxious inquiry, consideration and self-exposure.

The late afternoon sun was coming through the window, and so also the noise of the traffic. The parrots, bright green flashes of light, were returning from their day's outing to settle for the night in safety among the trees of the town, those very large trees that are found along roads and in private gardens. As they flew, the parrots uttered hideous screeches. They never flew in a straight line but dropped, rose, or moved sideways, always chattering and calling. Their flight and their cries were in contradiction to their own beauty. Far away on the sea there was a single white sail. A small group of people filled the room, a contrast of colour and thought. A little dog came in, looked around and went out, scarcely noticed; and a temple bell was ringing.

"Why is there contradiction in our life?" he asked. "We talk of the ideals of peace, of non-violence, and yet lay the foundation stone of war. We must be realists and not dreamers. We want peace, and yet our daily activities ultimately lead to war; we want light, and yet we close the window. Our very thought process is a contradiction, want and not-want. This contradiction is probably inherent in our nature, and it is therefore rather hopeless to try to be integrated, to be whole. Love and hate always seem to go together. Why is there this contradiction? Is it inevitable? Can one avoid it? Can the modern State be wholly for peace? Can it afford to be entirely one thing? It must work for peace and yet prepare for war; the goal is peace through preparedness for war."

Why do we have a fixed point, an ideal, since deviation from it creates contradiction? If there were no fixed point, no conclusion, there would be no contradiction. We establish a fixed point, and then wander away from it, which is considered a contradiction. We come to a conclusion through devious ways and at different levels, and then try to live in accordance with that conclusion or ideal. As we cannot, a contradiction is created; and then we try to build a bridge between the fixed, the ideal, the conclusion, and the thought or act which contradicts it. This bridging is called consistency. And how we admire a man who is consistent, who sticks to his conclusion, to his ideal! Such a man we consider a saint. But the insane are also consistent, they also stick to their conclusions. There is no contradiction in a man who feels himself to be Napoleon, he is the embodiment of his conclusion; and a man who is completely identified with his ideal is obviously unbalanced.

The conclusion which we call an ideal may be established at any level, and it may be conscious or unconscious; and having established it, we try to approximate our action to it, which creates contradiction. What is important is not how to be consistent with the pattern, with the ideal, but to discover why we have cultivated this fixed point, this conclusion; for if we had no pattern, then contradiction would disappear. So, why have we the ideal, the conclusion? Does not the ideal prevent action? Does not the ideal come into being to modify action, to control action? Is it not possible to act without the ideal? The ideal is the response of the background, of conditioning, and so it can never be the means of liberating man from conflict and confusion. On the contrary, the ideal, the conclusion, increases division between man and man and so hastens the process of disintegration.

If there is no fixed point, no ideal from which to deviate, there is no contradiction with its urge to be consistent; then there is only action from moment to moment, and that action will always be complete and true. The true is not an ideal, a myth, but the actual. The actual can be understood and dealt with. The understanding of the actual cannot breed enmity, whereas ideals do. Ideals can never bring about a fundamental revolution, but only a modified continuity of the old. There is fundamental and constant revolution only in action from moment to moment which is not based on an ideal and so is free of conclusion.

"But a State cannot be run on this principle. There must be a goal, a planned action, a concentrated effort on a particular issue. What you say may be applicable to the individual, and I see in it great possibilities for myself; but it will not work in collective action."

Planned action needs constant modification, there must be adjustment to changing circumstances. Action according to a fixed blueprint will inevitably fail if you do not take into consideration the physical facts and psychological pressures. If you plan to build a bridge, you must not only make a blueprint of it, but you have to study the soil, the terrain where it is going to be built, otherwise your planning will not be adequate. There can be complete action only when all the physical facts and psychological stresses of man's total process are understood, and this understanding does not depend on any blueprint. It demands swift adjustment, which is intelligence; and it is only when there is no intelligence that we resort to conclusions, ideals, goals. The State is not static; its leaders may be, but the State, like the individual, is living, dynamic, and what is dynamic cannot be put in the strait-jacket of a blueprint. We generally build walls around the State, walls of conclusions, ideals, hoping to tie it down; but a living thing cannot be tied down without killing it, so we proceed to kill the State and then mould it according to our blueprint, according to the ideal. Only a dead thing can be forced to conform to a pattern; and as life is in constant movement, there is contradiction the moment we try to fit life into a fixed pattern or conclusion. Conformity to a pattern is the disintegration of the individual and so of the State. The ideal is not superior to life, and when we make it so there is confusion, antagonism and misery.

JEALOUSY

THE SUN WAS bright on the white wall opposite, and its glare made the faces obscure. A little child, without the prompting of the mother, came and sat close by, wide-eyed and wondering what it was all about. She was freshly washed and clothed and had some flowers in her hair. She was keenly observing everything, as children do, without recording too much. Her eyes were sparkling, and she did not quite know what to do, whether to cry, to laugh or to jump; instead, she took my hand and looked at it with absorbing interest. Presently she forgot all those people in the room, relaxed and went to sleep with her head in my lap. Her head was of good shape and well balanced; she was spotlessly clean. Her future was as confused and as miserable as that of the others in the room. Her conflict and sorrow were as inevitable as that sun on the wall; for to be free of pain and misery needs supreme intelligence, and her education and the influences about her would see to it that she was denied this intelligence. Love is so rare in this world, that flame without smoke; the smoke is overpowering, all-suffocating, bringing anguish and tears. Through the smoke, the flame is rarely seen; and when the smoke becomes all-important, the flame dies. Without that flame of love, life has no meaning, it becomes dull and weary; but the flame cannot be in the darkening smoke. The two cannot exist together; the smoke must cease for the clear flame to be. The flame is not a rival of the smoke; it has no rival. The smoke is not the flame, it cannot contain the flame; nor does the smoke indicate the presence of the flame, for the flame is free of smoke.

"Cannot love and hate exist together? Is not jealousy an indication of love? We hold hands, and then the next minute scold; we say hard things, but soon embrace. We quarrel, then kiss and are reconciled. Is not all this love? The very expression of jealousy is an indication of love; they seem to go together, like light and darkness. The swift anger and the caress—are these not

131

the fullness of love? The river is both turbulent and calm; it flows through shadow and sunlight, and therein lies the beauty of the river."

What is it that we call love? It is this whole field of jealousy, of lust, of harsh words, of caress, of holding hands, of quarrelling and making up. These are the facts in this field of so-called love. Anger and caress are everyday facts in this field, are they not? And we try to establish a relationship between the various facts, or we compare one fact with another. We use one fact to condemn or justify another within this same field, or we try to establish a relationship between a fact within the field and something outside of it. We do not take each fact separately, but try to find an interrelationship between them. Why do we do this? We can understand a fact only when we do not use another fact in the same field as a medium of understanding, which merely creates conflict and confusion. But why do we compare the various facts in the same field? Why do we carry over the significance of one fact to offset or to explain another?

"I am beginning to grasp what you mean. But why do we do this?"

Do we understand a fact through the screen of idea, through the screen of memory? Do I understand jealousy because I have held your hand? The holding of the hand is a fact, as jealousy is a fact; but do I understand the process of jealousy because I have a remembrance of holding your hand? Is memory an aid to understanding? Memory compares, modifies, condemns, justifies, or identifies; but it cannot bring understanding. We approach the facts in the field of so-called love with idea, with conclusion. We do not take the fact of jealousy as it is and silently observe it, but we want to twist the fact according to the pattern, to the conclusion; and we approach it in this way because we really do not wish to understand the fact of jealousy. The sensations of jealousy are as stimulating as a caress; but we want stimulation without the pain and discomfort that invariably go with it. So there is conflict, confusion and antagonism within this field which we call love. But is it love? Is love an idea, a sensation, a stimulation? Is love jealousy?

"Is not reality held in illusion? Does not darkness encompass or hide light? Is not God held in bondage?"

These are mere ideas, opinions, and so they have no validity. Such ideas only breed enmity, they do not cover or hold reality. Where there is light, darkness is not. Darkness cannot conceal light; if it does, there is no light. Where jealousy is, love is not. Idea cannot cover love. To commune, there must be relationship. Love is not related to idea, and so idea cannot commune with love. Love is a flame without smoke.

SPONTANEITY

SHE WAS AMONG a group of people who had come to discuss some serious matter. She must have come out of curiosity, or was brought along by a friend. Well dressed, she held herself with some dignity, and she evidently considered herself very good looking. She was completely self-conscious : conscious of her body, of her looks, of her hair and the impression she was making on others. Her gestures were studied, and from time to time she took different attitudes which she must have thought out with great care. Her whole appearance had about it the air of a long-cultivated pose into which she was determined to fit, whatever might happen. The others began to talk of serious things, and during the whole hour or more she maintained her pose. One saw among all those serious and intent faces this self-conscious girl, trying to follow what was being said and to join in the discussion; but no words came out of her. She wanted to show that she too was aware of the problem that was being discussed; but there was bewilderment in her eyes, for she was incapable of taking part in the serious conversation. One saw her quickly withdraw into herself, still maintaining the long-cultivated pose. All spontaneity was being sedulously destroyed.

Each one cultivates a pose. There is the walk and the pose of a prosperous business man, the smile of one who has arrived; there is the look and the pose of an artist; there is the pose of a respectful disciple, and the pose of a disciplined ascetic. Like that self-conscious girl, the so-called religious man assumes a pose, the pose of self-discipline which he has sedulously cultivated through denials and sacrifices. She sacrifices spontaneity for effect, and he immolates himself to achieve an end. Both are concerned with a result, though at different levels; and while his result may be considered socially more beneficial than hers, fundamentally they are similar, one is not superior to the other. Both are unintelligent, for both indicate pettiness of mind. A petty mind is always petty; it cannot be made rich, abundant. Though such a mind may adorn itself or seek to acquire virtue, it remains what it is, a petty, shallow thing, and through so-called growth, experience, it can only be enriched in its own pettiness. An ugly thing cannot be made beautiful. The god of a petty mind is a petty god. A shallow mind does not become fathomless by adorning itself with knowledge and clever phrases, by quoting words of wisdom, or by decorating its outward appearance. Adornments, whether inward or outward, do not make a fathomless mind; and it is this fathomlessness of the mind that gives beauty, not the jewel or the acquired virtue. For beauty to come into being, the mind must be choicelessly aware of its own pettiness; there must be an awareness in which comparison has wholly ceased.

The cultivated pose of the girl, and the disciplined pose of the so-called religious ascetic, are equally the tortured results of a petty mind, for both deny essential spontaneity. Both are fearful of the spontaneous, for it reveals them as they are, to themselves and to others; both are bent on destroying it, and the measure of their success is the completeness of their conformity to a chosen pattern or conclusion. But spontaneity is the only key that opens the door to what *is*. The spontaneous response uncovers the mind as it is; but what is discovered is immediately adorned or destroyed, and so spontaneity is put an end to. The killing of spontaneity is the way of a petty mind, which then decorates the outer, at whatever level; and this decoration is the worship of itself. Only in spontaneity, in freedom, can there be discovery. A disciplined mind cannot discover; it may function effectively and hence ruthlessly, but it cannot uncover the fathomless. It is fear that creates the resistance called discipline; but the spontaneous discovery of fear is freedom from fear. Conformity to a pattern, at whatever level, is fear, which only breeds conflict, confusion and antagonism; but a mind that is in revolt is not fearless, for the opposite can never know the spontaneous, the free.

Without spontaneity, there can be no self-knowledge; without self-knowledge, the mind is shaped by passing influences. These passing influences can make the mind narrow or expansive, but it is still within the sphere of influence. What is put together can be unmade, and that which is not put together can be known only through self-knowledge. The self is put together, and it is only in undoing the self that that which is not the result of influence, which has no cause, can be known.

The Conscious and the Unconscious

HE WAS A business man as well as a politician, and was very successful in both. He laughingly said that business and politics were a good combination; yet he was an earnest man in an odd, superstitious way. Whenever he had time he would read sacred books and repeat over and over again certain words which he considered beneficial. They brought peace to the soul, he said. He was advanced in years and very wealthy, but he was not generous either with the hand or with the heart. One could see that he was cunning and calculating, and yet there was an urge for something more than physical success. Life had scarcely touched him, for he had very studiously guarded himself against any exposure; he had made himself invulnerable, physically as well as psychologically. Psychologically he had refused to see himself as he was, and he could well afford to do this; but it was beginning to tell on him. When he was not watchful, there was about him a deep haunted look. Financially he was safe, at least as long as the present Government lasted and there was no revolution. He also wanted a safe investment in the so-called spiritual world, and that was why he played with ideas, mistaking ideas for something spiritual, real. He had no love except for his many possessions; he clung to them as a child clings to its mother, for he had nothing else. It was slowly dawning on him that he was a very sad man. Even this realization he was avoiding as long as he could; but life was pressing him.

When a problem is not consciously soluble, does the unconscious take over and help to solve it? What is the conscious and what is the unconscious? Is there a definite line where the one ends and the other begins? Has the conscious a limit, beyond which it cannot go? Can it limit itself to its own boundaries? Is the unconscious something apart from the conscious? Are they dissimilar? When one fails, does the other begin to function?

What is it that we call the conscious? To understand what it is made up of, we must observe how we consciously approach a problem. Most of us try to seek an answer to the problem; we are concerned with the solution, and not with the problem. We want a conclusion, we are looking for a way out of the problem; we want to avoid the problem through an answer, through a solution. We do not observe the problem itself, but grope for a satisfactory answer. Our whole conscious concern is with the finding of a solution, a satisfying conclusion. Often we do find an answer that gratifies us, and then we think we have solved the problem. What we have actually done is to cover over the problem with a conclusion, with a satisfactory answer; but under the weight of the conclusion, which has temporarily smothered it, the problem is still there. The search for an answer is an evasion of the problem. When there is no satisfactory answer, the conscious or upper mind stops looking; and then the so-called unconscious, the deeper mind, takes over and finds an answer.

The conscious mind is obviously seeking a way out of the problem, and the way out is a satisfying conclusion. Is not the conscious mind itself made up of conclusions, whether positive or negative, and is it capable of seeking anything else? Is not the upper mind a storehouse of conclusions which are the residue of experiences, the imprints of the past? Surely, the conscious mind is made up of the past, it is founded on the past, for memory is a fabric of conclusions; and with these conclusions, the mind approaches a problem. It is incapable of looking at the problem without the screen of its conclusions; it cannot study, be silently aware of the problem itself. It knows only conclusions, pleasant or unpleasant, and it can only add to itself further conclusions, further ideas, further fixations. Any conclusion is a fixation, and the conscious mind inevitably seeks a conclusion.

When it cannot find a satisfactory conclusion, the conscious mind gives up the search, and thereby it becomes quiet; and into the quiet upper mind, the unconscious pops an answer. Now, is the unconscious, the deeper mind, different in its make-up from the conscious mind? Is not the unconscious also made up of racial, group and social conclusions, memories? Surely, the unconscious is also the result of the past, of time, only it is submerged and waiting; and when called upon it throws up its own hidden conclusions. If they are satisfactory, the upper mind accepts them; and if they are not, it flounders about, hoping by some miracle to find an answer. If it does not find an answer, it wearily puts up with the problem, which gradually corrodes the mind. Disease and insanity follow.

The upper and the deeper mind are not dissimilar; they are both made up of conclusions, memories, they are both the outcome of the past. They can supply an answer, a conclusion, but they are incapable of dissolving the problem. The problem is dissolved only when both the upper and the deeper mind are silent, when they are not projecting positive or negative conclusions. There is freedom from the problem only when the whole mind is utterly still, choicelessly aware of the problem; for only then the maker of the problem is not.

CHALLENGE AND RESPONSE

THE RIVER WAS full and sweeping, in some places several miles wide, and to see so much water was a delight. To the north were the green hills, fresh after the storm. It was splendid to see the great curve of the river with the white sails on it. The sails were large and triangular, and in the early morning light there was an enchantment about them, they seemed to come out of the water. The noise of the day had not yet begun, and the song of a boatman almost on the other side of the river came floating across the waters. At that hour his song seemed to fill the earth, and all other sounds were silenced; even the whistle of a train became soft and bearable.

Gradually the noise of the village began : the loud quarrels at the water fountain, the bleating of goats, the cows asking to be milked, the heavy carts on the road, the shrill call of the crows, the cries and laughter of children. And so another day was born. The sun was over the palm trees, and the monkeys were sitting on the wall, their long tails almost touching the earth. They were large, but very timid; you called to them, and they jumped to the ground and ran to a big tree in the field. They were black-faced and black-pawed, and they looked intelligent, but they were not as clever and mischievous as the little ones.

"Why is thought so persistent? It seems so restless, so exasperatingly insistent. Do what you will, it is always active, like those monkeys, and its very activity is exhausting. You cannot escape from it, it pursues you relentlessly. You try to suppress it, and a few seconds later it pops up again. It is never quiet, never in repose; it is always pursuing, always analysing, always torturing itself. Sleeping or waking, thought is in constant turmoil, and it seems to have no peace, no rest."

Can thought ever be at peace? It can think about peace and attempt to be peaceful, forcing itself to be still; but can thought in itself be tranquil? Is not thought in its very nature restless? Is not thought the constant response to constant challenge? There can be no cessation to challenge, because every movement of life is a challenge; and if there is no awareness of challenge, then there is decay, death. Challenge-and-response is the very way of life. Response can be adequate or inadequate; and it is inadequacy of response to challenge that provokes thought, with its restlessness. Challenge demands action, not verbalization. Verbalization is thought. The word, the symbol, retards action;

and idea is the word, as memory is the word. There is no memory without the symbol, without the word. Memory is word, thought, and can thought be the true response to challenge? Is challenge an idea? Challenge is always new, fresh; and can thought, idea, ever be new? When thought meets the challenge, which is ever new, is not that response the outcome of the old, the past?

When the old meets the new, inevitably the meeting is incomplete; and this incompleteness is thought in its restless search for completeness. Can thought, idea, ever be complete? Thought, idea, is the response of memory; and memory is ever incomplete. Experience is the response to challenge. This response is conditioned by the past, by memory; such response only strengthens the conditioning. Experience does not liberate, it strengthens belief, memory, and it is this memory that responds to challenge; so experience is the conditioner.

"But what place has thought?"

Do you mean what place has thought in action? Has idea any function in action? Idea becomes a factor in action in order to modify it, to control it, to shape it; but idea is not action. Idea, belief, is a safeguard against action; it has a place as a controller, modifying and shaping action. Idea is the pattern for action.

"Can there be action without the pattern?"

Not if one is seeking a result. Action towards a predetermined goal is not action at all, but conformity to belief, to idea. If one is seeking conformity, then thought, idea, has a place. The function of thought is to create a pattern for so-called action, and thereby to kill action. Most of us are concerned with the killing of action; and idea, belief, dogma, help to destroy it. Action implies insecurity, vulnerability to the unknown; and thought, belief, which is the known, is an effective barrier to the unknown. Thought can never penetrate into the unknown; it must cease for the unknown to be. The action of the unknown is beyond the action of thought; and thought, being aware of this, consciously or unconsciously clings to the known. The known is ever responding to the unknown, to the challenge; and from this inadequate response arise conflict, confusion and misery. It is only when the known, the idea, ceases that there can be the action of the unknown, which is measureless.

POSSESSIVENESS

HE HAD BROUGHT along his wife, for he said that it was their mutual problem. She had bright eyes and was small, sprightly, and rather disturbed. They were simple, friendly people; he spoke English fairly well, and she could just manage to understand it and ask simple questions. When it got a little difficult, she would turn to her husband and he would explain in their own language. He said that they had been married for over twenty-five years, and had several children; and that their problem was not the children, but the struggle between themselves. He explained that he had a job which gave him a modest income, and went on to say how difficult it was to live peacefully in this world, especially when you are married; he wasn't grumbling, he added, but there it was. He had been everything that a husband should be, at least he hoped so, but it was not always easy.

It was difficult for them to come to the point, and they talked for some time about various things: the education of their children, the marriage of their daughters, the waste of money on ceremonies, a recent death in the family, and so on. They felt at ease and unhurried, for it was good to talk to someone who would listen and who perhaps might understand.

Who cares to listen to the troubles of another? We have so many problems of our own that we have no time for those of others. To make another listen you have to pay either in coin, in prayer, or in belief. The professional will listen, it is his job, but in that there is no lasting release. We want to unburden ourselves freely, spontaneously, without any regrets afterwards. The purification of confession does not depend on the one who listens, but on him who desires to open his heart. To open one's heart is important, and it will find someone, a beggar perhaps, to whom it can pour itself out. Introspective talk can never open the heart; it is enclosing, depressing and utterly useless. To be open is to listen, not only to yourself, but to every influence, to every movement about you. It may or may not be possible to do something tangibly about what you hear, but the very fact of being open brings about its own action. Such hearing purifies your own heart, cleansing it of the things of the mind. Hearing with the mind is gossip, and in it there is no release either for you or for the other; it is merely a continuation of pain, which is stupidity.

Unhurriedly they were coming to the point.

"We have come to talk about our problem. We are jealous—I am not, but she is. Though she used not to be as openly jealous as she is now, there has always been a whisper of it. I don't think I have ever given her any reason to be jealous, but she finds a reason."

Do you think there is any reason to be jealous? Is there a cause for jealousy? And will jealousy disappear when the cause is known? Have you not noticed that even when you know the cause, jealousy continues? Do not let us look for the reason, but let us understand jealousy itself. As you say, one might pick up almost anything to be envious about; envy is the thing to understand, and not what it is about.

"Jealousy has been with me for a long time. I didn't know my husband very well when we married, and you know how it all happens; jealousy gradually crept in, like smoke in the kitchen."

Jealousy is one of the ways of holding the man or the woman, is it not? The more we are jealous, the greater the feeling of possession. To possess something makes us happy; to call something, even a dog, exclusively our own makes us feel warm and comfortable. To be exclusive in our possession gives assurance and certainty to ourselves. To own something makes us important; it is this importance we cling to. To think that we own, not a pencil or a house, but a human being, makes us feel strong and strangely content. Envy is not because of the other, but because of the worth, the importance of ourselves.

"But I am not important, I am nobody; my husband is all that I have. Even my children don't count."

We all have only one thing to which we cling, though it takes different forms. You cling to your husband, others to their children, and yet others to some belief; but the intention is the same. Without the object to which we cling we feel so hopelessly lost, do we not? We are afraid to feel all alone. This fear is jealousy, hate, pain. There is not much difference between envy and hate.

"But we love each other."

Then how can you be jealous? We do not love, and that is the unfortunate part of it. You are using your husband, as he is using you, to be happy, to have a companion, not to feel alone; you may not possess much, but at least you have someone to be with. This mutual need and use we call love.

"But this is dreadful."

It is not dreadful, only we never look at it. We call it dreadful, give it a name and quickly look away—which is what you are doing.

"I know, but I don't want to look. I want to carry on as I am, even though it means being jealous, because I cannot see anything else in life."

If you saw something else you would no longer be jealous of your husband, would you? But you would cling to the other thing as now you are clinging to your husband, so you would be jealous of that too. You want to find a substitute for your husband, and not freedom from jealousy. We are all like that: before we give up one thing, we want to be very sure of another. When you are completely uncertain, then only is there no place for envy. There is envy when there is certainty, when you feel that you have something. Exclusiveness is this feeling of certainty; to own is to be envious. Ownership breeds hatred. We really hate what we possess, which is shown in jealousy. Where there is possession there can never be love; to possess is to destroy love.

"I am beginning to see. I have really never loved my husband, have I? I am beginning to understand."

And she wept.

SHE HAD COME with three of her friends; they were all earnest and had the dignity of intelligence. One was quick to grasp, another was impatient in his quickness, and the third was eager, but the eagerness was not sustained. They made a good group, for they all shared the problem of their friend, and no one offered advice or weighty opinions. They all wanted to help her do whatever she thought was the right thing, and not merely act according to tradition, public opinion or personal inclination. The difficulty was, what was the right thing to do? She herself was not sure, she felt disturbed and confused. But there was much pressure for immediate action; a decision had to be made, and she could not postpone it any longer. It was a question of freedom from a particular relationship. She wanted to be free, and she repeated this several times.

There was quietness in the room; the nervous agitation had subsided, and they were all eager to go into the problem without expecting a result, a definition of the right thing to do. The right action would emerge, naturally and fully, as the problem was exposed. The discovery of the content of the problem was important, and not the end-result; for any answer would only be another conclusion, another opinion, another piece of advice, which would in no way solve the problem. The problem itself had to be understood, and not how to respond to the problem or what to do about it. The right approach to the problem was important, because the problem itself held the right action.

The waters of the river were dancing, for the sun had made on them a path of light. A white sail crossed the path, but the dance was not disturbed. It was a dance of pure delight. The trees were full of birds, scolding, preening, flying away only to come back again. Several monkeys were tearing off the tender leaves and stuffing them in their mouths; their weight bent the delicate branches into long curves, yet they held on lightly and were unafraid. With what ease they moved from branch to branch; though they jumped, it was a flow, the taking off and the landing were one movement. They would sit with their tails hanging and reach for the leaves. They were high up, and took no notice of the people passing below. As darkness approached, the parrots came by the hundred to settle down for the night among the thick leaves. One saw them come and disappear into the foliage. The new moon was just visible. Far away a train whistled as it was crossing the long bridge around the curve of the river. This river was sacred, and people came from far distances to bathe in it, that their sins might be washed away. Every river is lovely and sacred, and the beauty of this one was its wide, sweeping curve and the islands of sand between deep stretches of water; and those silent white sails that went up and down the river every day.

"I want to be free from a particular relationship," she said.

What do you mean by wanting to be free? When you say, "I want to be free," you imply that you are *not* free. In what way are you not free?

"I am free physically; I am free to come and go, because physically I am no longer the wife. But I want to be completely free; I do not want to have anything to do with that particular person."

In what way are you related to that person, if you are already physically free? Are you related to him in any other way?

"I do not know, but I have great resentment against him. I do not want to have anything to do with him."

You want to be free, and yet you have resentment against him? Then you are not free of him. Why have you this resentment against him?

"I have recently discovered what he is : his meanness, his real lack of love, his complete selfishness. I cannot tell you what a horror I have discovered in him. To think that I was jealous of him, that I idolized him, that I submitted to him! Finding him to be stupid and cunning when I thought him an ideal husband, loving and kind, has made me resentful of him. To think I had anything to do with him makes me feel unclean. I want to be completely free from him."

144

You may be physically free from him, but as long as you have resentment against him, you are not free. If you hate him, you are tied to him; if you are ashamed of him, you are still enslaved by him. Are you angry with him, or with yourself? He is what he is, and why be angry with him? Is your resentment really against him? Or, having seen what *is*, are you ashamed of yourself for having been associated with it? Surely, you are resentful, not of him, but of your own judgment, of your own actions. You are ashamed of yourself. Being unwilling to see this, you blame him for what he is. When you realize that your resentment against him is an escape from your own romantic idolization, then he is out of the picture. You are not ashamed of him, but of yourself for being associated with him. It is with yourself that you are angry, and not with him.

"Yes, that is so."

If you really see this, experience it as a fact, then you are free of him. He is no longer the object of your enmity. Hate binds as love does.

"But how am I to be free from my own shame, from my own stupidity? I see very clearly that he is what he is, and is not to be blamed; but how am I to be free of this shame, this resentment which has been slowly ripening in me and has come to fullness in this crisis? How am I to wipe out the past?"

Why you desire to wipe out the past is of more significance than knowing how to wipe it out. The intention with which you approach the problem is more important than knowing what to do about it. Why do you want to wipe out the memory of that association?

"I dislike the memory of all those years. It has left a very bad taste in my mouth. Is that not a good enough reason?"

Not quite, is it? Why do you want to wipe out those past memories? Surely, not because they leave a bad taste in your mouth. Even if you were able through some means to wipe out the past, you might again be caught in actions that you would be ashamed of. Merely wiping out the unpleasant memories does not solve the problem, does it?

"I thought it did; but what is the problem then? Are you not making it unnecessarily complex? It is already complex enough, at least my life is. Why add another burden to it?"

Are we adding a further burden, or are we trying to understand what *is* and be free of it? Please have a little patience. What is the urge that is prompting you to wipe out the past? It may be unpleasant, but why do you want to wipe it out? You have a certain idea or picture of yourself which these memories contradict, and so you want to get rid of them. You have a certain estimation of yourself, have you not?

"Of course, otherwise . . ."

We all place ourselves at various levels, and we are constantly falling from these heights. It is the falls we are ashamed of. Self-esteem is the cause of our shame, of our fall. It is this self-esteem that must be understood, and not the fall. If there is no pedestal on which you have put yourself, how can there be any fall? Why have you put yourself on a pedestal called self-esteem, human dignity, the ideal, and so on? If you can understand this, then there will be no shame of the past; it will have completely gone. You will be what you are without the pedestal. If the pedestal is not there, the height that makes you look down or look up, then you *are* what you have always avoided. It is this avoidance of what *is*, of what you are, that brings about confusion and antagonism, shame and resentment. You do not have to tell me or another what you are, but be aware of what you are, whatever it is, pleasant or unpleasant: live with it without justifying or resisting it. Live with it without naming it; for the very term is a condemnation or an identification. Live with it without fear, for fear prevents communion, and without communion you cannot live with it. To be in communion is to love. Without love, you cannot wipe out the past; with love, there is no past. Love, and time is not.

FEAR

SHE HAD TRAVELLED a long way, half across the world. There was a wary look about her, a guarded approach, a tentative opening that would close up at any suggestion of too deep an inquiry. She was not timid; but she was unwilling, though not consciously, to expose her inward state. Yet she wanted to talk about herself and her problems, and had come all that distance expressly to do so. She was hesitant, uncertain of her words, aloof, and at the same time eager to talk about herself. She had read many books on psychology, and while she had never been analysed, she was entirely capable of analysing herself; in fact, she said that from childhood she was used to analysing her own thoughts and feelings.

Why are you so intent upon analysing yourself?

"I do not know, but I have always done it ever since I can remember."

Is analysis a way of protecting yourself against yourself, against emotional explosions and consequent regrets?

"I am pretty sure that is why I analyse, constantly interrogate. I do not want to get caught up in all the mess about me, personal and general. It is too hideous, and I want to keep out of it. I see now that I have used analysis as a means of keeping myself intact, of not getting caught in the social and family turmoil."

Have you been able to avoid getting caught?

"I am not at all sure. I have succeeded in some directions, but in others I do not think I have. In talking about all this, I see what an extraordinary thing I have done. I have never looked at it all so clearly before."

Why are you protecting yourself so cleverly, and against what? You say, against the mess around you; but what is there in the mess against which you have to protect yourself? If it is a mess and you see it clearly as such, then you do not have to guard yourself against it. One guards oneself only when there is fear and not understanding. So what are you afraid of?

"I do not think I am afraid; I simply do not want to get entangled in the miseries of existence. I have a profession that supports me, but I want to be free of the rest of the entanglements, and I think I am."

If you are not afraid, then why do you resist entanglements? One resists something only when one does not know how to deal with it. If you know how a motor works, you are free of it; if anything goes wrong, you can put it right. We resist that which we do not understand; we resist confusion, evil, misery, only when we do not know its structure, how it is put together. You resist confusion because you are not aware of its structure, of its make-up. Why are you not aware of it?

"But I have never thought about it that way."

It is only when you are in direct relationship with the structure of confusion that you can be aware of the working of its mechanism. It is only when there is communion between two people that they understand each other; if they resist each other, there is no understanding. Communion or relationship can exist only when there is no fear.

"I see what you mean."

Then what are you afraid of?

"What do you mean by fear?"

Fear can exist only in relationship; fear cannot exist by itself, in isolation. There is no such thing as abstract fear; there is fear of the known or the unknown, fear of what one has done or what one may do; fear of the past or of the future. The relationship between what one is and what one desires to be causes fear. Fear arises when one interprets the fact of what one is in terms of reward and punishment. Fear comes with responsibility and the desire to be free from it. There is fear in the contrast between pain and pleasure. Fear exists in the conflict of the opposites. The worship of success brings the fear of failure. Fear is the process of the mind in the struggle of becoming. In becoming good, there is the fear of evil; in becoming complete, there is the fear of loneliness; in becoming great, there is the fear of being small. Comparison is not understanding; it is prompted by fear of the unknown in relation to the known. Fear is uncertainty in search of security.

The effort to become is the beginning of fear, the fear of being or not being. The mind, the residue of experience, is always in fear of the unnamed, the challenge. The mind, which is name, word, memory, can function only within the field of the known; and the unknown, which is challenge from moment to moment, is resisted or translated by the mind in terms of the known. This resistance or translation of the challenge is fear; for the mind can have no communion with the unknown. The known cannot commune with the unknown; the known must cease for the unknown to be.

The mind is the maker of fear; and when it analyses fear, seeking its cause in order to be free from it, the mind only further isolates itself and thereby increases fear. When you use analysis to resist confusion, you are increasing the power of resistance; and resistance of confusion only increases the fear of it, which hinders freedom. In communion there is freedom, but not in fear.

"How am I to Love?"

WE WERE HIGH up on the side of a mountain overlooking the valley, and the large stream was a silver ribbon in the sun. Here and there the sun came through the thick foliage, and there was the scent of many flowers. It was a delicious morning, and the dew was still heavy on the ground. The scented breeze was coming across the valley, bringing the distant noise of people, the sound of bells and of an occasional water-horn. In the valley the smoke was going straight up, and the breeze was not strong enough to disperse it. The column of smoke was a lovely thing to watch; it rose from the bottom of the valley and tried to reach up to the very heavens, like that ancient pine. A large black squirrel which had been scolding us gave it up at last and came down the tree to investigate further, and then, partially satisfied, went bounding away. A tiny cloud was forming, but otherwise the sky was clear, a soft, pale blue.

He had no eyes for all this. He was consumed with his immediate problem, as he had been consumed with his problems before. The problems moved and had their being around himself. He was a very rich man; he was lean and hard, but had an easy air with a ready smile. He was now looking across the valley, but the quickening beauty had not touched him; there was no softening of the face, the lines were still hard and determined.

He was still hunting, not for money, but for what he called God. He was forever talking about love and God. He had hunted far and wide, and had been to many teachers; and as he was getting on in years, the hunt was becoming more keen. He had come several times to talk over these matters, but there was always a look of cunning and calculation; he was constantly weighing how much it would cost to find his God, how expensive the journey would be. He knew that he could not take with him what he had; but could he take something else, a coin that had value where he was going? He was a hard man, and there was never a gesture of generosity either of the heart or of the hand. He was always very hesitant to give the little extra; he felt everyone must be worthy of his reward, as he had been worthy. But he was there that morning to further expose himself; for there was trouble brewing, serious disturbances were taking place in his otherwise successful life. The goddess of success was not with him altogether.

"I am beginning to realize what I am," he said. "I have these many years subtly opposed and resisted you. You talk against the rich, you say hard things about us, and I have been angry with you; but I have been unable to hit you back, for I cannot get at you. I have tried in different ways, but I cannot lay my hands on you. But what do you want me to do? I wish to God I had never listened to you or come anywhere near you. I now have sleepless nights, and I always slept so well before; I have torturing dreams, and I rarely used to dream at all. I have been afraid of you, I have silently cursed you—but I cannot go back. What am I to do? I have no friends, as you pointed out, nor can I buy them as I used to—I am too exposed by what has happened. Perhaps I can be *your* friend. You have offered help, and here I am. What am I to do?"

To be exposed is not easy; and has one exposed oneself? Has one opened that cupboard which one has so carefully locked, stuffing into it the things which one does not want to see? Does one want to open it and see what is there?

"I do, but how am I to go about it?"

Does one really want to, or is one merely playing with the

intention? Once open, however little, it cannot be closed again. The door will always remain open; day and night, its contents will be spilling out. One may try to run away, as one always does; but it will be there, waiting and watching. Does one really want to open it?

"Of course I do, that is why I have come. I must face it, for I am coming to the end of things. What am I to do?"

Open and look. To accumulate wealth one must injure, be cruel, ungenerous; there must be ruthlessness, cunning calculation, dishonesty; there must be the search for power, that egocentric action which is merely covered over by such pleasant-sounding words as responsibility, duty, efficiency, rights.

"Yes, that is all true, and more. There has been no consideration of anyone; the religious pursuits have been mere cloaks of respectability. Now that I look at it, I see that everything revolved around me. I was the centre, though I pretended not to be. I see all that. But what am I to do?"

First one must recognize things for what they are. But beyond all this, how can one wipe these things away if there is no affection, no love, that flame without smoke? It is this flame alone that will wipe away the contents of the cupboard, and nothing else; no analysis, no sacrifice, no renunciation can do it. When there is this flame, then it will no longer be a sacrifice, a renunciation; then you will meet the storm without waiting for it.

"But how am I to love? I know I have no warmth for people; I have been ruthless, and they are not with me who should be with me. I am utterly alone, and how am I to know love? I am not a fool to think that I can get it by some conscious act, buy it through some sacrifice, some denial. I know I have never loved, and I see that if I had, I would not be in this situation. What am I to do? Should I give up my properties, my wealth?"

If you find the garden that you have so carefully cultivated has produced only poisonous weeds, you have to tear them out by the roots; you have to pull down the walls that have sheltered them. You may or may not do it, for you have extensive gardens, cunningly walled-in and well-guarded. You will do it only when there is no bartering; but it must be done, for to die rich is to have lived in vain. But beyond all this, there must be the flame that cleanses the mind and the heart, making all things new. That flame is not of the mind, it is not a thing to be cultivated. The show of kindliness can be made to shine, but it is not the flame; the activity called service, though beneficial and necessary, is not love; the much-practised and disciplined tolerance, the cultivated compassion of the church and temple, the gentle speech, the soft manner, the worship of the saviour, of the image, of the ideal—none of this is love.

"I have listened and observed, and I am aware that there is no love in any of these things. But my heart is empty, and how is it to be filled? What am I to do?"

Attachment denies love. Love is not to be found in suffering; though jealousy is strong, it cannot bind love. Sensation and its gratification is ever coming to an end; but love is inexhaustible.

"These are mere words to me. I am starving : feed me."

To be fed, there must be hunger. If you are hungry, you will find food. Are you hungry, or merely greedy for the taste of some other food? If you are greedy, you will find that which will gratify; but it will soon come to an end, and it will not be love.

"But what am I to do?"

You keep on repeating that question. What you are to do is not important; but it is essential to be aware of what you *are* doing. You are concerned with future action, and that is one way of avoiding immediate action. You do not want to act, and so you keep on asking what you are to do. You are again being cunning, deceiving yourself, and so your heart is empty. You want to fill it with the things of the mind; but love is not of the mind. Let your heart be empty. Do not fill it with words, with the actions of the mind. Let your heart be wholly empty; then only will it be filled.

THE FUTILITY OF RESULT

THEY HAD COME from different parts of the world, and had been discussing some of the problems that confront most of us. It is good to talk things over; but mere words, clever arguments and wide knowledge do not bring freedom from aching problems. Cleverness and knowledge may and often do show their own futility, and the discovery of their futility makes the mind silent. In that silence, understanding of the problem comes; but to seek that silence is to breed another problem, another conflict. Explanations, the uncovering of causes, analytical dissections of the problem, do not in any way resolve it; for it cannot be resolved by the ways of the mind. The mind can only breed further problems. It can run away from the problem through explanations, ideals, intentions; but do what it will, the mind cannot free itself from the problem. The mind itself is the field in which problems, conflicts, grow and multiply. Thought cannot silence itself; it can put on a cloak of silence, but that is only concealment and pose. Thought can kill itself by disciplined action towards a predetermined end; but death is not silent. Death is more vociferous than life. Any movement of the mind is a hindrance to silence.

Through the open windows came a confusion of sounds : the loud talk and quarrelling in the village, an engine letting off steam, the cries of children and their free laughter, the rumble of a passing lorry, the buzzing of bees, the strident call of the crows. And amidst all this noise, a silence was creeping into the room, unsought and uninvited. Through words and arguments, through misunderstandings and struggles, that silence was spreading its wings. The quality of that silence is not the cessation of noise, of chatter and word; to include that silence, the mind must lose its capacity to expand. That silence is free from all compulsions, conformities, efforts; it is inexhaustible and so ever new, ever fresh. But the word is not that silence.

Why is it that we seek results, goals? Why is it that the mind is ever pursuing an end? And why should it *not* pursue an end? In coming here, are we not seeking something, some experience, some delight? We are tired and fed up with the many things that we have been playing with; we have turned away from them, and now we want a new toy to play with. We go from one thing to another, like a woman who goes window shopping, till we find something that is entirely satisfying; and then we settle down to stagnate. We are forever craving something; and having tasted many things which were mostly unsatisfactory, we now want the ultimate thing : God, truth, or what you will. We want a result, a new experience, a new sensation that will endure in spite of everything. We never see the futility of result, but only of a particular result; so we wander from one result to another, hoping always to find the one that will end all search.

The search for result, for success, is binding, limiting; it is ever coming to an end. Gaining is a process of ending. To arrive is death. Yet that is what we are seeking, is it not? We are seeking death, only we call it result, goal, purpose. We want to arrive. We are tired of this everlasting struggle, and we want to get there—"there" placed at whatever level. We do not see the wasteful destructiveness of struggle, but desire to be free of it through gaining a result. We do not see the truth of struggle, of conflict, and so we use it as a means of getting what we want, the most satisfying thing; and that which is most satisfying is determined by the intensity of our discontent. This desire for result always ends in gain; but we want a never-ending result. So, what is our problem? How to be free from the craving for results, is that it?

"I think that is it. The very desire to be free is also a desire for a result, is it not?"

We shall get thoroughly entangled if we pursue that line. Is it that we cannot see the futility of result, at whatever level we may place it? Is that our problem? Let us see our problem clearly, and then perhaps we shall be able to understand it. Is it a question of seeing the futility of one result and so discarding all desire for results? If we perceive the uselessness of one escape, then all escapes are vain. Is that our problem? Surely, it is not quite that, is it? Perhaps we can approach it differently.

Is not experience a result also? If we are to be free from results, must we not also be free from experience? For is not experience an outcome, an end?

"The end of what?"

The end of experiencing. Experience is the memory of experiencing, is it not? When experiencing ends there is experience, the result. While experiencing, there is no experience; experience is but the memory of having experienced. As the state of experiencing fades, experience begins. Experience is ever hindering experiencing, living. Results, experiences, come to an end; but experiencing is inexhaustible. When the inexhaustible is hindered by memory, then the search for results begins. The mind, the result, is always seeking an end, a purpose, and that is death. Death is not when the experiencer is not. Only then is there the inexhaustible.

THE DESIRE FOR BLISS

THE SINGLE TREE on the wide green lawn was the centre of the little world which included the woods, the house and the small lake; the whole surrounding area seemed to flow towards the tree, which was high and spreading. It must have been very old, but there was a freshness about it, as though it had just come into being; there were hardly any dead branches, and its leaves were spotless, glistening in the morning sun. Because it was alone, all things seemed to come to it. Deer and pheasants, rabbits and cattle congregated in its shade, especially at midday. The symmetrical beauty of that tree gave a shape to the sky, and in the early morning light the tree appeared to be the only thing that was living. From the woods, the tree seemed far away; but from the tree, the woods, the house and even the sky seemed close—one often felt one could touch the passing clouds.

We had been seated under the tree for some time, when he

came to join us. He was seriously interested in meditation, and said that he had practised it for many years. He did not belong to any particular school of thought, and though he had read many of the Christian mystics, he was more attracted to the meditations and disciplines of the Hindu and Buddhist saints. He had realized early, he continued, the immaturity of asceticism, with its peculiar fascination and cultivation of power through abstinence, and he had from the beginning avoided all extremes. He had, however, practised discipline, an unvarying self-control, and was determined to realize that which lay through and beyond meditation. He had led what was considered to be a strict moral life, but that was only a minor incident, nor was he attracted to the ways of the world. He had once played with worldly things, but the play was over some years ago. He had a job of sorts, but that too was quite incidental.

The end of meditation is meditation itself. The search for something through and beyond meditation is end-gaining; and that which is gained is again lost. Seeking a result is the continuation of self-projection; result, however lofty, is the projection of desire. Meditation as a means to arrive, to gain, to discover, only gives strength to the meditator. The meditator is the meditation; meditation is the understanding of the meditator.

"I meditate to find ultimate reality, or to allow that reality to manifest itself. It is not exactly a result I am seeking, but that bliss which occasionally one senses. It is there; and as a thirsty man craves for water, I want that inexpressible happiness. That bliss is infinitely greater than all joy, and I pursue it as my most cherished desire."

That is, you meditate to gain what you want. To attain what you desire, you strictly discipline yourself, follow certain rules and regulations; you lay out and follow a course in order to have that which is at the end of it. You hope to achieve certain results, certain well-marked stages, depending upon your persistence of effort, and progressively experience greater and greater joy. This well-laid-out course assures you of the final result. So your meditation is a very calculated affair, is it not?

"When you put it that way, it does seem, in the superficial

sense, rather absurd; but deeply, what is wrong with it? What is wrong essentially with seeking that bliss? I suppose I do want a result for all my efforts; but again, why shouldn't one?"

This desire for bliss implies that bliss is something final, everlasting, does it not? All other results have been unsatisfactory; one has ardently pursued worldly goals and has seen their transient nature, and now one wants the everlasting state, an end that has no ending. The mind is seeking a final and imperishable refuge; so it disciplines and trains itself, practises certain virtues to gain what it wants. It may once have experienced that bliss, and now it is panting after it. Like other pursuers of results, you are pursuing yours, only you have placed it at a different level; you may call it higher, but that is irrelevant. A result means an ending; arrival implies another effort to become. The mind is never at rest, it is always striving, always achieving, always gaining—and, of course, always in fear of losing. This process is called meditation. Can a mind which is caught in endless becoming be aware of bliss? Can a mind that has imposed discipline upon itself ever be free to receive that bliss? Through effort and struggle, through resistance and denials, the mind makes itself insensitive; and can such a mind be open and vulnerable? Through the desire for that bliss, have you not built a wall around yourself which the imponderable, the unknown, cannot penetrate? Have you not effectively shut yourself off from the new? Out of the old, you have made a path for the new; and can the new be contained in the old?

The mind can never create the new; the mind itself is a result, and all results are the outcome of the old. Results can never be new; the pursuit of a result can never be spontaneous; that which is free cannot pursue an end. The goal, the ideal, is always a projection of the mind, and surely that is not meditation. Meditation is the freeing of the meditator; in freedom alone is there discovery, sensitivity to receive. Without freedom, there can be no bliss; but freedom does not come through discipline. Discipline makes the pattern of freedom, but the pattern is not freedom. The pattern must be broken for freedom to be. The breaking of the mould is meditation. But this breaking of the mould is not a goal, an ideal. The mould is broken from moment to moment. The broken moment is the forgotten moment. It is the remembered moment that gives shape to the mould, and only then does the maker of the mould come into being, the creator of all problems, conflicts, miseries.

Meditation is freeing the mind of its own thoughts at all levels. Thought creates the thinker. The thinker is not separate from thought; they are a unitary process, and not two separate processes. The separate processes only lead to ignorance and illusion. The meditator is the meditation. Then the mind is alone, not *made* alone; it is silent, not *made* silent. Only to the alone can the causeless come, only to the alone is there bliss.

THOUGHT AND CONSCIOUSNESS

ALL THINGS WERE withdrawing into themselves. The trees were enclosing themselves in their own being; the birds were folding their wings to brood over their day's wanderings; the river had lost its glow, and the waters were no longer dancing but quiet and closed. The mountains were distant and unapproachable, and man had withdrawn into his house. Night had come, and there was the stillness of isolation. There was no communion; each thing had closed itself, set itself apart. The flower, the sound, the talk—everything was unexposed, invulnerable. There was laughter, but it was isolated and distant; the talk was muffled and from within. Only the stars were inviting, open and communicating; but they too were very far away.

Thought is always an outward response, it can never respond deeply. Thought is always the outer; thought is always an effect, and thinking is the reconciliation of effects. Thought is always superficial, though it may place itself at different levels. Thought can never penetrate the profound, the implicit. Thought cannot go beyond itself, and every attempt to do so is its own frustration.

"What do you mean by thought?"

Thought is response to any challenge; thought is not action, doing. Thought is an outcome, the result of a result; it is the result of memory. Memory is thought, and thought is the verbalization of memory. Memory is experience. The thinking process is the conscious process, the hidden as well as the open. This whole thinking process is consciousness; the waking and the sleeping, the upper and the deeper levels are all part of memory, experience. Thought is not independent. There is no independent thinking; "independent thinking" is a contradiction in terms. Thought, being a result, opposes or agrees, compares or adjusts, condemns or justifies, and therefore it can never be free. A result can never be free; it can twist about, manipulate, wander, go a certain distance, but it cannot be free from its own mooring. Thought is anchored to memory, and it can never be free to discover the truth of any problem.

"Do you mean to say that thought has no value at all?"

It has value in the reconciliation of effects, but it has no value in itself as a means to action. Action is revolution, not the reconciliation of effects. Action freed from thought, idea, belief, is never within a pattern. There can be activity within the pattern, and that activity is either violent, bloody, or the opposite; but it is not action. The opposite is not action, it is a modified continuation of activity. The opposite is still within the field of result, and in pursuing the opposite, thought is caught within the net of its own responses. Action is not the result of thought; action has no relation to thought. Thought, the result, can never create the new; the new is from moment to moment, and thought is always the old, the past, the conditioned. It has value but no freedom. All value is limitation, it binds. Thought is binding, for it is cherished.

"What relationship is there between consciousness and thought?"

Are they not the same? Is there any difference between thinking and being conscious? Thinking is a response; and is being conscious not also a response? When one is conscious of that chair, it is a response to a stimulus; and is not thought the response of memory to a challenge? It is this response that we call experience. Experiencing is challenge and response; and this experiencing, together with the naming or recording of it—this total process, at different levels, is consciousness, is it not? Experience is the result, the outcome of experiencing. The result is given a term; the term itself is a conclusion, one of the many conclusions which constitute memory. This concluding process is consciousness. The conclusion, the result, is self-consciousness. The self is memory, the many conclusions; and thought is the response of memory. Thought is always a conclusion; thinking is concluding, and therefore it can never be free.

Thought is always the superficial, the conclusion. Consciousness is the recording of the superficial. The superficial separates itself as the outer and the inner, but this separation does not make thought any the less superficial.

"But is there not something which is beyond thought, beyond time, something that is not created by the mind?"

Either you have been told about that state, have read about it, or there is the experiencing of it. The experiencing of it can never be an experience, a result; it cannot be thought about—and if it is, it is a remembrance and not experiencing. You can repeat what you have read or heard, but the word is not the thing; and the word, the very repetition, prevents the state of experiencing. That state of experiencing cannot be as long as there is thinking; thought, the result, the effect, can never know the state of experiencing.

"Then how is thought to come to an end?"

See the truth that thought, the outcome of the known, can never be in the state of experiencing. Experiencing is always the new; thinking is always of the old. See the truth of this, and truth brings freedom—freedom from thought, the result. Then there is that which is beyond consciousness, which is neither sleeping nor waking, which is nameless : it *is*.

SELF-SACRIFICE

HE WAS RATHER fat and very pleased with himself. He had been to prison several times and had been beaten by the police, and now he was a well-known politician on his way to becoming a minister. He was at several of the meetings, sitting unobtrusively, one among the many; but the many were aware of him, and he was conscious of them. When he spoke, he had the authoritative voice of the platform; many of the people looked at him, and his voice came down to their level. Though he was among them, he had set himself apart; he was the big politician, known and looked up to; but the regard only went to a certain point, and no further. One was aware of all this as the discussion began, and there was that peculiar atmosphere that comes when a well-known figure is among the audience, an atmosphere of surprise and expectation, of camaraderie and suspicion, of condescending aloofness and pleasure.

He had come with a friend, and the friend began to explain who he was : the number of times he had been to prison, the beatings he had had, and the immense sacrifices he had made for the cause of the freedom of his country. He had been a wealthy man, thoroughly Europeanized, with a large house and gardens, several cars, and so on. As the friend was narrating the big man's exploits, his voice became more and more admiring and respectful; but there was an undercurrent, a thought that seemed to say, "He may not be all that he should be, but after all, look at the sacrifices he has made, at least that is something." The big man himself talked of improvement, of hydro-electrical development, of bringing prosperity to the people, of the current threat of Communism, of vast schemes and goals. Man was forgotten, but plans and ideologies remained.

Renunciation to gain an end is barter; in it there is no giving up, but only exchange. Self-sacrifice is an extension of the self. The sacrifice of the self is a refinement of the self, and however subtle the self may make itself, it is still enclosed, petty, limited.

Renunciation for a cause, however great, however extensive and significant, is substitution of the cause for the self; the cause or the idea becomes the self, the "me" and the "mine." Conscious sacrifice is the expansion of the self, giving up in order to gather again; conscious sacrifice is negative assertion of the self. To give up is another form of acquisition. You renounce *this* in order to gain *that*. *This* is put at a lower level, *that* at a higher level; and to gain the higher, you "give up" the lower. In this process, there is no giving up, but only a gaining of greater satisfaction; and the search for greater satisfaction has no element of sacrifice. Why use a righteous-sounding word for a gratifying activity in which all indulge? You "gave up" your social position in order to gain a different kind of position, and presumably you have it now; so your sacrifice has brought you the desired reward. Some want their reward in heaven, others here and now.

"This reward has come in the course of events, but consciously I never sought reward when I first joined the movement."

The very joining of a popular or an unpopular movement is its own reward, is it not? One may not consciously join for a reward, but the inward promptings that compel one to join are complex, and without understanding them one can hardly say that one has not sought reward. Surely, what is important is to understand this urge to renounce, to sacrifice, is it not? Why do we want to give up? To answer that, must we not first find out why we are attached? It is only when we are attached that we talk about detachment; there would be no struggle to be detached if there were no attachment. There would be no renunciation if there were no possession. We possess, and then renounce in order to possess something else. This progressive renunciation is looked upon as being noble and edifying.

"Yes, that is so. If there were no possession, of course there would be no need of renunciation."

So, renunciation, self-sacrifice, is not a gesture of greatness, to be praised and copied. We possess because without possession we are not. Possessions are many and varied. One who possesses no worldly things may be attached to knowledge, to ideas; another may be attached to virtue, another to experience, another to name and fame, and so on. Without possessions, the "me" is not; the "me" *is* the possession, the furniture, the virtue, the name. In its fear of not being, the mind is attached to name, to furniture, to value; and it will drop these in order to be at a higher level, the higher being the more gratifying, the more permanent. The fear of úncertainty, of not being, makes for attachment, for possession. When the possession is unsatisfactory or painful, we renounce it for a more pleasurable attachment. The ultimate gratifying possession is the word God, or its substitute, the State.

"But it is a natural thing to be afraid of being nothing. You are suggesting, I take it, that one should love to be nothing."

As long as you are attempting to become something, as long as you are possessed by something, there will inevitably be conflict, confusion and increasing misery. You may think that you yourself, in your achievement and success, will not be caught in this mounting disintegration; but you cannot escape it, for you are of it. Your activities, your thoughts, the very structure of your existence is based on conflict and confusion, and therefore on the process of disintegration. As long as you are unwilling to be nothing, which in fact you are, you must inevitably breed sorrow and antagonism. The willingness to be nothing is not a matter of renunciation, of enforcement, inner or outer, but of seeing the truth of what *is*. Seeing the truth of what *is* brings freedom from the fear of insecurity, the fear which breeds attachment and leads to the illusion of detachment, renunciation. The love of what *is* is the beginning of wisdom. Love alone shares, it alone can commune; but renunciation and self-sacrifice are the ways of isolation and illusion.

THE FLAME AND THE SMOKE

IT HAD BEEN warm all day and it was a trial to be out. The glare of the road and of the water, already harsh and penetrating, was made more intense by the white houses; and the earth that had been green was now bright golden and parched. The rains

163

would not come for many months. The little stream had dried up and was now a winding ribbon of sand. Some cattle were in the shade of the trees, and the boy who was looking after them sat apart, flinging stones and singing in his loneliness. The village was some miles away, and he was by himself; he was thin and underfed, but cheerful, and his song was not too sad.

Beyond the hill was the house, and we reached it as the sun was going down. From the roof one could see the green tops of the palms, stretching in an unending wave to the yellow sands. The palms cast a yellow shade, and their green was golden. Beyond the yellow sands was the green-grey sea. White waves were crowding on to the beach, but the deep waters were quiet. The clouds over the sea were taking on colour, though the sun was setting far away from them. The evening star was just showing herself. A cool breeze had come up, but the roof was still warm. A small group had gathered, and they must have been there for some time.

"I am married and the mother of several children, but I have never felt love. I am beginning to wonder if it exists at all. We know sensations, passions, excitements and satisfying pleasures, but I wonder if we know love. We often say that we love, but there is always a withholding. Physically we may not withhold, we may give ourselves completely at first; but even then there is a withholding. The giving is a gift of the senses, but that which alone can give is unawakened, far away. We meet and get lost in the smoke, but that is not the flame. Why is it that we have not got the flame? Why is the flame not burning without smoke? I wonder if we have become too clever, too knowing to have that perfume. I suppose I am too well read, too modern and stupidly superficial. In spite of clever talk, I suppose I am really dull."

But is it a matter of dullness? Is love a bright ideal, the unattainable which becomes attainable only if the conditions are fulfilled? Has one the time to fulfil all the conditions? We talk about beauty, write about it, paint it, dance it, preach it, but we are not beautiful, nor do we know love. We know only the words.

To be open and vulnerable is to be sensitive; where there is a withholding, there is insensitivity. The vulnerable is the insecure, the free from tomorrow; the open is the implicit, the unknown. That which is open and vulnerable is beautiful; the enclosed is dull and insensitive. Dullness, like cleverness, is a form of self-protection. We open this door, but keep that one closed, for we want the fresh breeze only through a particular opening. We never go outside or open all the doors and windows at the same time. Sensitivity is not a thing you get in time. The dull can never become the sensitive; the dull is always the dull. Stupidity can never become intelligent. The attempt to become intelligent is stupid. That is one of our difficulties, is it not? We are always trying to become something—and dullness remains.

"Then what is one to do?"

Do nothing but be what you are, insensitive. To do is to avoid what *is*, and the avoidance of what *is* is the grossest form of stupidity. Whatever it does, stupidity is still stupidity. The insensitive cannot become the sensitive; all it can do is to be aware of what it is, to let the story of what it is unfold. Do not interfere with insensitivity, for that which interferes is the insensitive, the stupid. Listen, and it will tell you its story; do not translate or act, but listen without interruption or interpretation right to the end of the story. Then only will there be action. The doing is not important, but the listening is.

To give, there must be the inexhaustible. The withholding that gives is the fear of ending, and only in ending is there the inexhaustible. Giving is not ending. Giving is from the much or the little; and the much or the little is the limited, the smoke, the giving and taking. The smoke is desire as jealousy, anger, disappointment; the smoke is the fear of time; the smoke is memory, experience. There is no giving, but only extending the smoke. Withholding is inevitable, for there is nothing to give. Sharing is not giving; the consciousness of sharing or giving puts an end to communion. The smoke is not the flame, but we mistake it for the flame. Be aware of the smoke, that which *is*, without blowing away the smoke to see the flame.

"Is it possible to have that flame, or is it only for the few?"

Whether it is for the few or the many is not the point, is it? If we pursue that path it can only lead to ignorance and illusion. Our concern is with the flame. Can you have that flame, that flame without smoke? Find out; observe the smoke silently and patiently. You cannot dispel the smoke, for you *are* the smoke. As the smoke goes, the flame will come. This flame is inexhaustible. Everything has a beginning and an ending, it is soon exhausted, worn out. When the heart is empty of the things of the mind, and the mind is empty of thought, then is there love. That which is empty is inexhaustible.

The battle is not between the flame and the smoke, but between the different responses within the smoke. The flame and the smoke can never be in conflict with each other. To be in conflict, they must be in relationship; and how can there be relationship between them? The one is when the other is not.

Occupation of the Mind

It was a narrow street, fairly crowded, but without too much traffic. When a bus or a car passed, one had to go to the very edge, almost into the gutter. There were a few very small shops, and a small temple without doors. This temple was exceptionally clean, and the local people were there, though not in large numbers. At the side of one of the shops a boy was sitting on the ground making garlands and small bouquets of flowers; he must have been twelve or fourteen. The thread was in a small jar of water, and in front of him, spread in little heaps on a damp cloth, were jasmine, a few roses, marigold and other flowers. With the string in one hand he would pick up with the other an assortment of flowers, and with a quick, deft twist of the string they would be tied and a bouquet would be made. He was paying hardly any attention to what his hands were doing; his eyes would wander over to the passing people, smile in recognition of someone, come back to his hands, and wander off again. Presently he was joined by another boy, and they began talking and laughing, but his hands never left off their task. By now there was quite a pile of tied flowers, but it was a little too early to sell them. The boy stopped, got up and went off, but soon returned with another boy smaller than himself, perhaps his brother. Then he resumed his pleasant work with the same ease and rapidity. Now people were coming to buy, one by one or in groups. They must have been his regular customers, for there were smiles, and a few words were exchanged. From then on he never moved from his place for over an hour. There was the fragrance of many flowers, and we smiled at each other.

The road led to a path, and the path to the house.

How we are bound to the past! But we are not bound to the past : we *are* the past. And what a complicated thing the past is, layer upon layer of undigested memories, both cherished and sorrowful. It pursues us day and night, and occasionally there is a break-through, revealing a clear light. The past is like a shadow, making things dull and weary; in that shadow, the present loses its clarity, its freshness, and tomorrow is the continuation of the shadow. The past, the present and the future are tied together by the long string of memory; the whole bundle is memory, with little fragrance. Thought moves through the present to the future and back again; like a restless animal tied to a post, it moves within its own radius, narrow or wide, but it is never free of its own shadow. This movement is the occupation of the mind with the past, the present and the future. The mind *is* the occupation. If the mind is not occupied, it ceases to exist; its very occupation is its existence. The occupation with insult and flattery, with God and drink, with virtue and passion, with work and expression, with storing up and giving, is all the same; it is still occupation, worry, restlessness. To be occupied with something, whether with furniture or God, is a state of pettiness, shallowness.

Occupation gives, to the mind a feeling of activity, of being alive. That is why the mind stores up, or renounces; it sustains itself with occupation. The mind must be busy with something. What it is busy with is of little importance; the important thing is that it be occupied, and the better occupations have social significance. To be occupied with something is the nature of the mind, and its activity springs from this. To be occupied with God, with the State, with knowledge, is the activity of a petty mind. Occupation with something implies limitation, and the God of the mind is a petty god, however high it may place him. Without occupation, the mind is not; and the fear of not being makes the mind restless and active. This restless activity has the appearance of life, but it is not life; it leads always to death —a death which is the same activity in another form.

The dream is another occupation of the mind, a symbol of its restlessness. Dreaming is the continuation of the conscious state, the extension of what is not active during the waking hours. The activity of both the upper and the deeper mind is occupational. Such a mind can be aware of an end only as a continued beginning; it can never be aware of ending, but only of a result, and result is ever continuous. The search for a result is the search for continuity. The mind, the occupation, has no ending; and only to that which ends can there be the new, only to that which dies can there be life. The death of occupation, of the mind, is the beginning of silence, of total silence. There is no relationship between this imponderable silence and the activity of the mind. To have relationship, there must be contact, communion; but there is no contact between silence and the mind. The mind cannot commune with silence; it can have contact only with its own self-projected state which it calls silence. But this silence is not silence, it is merely another form of occupation. Occupation is not silence. There is silence only with the death of the mind's occupation with silence.

Silence is beyond the dream, beyond the occupation of the deeper mind. The deeper mind is a residue, the residue of the past, open or hidden. This residual past cannot experience silence; it can dream about it, as it often does, but the dream is not the real. The dream is often taken for the real, but the dream and the dreamer are the occupation of the mind. The mind is a total process, and not an exclusive part. The total process of activity, residual and acquiring, cannot commune with that silence which is inexhaustible.

CESSATION OF THOUGHT

HE WAS A scholar, well versed in the ancient literature, and made a practice of quoting from the ancients to top off his own thoughts. One wondered if he really had any thoughts independent of the books. Of course, there is no independent thought; all thought is dependent, conditioned. Thought is the verbalization of influences. To think is to be dependent; thought can never be free. But he was concerned with learning; he was burdened with knowledge and carried it highly. He began right away talking in Sanskrit, and was very surprised and even somewhat shocked to find that Sanskrit was not at all understood. He could hardly believe it. "What you say at the various meetings shows that you have either read extensively in Sanskrit, or have studied the translations of some of the great teachers," he said. When he found it was not so, and that there had not been any reading of religious, philosophical or psychological books, he was openly incredulous.

It is odd what importance we give to the printed word, to so-called sacred books. The scholars, as the laymen, are gramophones; they go on repeating, however often the records may be changed. They are concerned with knowledge, and not with experiencing. Knowledge is an impediment to experiencing. But knowledge is a safe haven, the preserve of a few; and as the ignorant are impressed by knowledge, the knower is respected and honoured. Knowledge is an addiction, as drink; knowledge does not bring understanding. Knowledge can be taught, but not wisdom; there must be freedom from knowledge for the coming of wisdom. Knowledge is not the coin for the purchase of wisdom; but the man who has entered the refuge of knowledge does not venture out, for the word feeds his thought and he is gratified with thinking. Thinking is an impediment to experiencing; and there is no wisdom without experiencing. Knowledge, idea, belief, stand in the way of wisdom.

An occupied mind is not free, spontaneous, and only in

spontaneity can there be discovery. An occupied mind is self-enclosing; it is unapproachable, not vulnerable, and therein lies its security. Thought, by its very structure, is self-isolating; it cannot be made vulnerable. Thought cannot be spontaneous, it can never be free. Thought is the continuation of the past, and that which continues cannot be free. There is freedom only in ending.

An occupied mind creates what it is working on. It can turn out the bullock cart or the jet plane. We can think we are stupid, and we are stupid. We can think we are God, and we are our own conception : "I am That."

"But surely it is better to be occupied with the things of God than with the things of the world, is it not?"

What we think, we are; but it is the understanding of the process of thought that is important, and not what we think about. Whether we think about God, or about drink, is not important; each has its particular effect, but in both cases thought is occupied with its own self-projection. Ideas, ideals, goals, and so on, are all the projections or extensions of thought. To be occupied with one's own projections, at whatever level, is to worship the self. The Self with a capital "S" is still a projection of thought. Whatever thought is occupied with, that it is; and what it is, is nothing else but thought. So it is important to understand the thought process.

Thought is response to challenge, is it not? Without challenge, there is no thought. The process of challenge and response is experience; and experience verbalized is thought. Experience is not only of the past, but also of the past in conjunction with the present; it is the conscious as well as the hidden. This residue of experience is memory, influence; and the response of memory, of the past, is thought.

"But is that all there is to thought? Are there not greater depths to thought than the mere response of memory?"

Thought can and does place itself at different levels, the stupid and the profound, the noble and the base; but it is still thought, is it not? The God of thought is still of the mind, of the word. The thought of God is not God, it is merely the response of memory. Memory is long-lasting, and so may appear to be deep; but by its very structure it can never be deep. Memory may be concealed, not in immediate view, but that does not make it profound. Thought can never be profound, or anything more than what it is. Thought can give to itself greater value, but it remains thought. When the mind is occupied with its own self-projection, it has not gone beyond thought, it has only assumed a new role, a new pose; under the cloak it is still thought.

"But how can one go beyond thought?"

That is not the point, is it? One cannot go beyond thought, for the "one," the maker of effort, is the result of thought. In uncovering the thought process, which is self-knowledge, the truth of what *is* puts an end to the thought process. The truth of what *is* is not to be found in any book, ancient or modern. What is found is the word, but not truth.

"Then how is one to find truth?"

One cannot find it. The effort to find truth brings about a self-projected end; and that end is not truth. A result is not truth; result is the continuation of thought, extended or projected. Only when thought ends is there truth. There is no ending of thought through compulsion, through discipline, through any form of resistance. Listening to the story of what *is* brings its own liberation. It is truth that liberates, not the effort to be free.

DESIRE AND CONFLICT

IT WAS A pleasant group; most of them were eager, and there were a few who listened to refute. Listening is an art not easily come by, but in it there is beauty and great understanding. We listen with the various depths of our being, but our listening is always with a preconception or from a particular point of view. We do not listen simply; there is always the intervening screen of our own thoughts, conclusions and prejudices. We listen with pleasure or resistance, with grasping or rejection, but there is no listening. To listen there must be an inward quietness, a freedom from the strain of acquiring, a relaxed attention. This alert yet passive state is able to hear what is beyond the verbal conclusion. Words confuse, they are only the outward means of communication; but to commune beyond the noise of words, there must be in listening an alert passivity. Those who love may listen; but it is extremely rare to find a listener. Most of us are after results, achieving goals, we are forever overcoming and conquering, and so there is no listening. It is only in listening that one hears the song of the words.

"Is it possible to be free of all desire? Without desire, is there life? Is not desire life itself? To seek to be free of desire is to invite death, is it not?"

What is desire? When are we aware of it? When do we say we desire? Desire is not an abstraction, it exists only in relationship. Desire arises in contact, in relationship. Without contact, there is no desire. Contact may be at any level, but without it there is no sensation, no response, no desire. We know the process of desire, the way it comes into being: perception, contact, sensation, desire. But when are we aware of desire? When do I say I have a desire? Only when there is the disturbance of pleasure or of pain. It is when there is an awareness of conflict, of disturbance, that there is the cognizance of desire. Desire is the inadequate response to challenge. The perception of a beautiful car gives rise to the disturbance of pleasure. This disturbance is the consciousness of desire; the focusing of disturbance, caused by pain or by pleasure, is self-consciousness. Self-consciousness is desire. We are conscious when there is the disturbance of inadequate response to challenge. Conflict is self-consciousness. Can there be freedom from this disturbance, from the conflict of desire?

"Do you mean freedom from the conflict of desire, or from desire itself?"

Are conflict and desire two separate states? If they are, our inquiry must lead to illusion. If there were no disturbance of pleasure or pain, of wanting, seeking, fulfilling, either negatively or positively, would there be desire? And do we want to get rid of disturbance? If we can understand this, then we may be able to grasp the significance of desire. Conflict is self-consciousness; the focusing of attention through disturbance is desire. Is it that you want to get rid of the conflicting element in desire, and keep the pleasurable element? Both pleasure and conflict are disturbing, are they not? Or do you think pleasure does not disturb?

"Pleasure is not disturbing."

Is that true? Have you never noticed the pain of pleasure? Is not the craving for pleasure ever on the increase, ever demanding more and more? Is not the craving for more as disturbing as the urgency of avoidance? Both bring about conflict. We want to keep the pleasurable desire, and avoid the painful; but if we look closely, both are disturbing. But do you want to be free from disturbance?

"If we have no desire we will die; if we have no conflict we will go to sleep."

Are you speaking from experience, or have you merely an idea about it? We are imagining what it would be like to have no conflict and so are preventing the experiencing of whatever that state is in which all conflict has ceased. Our problem is, what causes conflict? Can we not see a beautiful or an ugly thing without conflict coming into being? Can we not observe, listen without self-consciousness? Can we not live without disturbance? Can we not be without desire? Surely, we must understand the disturbance, and not seek a way of overcoming or exalting desire. Conflict must be understood, not ennobled or suppressed.

What causes conflict? Conflict arises when the response is not adequate to the challenge; and this conflict is the focusing of consciousness as the self. The self, the consciousness focused through conflict, is experience. Experience is response to a stimulus or challenge; without terming or naming, there is no experience. Naming is out of the storehouse, memory; and this naming is the process of verbalizing, the making of symbols, images, words, which strengthens memory. Consciousness, the focusing of the self through conflict, is this total process of experience, of naming, of recording.

"In this process, what is it that gives rise to conflict? Can we be free from conflict? And what is beyond conflict?"

It is naming that gives rise to conflict, is it not? You approach the challenge, at whatever level, with a record, with an idea, with a conclusion, with prejudice; that is, you name the experience. This terming gives quality to experience, the quality arising out of naming. Naming is the recording of memory. The past meets the new; challenge is met by memory, the past. The responses of the past cannot understand the living, the new, the challenge; the responses of the past are inadequate, and from this arises conflict, which is self-consciousness. Conflict ceases when there is no process of naming. You can watch in yourself how the naming is almost simultaneous with the response. The interval between response and naming is experiencing. Experiencing, in which there is neither the experiencer nor the experienced, is beyond conflict. Conflict is the focusing of the self, and with the cessation of conflict there is the ending of all thought and the beginning of the inexhaustible.

ACTION WITHOUT PURPOSE

HE BELONGED TO various and widely different organizations, and was active in them all. He wrote and talked, collected money, organized. He was aggressive, insistent and effective. He was a very useful person, much in demand, and was forever going up and down the land. He had been through the political agitations, had gone to prison, followed the leaders, and now he was becoming an important person in his own right. He was all for the immediate carrying out of great schemes; and like all these educated people, he was versed in philosophy. He said he was a man of action, and not a contemplative; he used a Sanskrit phrase which was intended to convey a whole philosophy of action. The very assertion that he was a man of action implied that he was one of the essential elements of life—perhaps not he personally, but the type. He had classified himself and thereby blocked the understanding of himself.

Labels seem to give satisfaction. We accept the category to

which we are supposed to belong as a satisfying explanation of life. We are worshippers of words and labels; we never seem to go beyond the symbol, to comprehend the worth of the symbol. By calling ourselves this or that, we ensure ouselves against further disturbance, and settle back. One of the curses of ideologies and organized beliefs is the comfort, the deadly gratification they offer. They put us to sleep, and in the sleep we dream, and the dream becomes action. How easily we are distracted! And most of us want to be distracted; most of us are tired out with incessant conflict, and distractions become a necessity, they become more important than what *is*. We can play with distractions, but not with what *is*; distractions are illusions, and there is a perverse delight in them.

What is action? What is the process of action? Why do we act? Mere activity is not action, surely; to keep busy is not action, is it? The housewife is busy, and would you call that action?

"No, of course not. She is only concerned with everyday, petty affairs. A man of action is occupied with larger problems and responsibilities. Occupation with wider and deeper issues may be called action, not only political but spiritual. It demands capacity, efficiency, organized effort, a sustained drive towards a purpose. Such a man is not a contemplative, a mystic, a hermit, he is a man of action."

Occupation with wider issues you would call action. What are wider issues? Are they separate from everyday existence? Is action apart from the total process of life? Is there action when there is no integration of all the many layers of existence? Without understanding and so integrating the total process of life, is not action mere destructive activity? Man is a total process, and action must be the outcome of this totality.

"But that would imply not only inaction, but indefinite postponement. There is an urgency of action, and it is no good philosophizing about it."

We are not philosophizing, but only wondering if your so-called action is not doing infinite harm. Reform always needs further reform. Partial action is no action at all, it brings about

175

disintegration. If you will have the patience, we can find now, not in the future, that action which is total, integrated.

Can purposive action be called action? To have a purpose, an ideal, and work towards it—is that action? When action is for a result, is it action?

"How else can you act?"

You call action that which has a result, an end in view, do you not? You plan the end, or you have an idea, a belief, and work towards it. Working towards an object, an end, a goal, factual or psychological, is what is generally called action. This process can be understood in relation to some physical fact, such as building a bridge; but is it as easily understood with regard to psychological purposes? Surely, we are talking of the psychological purpose, the ideology, the ideal, or the belief towards which you are working. Would you call action this working towards a psychological purpose?

"Action without a purpose is no action at all, it is death. Inaction is death."

Inaction is not the opposite of action, it is quite a different state, but for the moment that is irrelevant; we may discuss that later, but let us come back to our point. Working towards an end, an ideal, is generally called action, is it not? But how does the ideal come into being? Is it entirely different from what *is*? Is antithesis different and apart from thesis? Is the ideal of non-violence wholly other than violence? Is not the ideal self-projected? Is it not home-made? In acting towards a purpose, an ideal, you are pursuing a self-projection, are you not?

"Is the ideal a self-projection?"

You are *this,* and you want to become *that.* Surely, *that* is the outcome of your thought. It may not be the outcome of your own thought, but it is born of thought, is it not? Thought projects the ideal; the ideal is part of thought. The ideal is not something beyond thought; it is thought itself.

"What's wrong with thought? Why shouldn't thought create the ideal?"

You are *this,* which does not satisfy, so you want to be *that.* If there were an understanding of *this,* would *that* come into being? Because you do not understand *this*, you create *that*, hoping through *that* to understand or to escape from *this*. Thought creates the ideal as well as the problem; the ideal is a self-projection, and your working towards that self-projection is what you call action, action with a purpose. So your action is within the limits of your own projection, whether God or the State. This movement within your own bounds is the activity of the dog chasing its tail; and is that action?

"But is it possible to act without a purpose?"

Of course it is. If you see the truth of action with a purpose, then there is just action. Such action is the only effective action, it is the only radical revolution.

"You mean action without the self, don't you?"

Yes, action without the idea. The idea is the self identified with God or with the State. Such identified action only creates more conflict, more confusion and misery. But it is hard for the man of so-called action to put aside the idea. Without the ideology he feels lost, and he is; so he is not a man of action, but a man caught in his own self-projections whose activities are the glorification of himself. His activities contribute to separation, to disintegration.

"Then what is one to do?"

Understand what your activity is, and only then is there action.

CAUSE AND EFFECT

"I KNOW YOU have healed," he said, "and will you not heal my son? He is nearly blind. I have seen a few doctors, and they can do nothing. They advise me to take him to Europe or America, but I am not a rich man and I cannot afford it. Will you not please do something? He is our only child, and my wife is heart-stricken."

He was a petty official, poor but educated, and like all of his group he knew Sanskrit and its literature. He kept on saying that it was the boy's karma that he should suffer, and theirs too. What had they done to deserve this punishment? What evil had they committed, in a previous life or in the earlier part of this one, to have to bear such pain? There must be a cause for this calamity, hidden in some past action.

There may be an immediate cause for this blindness which the physicians have not yet discovered; some inherited disease may have brought it about. If the doctors cannot discover the physical cause, why do you seek a metaphysical one in the distant past?

"By seeking the cause I may be better able to understand the effect."

Do you understand anything by knowing its cause? By knowing why one is afraid, is one free of fear? One may know the cause, but does that in itself bring understanding? When you say that you will understand the effect by knowing the cause, you mean that you will take comfort in knowing how this thing has come about, do you not?

"Of course, that is why I want to know what action in the past has produced this blindness. It will certainly be most comforting."

Then you want comfort and not understanding.

"But are they not the same thing? To understand is to find comfort. What is the good of understanding if there is no joy in it?"

Understanding a fact may cause disturbance, it does not necessarily bring joy. You want comfort, and that is what you are seeking. You are disturbed by the fact of your son's ailment, and you want to be pacified. This pacification you call understanding. You start out, not to understand, but to be comforted; your intention is to find a way to quiet your disturbance, and this you call the search for the cause. Your chief concern is to be put to sleep, to be undisturbed, and you are seeking a way to do it. We put ourselves to sleep through various ways : God, rituals, ideals, drink, and so on. We want to escape from disturbance, and one of the escapes is this search for the cause.

"Why shouldn't one seek freedom from disturbance? Why shouldn't one avoid suffering?"

Through avoidance is there freedom from suffering? You may

shut the door on some ugly thing, on some fear; but it is still there behind the door, is it not? What is suppressed, resisted, is not understood, is it? You may suppress or discipline your child, but surely that does not yield the understanding of him. You are seeking the cause in order to avoid the pain of disturbance; with that intention you look, and naturally you will find what you are seeking. There is a possibility of being free of suffering only when one observes its process, when one is aware of every phase of it, cognizant of its whole structure. To avoid suffering is only to strengthen it. The explanation of the cause is not the understanding of the cause. Through explanation you are not freed from suffering; the suffering is still there, only you have covered it over with words, with conclusions, either your own or those of another. The study of explanations is not the study of wisdom; when explanations cease, then only is wisdom possible. You are anxiously seeking explanations which will put you to sleep, and you find them; but explanation is not truth. Truth comes when there is observation without conclusions, without explanations, without words. The observer is built out of words, the self is made up of explanations, conclusions, condemnations, justifications, and so on. There is communion with the observed only when the observer is not; and only then is there understanding, freedom from the problem.

"I think I see this; but is there not such a thing as karma?"

What do you mean by that word?

"Present circumstances are the result of previous actions, immediately past or long removed. This process of cause and effect, with all its ramifications, is more or less what is meant by karma."

That is only an explanation, but let us go beyond the words. Is there a fixed cause producing a fixed effect? When cause and effect are fixed, is there not death? Anything static, rigid, specialized, must die. The specialized animals soon come to an end, do they not? Man is the unspecialized, and so there is a possibility of his continued existence. That which is pliable endures; that which is not pliable is broken. The acorn cannot become anything but an oak tree; the cause and the effect are in the acorn. But man is not so completely enclosed, specialized; hence, if he does not destroy himself through various ways, he can survive. Are cause and effect fixed, stationary? When you use the word "and" between cause and effect, does it not imply that both are stationary? But is cause ever stationary? Is effect always unchangeable? Surely, cause-effect is a continuous process, is it not? Today is the result of yesterday, and tomorrow is the result of today; what was cause becomes effect, and what was effect becomes cause. It is a chain-process, is it not? One thing flows into another, and at no point is there a halt. It is a constant movement, with no fixation. There are many factors that bring about this cause-effect-cause movement.

Explanations, conclusions, are stationary, whether they are of the right or of the left, or of the organized belief called religion. When you try to cover the living with explanations, there is death to the living, and that is what most of us desire; we want to be put to sleep by word, by idea, by thought. Rationalization is merely another way to quiet the disturbed state; but the very desire to be put to sleep, to find the cause, to seek conclusions, brings disturbance, and so thought is caught in a net of its own making. Thought cannot be free nor can it ever make itself free. Thought is the result of experience, and experience is always conditioning. Experience is not the measure of truth. Awareness of the false as the false is the freedom of truth.

DULLNESS

WHEN THE TRAIN started there was still light, but the shadows were lengthening. The town wound itself around the railway line. People came out to watch the train go by, and passengers waved to their friends. With a great roar we began to cross the bridge over a broad, curving river; it was several miles wide at this point, and the other shore was just visible in the fast-fading light. The train crossed the bridge very slowly, as though it were picking its way along; the spans were numbered, and there were fifty-eight of them between the two shores. How beautiful were those waters, silent, rich and deeply flowing! There were islands of sand that looked pleasantly cool in the distance. The town, with its noise, dust and squalor, was being left behind, and the clean evening air was coming in through the windows; but there would be dust again as soon as we left the long bridge.

The man in the lower berth was very talkative, and as we had a whole night before us, he felt he had a right to ask questions. He was a heavy-built man with large hands and feet. He began by talking about himself, his life, his troubles and his children. He was saying that India should become as prosperous as America; this over-population must be controlled, and the people must be made to feel their responsibility. He talked of the political situation and the war, and ended with an account of his own travels.

How insensitive we are, how lacking in swift and adequate response, how little free to observe! Without sensitivity, how can there be pliability and a quickening perception; how can there be receptivity, an understanding free of striving? The very striving prevents understanding. Understanding comes with high sensitivity, but sensitivity is not a thing to be cultivated. That which is cultivated is a pose, an artificial veneer; and this coating is not sensitivity, it is a mannerism, shallow or deep according to influence. Sensitivity is not a cultural effect, the result of influence; it is a state of being vulnerable, open. The open is the implicit, the unknown, the imponderable. But we take care not to be sensitive; it is too painful, too exacting, it demands constant adjustment, which is consideration. To consider is to be watchful; but we would rather be comforted, put to sleep, made dull. The newspapers, the magazines, the books, through our addiction to reading, leave their dulling imprint; for reading is a marvellous escape, like drink or a ceremony. We want to escape from the pain of life, and dullness is the most effective way: the dullness brought about by explanations, by following a leader or an ideal, by being identified with some achievement, some label or characteristic. Most of us want to be made dull, and habit is very effective in putting the mind to sleep. The habit of discipline, of practice, of sustained effort to become—these are respectable ways of being made insensitive.

"But what could one do in life if one were sensitive? We would all shrivel up, and there would be no effective action."

What do the dull and insensitive bring to the world? What is the outcome of their "effective" action? Wars, confusion within and without, ruthlessness and increasing misery for themselves and so for the world. The action of the unwatchful inevitably leads to destruction, to physical insecurity, to disintegration. But sensitivity is not easy to come by; sensitivity is the understanding of the simple, which is highly complex. It is not a withdrawal, a shrivelling up, an isolating process. To act with sensitivity is to be aware of the total process of the actor.

"To understand the total process of myself will take a long time, and meanwhile my business will go to ruin and my family will starve."

Your family will not starve; even if you have not saved up enough money, it is always possible to arrange that they shall be fed. Your business will undoubtedly go to ruin; but disintegration at other levels of existence is already taking place. You are only concerned with the outward break-up, you do not want to see or know what is happening within yourself. You disregard the inner and hope to build up the outer; yet the inner is always overcoming the outer. The outer cannot last without the fullness of the inner; but the fullness of the inner is not the repetitious sensation of organized religion nor the accumulation of facts called knowledge. The way of all these inner pursuits must be understood for the outer to survive, to be healthy. Do not say that you have no time, for you have plenty of time; it is not a matter of lack of time, but of disregard and disinclination. You have no inward richness, for you want the gratification of inner riches as you already have that of the outer. You are not seeking the wherewithal to feed your family, but the satisfaction of possessing. The man who possesses, whether property or knowledge, can never be sensitive, he can never be vulnerable or open. To possess is to be made dull, whether the possession is virtue or coins. To possess a person is to be unaware of that person; to seek and to possess reality is to deny it. When you try to become virtuous, you are no longer virtuous; your seeking virtue is only the attainment of gratification at a different level. Gratification is not virtue, but virtue is freedom.

How can the dull, the respectable, the unvirtuous be free? The freedom of aloneness is not the enclosing process of isolation. To be isolated in wealth or in poverty, in knowledge or in success, in idea or in virtue, is to be dull, insensitive. The dull, the respectable cannot commune; and when they do, it is with their own self-projections. To commune there must be sensitivity, vulnerability, the freedom from becoming, which is freedom from fear. Love is not a becoming, a state of "I shall be". That which is becoming cannot commune, for it is ever isolating itself. Love is the vulnerable; love is the open, the imponderable, the unknown.

CLARITY IN ACTION

IT WAS A lovely morning, pure after the rains. There were tender new leaves on the trees, and the breeze from the sea had set them dancing. The grass was green and lush, and the cattle were hungrily eating it up, for after a few months there would not be a blade of it left. The fragrance of the garden filled the room, and children were shouting and laughing. The palm trees had golden coco-nuts, and the banana leaves, large and swaying, were not yet torn by age and wind. How beautiful the earth was, and what a poem of colour! Past the village, beyond the big houses and the groves, was the sea, full of light and with thunderous waves. Far out there was a small boat, a few logs tied together, with a solitary man fishing.

She was quite young, in her twenties, and recently married, but the passing years were already leaving their mark upon her. She said she was of good family, cultured and hard working; she had taken her M.A. with honours, and one could see that she was bright and alert. Once started, she spoke easily and fluently, but she would suddenly become self-conscious and silent.

She wanted to unburden herself, for she said she had not talked to anyone about her problem, not even to her parents. Gradually, bit by bit, her sorrow was put into words. Words convey meaning only at a certain level; they have a way of distorting, of not giving fully the significance of their symbol, of creating a deception that is entirely unintentional. She wanted to convey much more than merely what the words meant, and she succeeded; she could not speak of certain things, however hard she tried, but her very silence conveyed those pains and unbearable indignities of a relationship that had become merely a contract. She had been struck and left alone by her husband, and her young children were hardly companions. What was she to do? They were now living apart, and should she go back?

What a strong hold respectability has on us! What will they say? Can one live alone, especially a woman, without their saying nasty things? Respectability is a cloak for the hypocrite; we commit every possible crime in thought, but outwardly we are irreproachable. She was courting respectability, and was confused. It is strange how, when one is clear within oneself, whatever may happen is right. When there is this inward clarity, the right is not according to one's desire, but whatever *is* is right. Contentment comes with the understanding of what *is*. But how difficult it is to be clear!

"How am I to be clear about what I should do?"

Action does not follow clarity: clarity *is* action. You are concerned with what you should do, and not with being clear. You are torn between respectability and what you should do, between the hope and what *is*. The dual desire for respectability and for some ideal action brings conflict and confusion, and only when you are capable of looking at what *is*, is there clarity. What *is* is not what *should* be, which is desire distorted to a particular pattern; what *is* is the actual, not the desirable but the fact. Probably you have never approached it this way; you have thought or cunningly calculated, weighing this against that, planning and counter-planning, which has obviously led to this confusion which makes you ask what you are to do. Whatever choice you may make in the state of confusion can only lead to further confusion. See this very simply and directly; if you do, then you will be able to observe what *is* without distortion. The implicit is its own action. If what *is* is clear, then you will see that there is no choice but only action, and the question of what you should do will never arise; such a question arises only when there is the uncertainty of choice. Action is not of choice; the action of choice is the action of confusion.

"I am beginning to see what you mean : I must be clear in myself, without the persuasion of respectability, without self-interested calculation, without the spirit of bargaining. I am clear, but it is difficult to maintain clarity, is it not?"

Not at all. To maintain is to resist. You are not maintaining clarity and opposing confusion : you are experiencing what is confusion, and you see that any action arising from it must inevitably be still more confusing. When you experience all this, not because another has said it but because you see it directly for yourself, then the clarity of what *is* is there; you do not maintain clarity, it is there.

"I quite see what you mean. Yes, I am clear; it is all right. But what of love? We don't know what love means. I thought I loved, but I see I do not."

From what you have told me, you married out of fear of loneliness and through physical urges and necessities; and you have found that all this is not love. You may have called it love to make it respectable, but actually it was a matter of convenience under the cloak of the word "love". To most people, this *is* love, with all its confusing smoke : the fear of insecurity, of loneliness, of frustration, of neglect in old age, and so on. But all this is merely a thought process, which is obviously not love. Thought makes for repetition, and repetition makes relationship stale. Thought is a wasteful process, it does not renew itself, it can only continue; and what has continuity cannot be the new, the fresh. Thought is sensation, thought is sensuous, thought is the sexual problem. Thought cannot end itself in order to be creative; thought cannot become something other than it is, which is sensation. Thought is always the stale, the past, the old; thought can never be new. As you have seen, love is not thought.

Love is when the thinker is not. The thinker is not an entity different from thought; thought and the thinker are one. The thinker is the thought.

Love is not sensation; it is a flame without smoke. You will know love when you as the thinker are not. You cannot sacrifice yourself, the thinker, for love. There can be no deliberate action for love, because love is not of the mind. The discipline, the will to love, is the thought of love; and the thought of love is sensation. Thought cannot think about love, for love is beyond the reaches of the mind. Thought is continuous, and love is inexhaustible. That which is inexhaustible is ever new, and that which has continuance is ever in the fear of ending. That which ends knows the eternal beginning of love.

IDEOLOGY

"ALL THIS TALK about psychology, the inner workings of the mind, is a waste of time; people want work and food. Are you not deliberately misleading your audiences when it is obvious that the economic situation must first be attacked? What you say may ultimately be effective, but what is the good of all this stuff when people are starving? You can't think or do anything without having a full stomach."

One must of course have something in the stomach to be able to carry on; but to have food for all, there must be a fundamental revolution in the ways of our thinking, and hence the importance of attacking the psychological front. To you, an ideology is far more important than the production of food. You may talk about feeding the poor and of having consideration for them, but are you not much more concerned with an idea, with an ideology?

"Yes, we are; but an ideology is only a means of gathering people together for collective action. Without an idea there can be no collective action; the idea, the plan comes first, and then action follows."

So you also are concerned with psychological factors first, and from that what you call action will follow. You do not mean, then, that to talk of psychological factors is deliberately to mislead the people. What you mean is that you have the only rational ideology, so why bother to consider further? You want to act collectively for your ideology, and that is why you say any further consideration of the psychological process is not only a waste of time but also a deviation from the main issue, which is the setting up of a classless society with work for all, and so on.

"Our ideology is the result of wide historical study, it is history interpreted according to facts; it is a factual ideology, not like the superstitious beliefs of religion. Our ideology has direct experience behind it, not mere visions and illusions."

The ideologies or dogmas of organized religions are also based on experience, perhaps that of the one who has given out the teachings. They also are founded on historical facts. Your ideology may be the outcome of study, of comparison, of accepting certain facts and denying others, and your conclusions may be the product of experience; but why reject the ideologies of others as being illusory when they also are the result of experience? You gather a group around your ideology, as do others around theirs; you want collective action, and so do they in a different way. In each case, what you call collective action springs from an idea; you are both concerned with ideas, positive or negative, to bring about collective action. Each ideology has experience behind it, only you refute the validity of their experience, and they refute the validity of yours. They say that your system is impractical, will lead to slavery, and so on, and you call them warmongers and say that their system must inevitably lead to economic disaster. So both of you are concerned with ideologies, not with feeding people or bringing about their happiness. The two ideologies are at war and man is forgotten.

"Man is forgotten to save man. We sacrifice the present man to save the future man."

You liquidate the present for the future. You assume the power of Providence in the name of the State as the Church has done in the name of God. You both have your gods and your holy book; you both have the true interpreters, the priests—and woe to anyone who deviates from the true and the authentic! There is not much difference between you, you are both very similar; your ideologies may vary, but the process is more or less the same. You both want to save the future man by sacrificing the present man—as though you knew all about the future, as though the future were a fixed thing and you had the monopoly of it! Yet you are both as uncertain of tomorrow as any other. There are so many imponderable facts in the present that make the future. You both promise a reward, a Utopia, a heaven in the future; but the future is not an ideological conclusion. Ideas are always concerned with the past or the future, but never with the present. You cannot have an idea about the present, for the present is action, the only action there is. All other action is delay, postponement, and so no action at all; it is an avoidance of action. Action based on an idea, either of the past or of the future, is inaction; action can only be in the present, in the now. Idea is of the past or of the future, and there can be no idea of the present. To an ideologist the past or the future is a fixed state, for he himself is of the past or of the future. An ideologist is never in the present; to him, life is always in the past or in the future, but never in the now. Idea is ever of the past, threading its way through the present to the future. For an ideologist the present is a passage to the future and so not important; the means do not matter at all, but only the end. Use any means to get to the end. The end is fixed, the future is known, therefore liquidate anyone who stands in the way of the end.

"Experience is essential for action, and ideas or explanations come from experience. Surely you do not deny experience. Action without the framework of idea is anarchical, it is chaos, leading straight to the asylum. Are you advocating action without the cohesive power of idea? How can you do anything without the idea first?"

As you say, the idea, the explanation, the conclusion, is the outcome of experience; without experience there can be no knowledge; without knowledge there can be no action. Does idea follow action, or is there idea first and then action? You say experience comes first, and then action, is that it? What do you mean by experience?

"Experience is the knowledge of a teacher, of a writer, of a revolutionary, the knowledge which he has gathered from his studies and from experiences, either his own or those of another. From knowledge or experience ideas are constructed, and from this ideological structure flows action."

Is experience the only criterion, the true standard of measurement? What do we mean by experience? Our talking together is an experience; you are responding to stimuli, and this response to challenge is experience, is it not? Challenge and response are almost a simultaneous process; they are a constant movement within the framework of a background. It is the background that responds to challenge, and this responding to challenge is experience, is it not? The response is from the background, from a conditioning. Experience is always conditioned, and so then is idea. Action based on idea is conditioned, limited action. Experience, idea, in opposition to another experience, idea, does not produce synthesis but only further opposition. Opposites can never produce a synthesis. An integration can take place only when there is no opposition; but ideas always breed opposition, the conflict of the opposites. Under no circumstances can conflict bring about a synthesis.

Experience is the response of the background to challenge. The background is the influence of the past, and the past is memory. The response of memory is idea. An ideology built out of memory, called experience, knowledge, can never be revolutionary. It may call itself revolutionary, but it is only a modified continuity of the past. An opposite ideology or doctrine is still idea, and idea must ever be of the past. No ideology is *the* ideology; but if you said that your ideology is limited, prejudiced, conditioned, like any other, no one would follow you. You must say it is the only ideology that can save the world; and as most of us are addicted to formulas, to conclusions, we follow and are thoroughly exploited, as the exploiter is also exploited.

Action based on an idea can never be a freeing action, but is always binding. Action towards an end, a goal, is in the long run inaction; in the short view it may assume the role of action, but such action is self-destructive, which is obvious in our daily life.

"But can one ever be free from all conditioning? We believe it is not possible."

Again, the idea, the belief imprisons you. You believe, another does not believe; you are both prisoners to your belief, you both experience according to your conditioning. One can find out if it is possible to be free only by inquiring into the whole process of conditioning, of influence. The understanding of this process is self-knowledge. Through self-knowledge alone is there freedom from bondage, and this freedom is devoid of all belief, all ideology.

BEAUTY

THE VILLAGE WAS dirty, but there was tidiness around each hut. The front steps were washed and decorated daily, and inside the hut was clean though somewhat smoky from the cooking. The whole family was there, father, mother and children, and the old lady must have been the grandmother. They all seemed so cheerful and strangely contented. Verbal communication was impossible, as we did not know their language. We sat down, and there was no embarrassment. They went on with their work, but the children came near, a boy and a girl, and sat down, smiling. The evening meal was nearly ready, and there was not too much of it. As we left, they all came out and watched; the sun was over the river, behind a vast, solitary cloud. The cloud was on fire and made the waters glow like remembered forest fires.

The long rows of huts were divided by a widish path, and on each side of the path were open, filthy gutters where every imaginable horror was being bred. One could see white worms struggling in the black slime. Children were playing on the path, completely absorbed in their games, laughing and shouting, indifferent to every passer-by. Along the embankment of the river, palms stood out against the burning sky. Pigs, goats and cattle were wandering about the huts, and the children would push a goat or a withered cow out of the way. The village was settling down for the coming darkness, and the children too were becoming quiet as their mothers called them.

The large house had a lovely garden with high, white walls all around it. The garden was full of colour and bloom, and a great deal of money and care must have gone into it. It was extraordinarily peaceful in that garden; everything was flourishing, and the beauty of the large tree seemed to protect all the other things that were growing. The fountain must have been a delight to the many birds, but now it was quietly singing to itself, undisturbed and alone. Everything was enclosing itself for the night.

She was a dancer, not by profession but by choice. She was considered by some to be a fairly good dancer. She must have felt proud of her art, for there was arrogance about her, not only the arrogance of achievement but also that of some inner recognition of her own spiritual worth. As another would be satisfied with outward success, she was gratified by her spiritual advancement. The advance of the spirit is a self-imposed deception, but it is very gratifying. She had jewels on, and her nails were red; her lips were painted the appropriate colour. She not only danced, but also gave talks on art, on beauty, and on spiritual achievement. Vanity and ambition were on her face; she wanted to be known both spiritually and as an artist, and now the spirit was gaining.

She said she had no personal problems, but wanted to talk about beauty and the spirit. She did not care about personal problems, which were stupid anyhow, but was concerned with wider issues. What was beauty? Was it inner or outer? Was it subjective or objective, or a combination of both? She was so sure of her ground, and surety is the denial of the beautiful. To be certain is to be self-enclosed and invulnerable. Without being open, how can there be sensitivity?

"What is beauty?"

Are you waiting for a definition, for a formula, or do you desire to inquire?

"But must one not have the instrument for inquiry? Without knowing, without explanations, how can one inquire? We must know where we are going before we can go."

Does not knowledge prevent inquiry? When you know, how can there be inquiry? Does not the very word "knowing" indicate a state in which inquiry has ceased? To know is not to inquire; so you are merely asking for a conclusion, a definition. Is there a measure for beauty? Is beauty the approximation to a known or an imaginary pattern? Is beauty an abstraction without a frame? Is beauty exclusive, and can the exclusive be the integrated? Can the outer be beautiful without inner freedom? Is beauty decoration, adornment? Is the outward show of beauty an indication of sensitivity? What is it that you are seeking? A combination of the outer and the inner? How can there be outer beauty without the inner? On which do you lay emphasis?

"I lay emphasis on both; without the perfect form, how can there be perfect life? Beauty is the combination of the outer and the inner."

So you have a formula for becoming beautiful. The formula is not beauty, but only a series of words. Being beautiful is not the process of becoming beautiful. What is it that you are seeking?

"The beauty of both form and spirit. There must be a lovely vase for the perfect flower."

Can there be inner harmony, and so perhaps outer harmony, without sensitivity? Is not sensitivity essential for perception either of the ugly or the beautiful? Is beauty the avoidance of the ugly?

"Of course it is."

Is virtue avoidance, resistance? If there is resistance, can there be sensitivity? Must there not be freedom for sensitivity? Can the self-enclosed be sensitive? Can the ambitious be sensitive, aware of beauty? Sensitivity, vulnerability to what *is*, is essential, is it not? We want to identify ourselves with what we call the beautiful and avoid what we call the ugly. We want to be identified with the lovely garden and shut our eyes to the smelly village. We want to resist and yet receive. Is not all identification resistance? To be aware of the village and the garden without resistance, without comparison, is to be sensitive. You want to be sensitive only to beauty, to virtue, and resist evil, the ugly. Sensitivity, vulnerability is a total process, it cannot be cut off at a particular gratifying level.

"But I am seeking beauty, sensitivity."

Is that really so? If it is, then all concern about beauty must cease. This consideration, this worship of beauty is an escape from what *is,* from yourself, is it not? How can you be sensitive if you are unaware of what you are, of what *is*? The ambitious, the crafty, the pursuers of beauty, are only worshipping their own self-projections. They are wholly self-enclosed, they have built a wall around themselves; and as nothing can live in isolation, there is misery. This search for beauty and the incessant talk of art are respectable and highly regarded escapes from life, which is oneself.

"But music is not an escape."

It is when it replaces the understanding of oneself. Without the understanding of oneself, all activity leads to confusion and pain. There is sensitivity only when there is the freedom which understanding brings—the understanding of the ways of the self, of thought.

INTEGRATION

THE LITTLE PUPPIES were plump and clean, and were playing in the warm sand. There were six of them, all white and light brown. The mother was lying a little away from them in the shade. She was thin and worn out, and so mangy that she had hardly a hair on her. There were several wounds on her body, but she wagged her tail and was so proud of those round puppies. She probably would not survive for more than a month or so. She was one of those dogs that prowl about, picking up what they can from the filthy streets or around a poor village, always hungry and always on the run. Human beings threw stones at her, chased her from their door, and they were to be avoided. But here in the shade the memories of yesterday were distant, and she was exhausted; besides, the puppies were being petted and talked to. It was late afternoon; the breeze from across the wide river was fresh and cooling, and for the moment there was contentment. Where she would get her next meal was another matter, but why struggle now?

Past the village, along the embankment, beyond the green fields and then down a dusty and noisy road, was the house in which people were waiting to talk things over. They were of every type: the thoughtful and the eager, the lazy and the argumentative, the quick-witted and those who lived according to definitions and conclusions. The thoughtful were patient, and the quick-witted were sharp with those who dragged; but the slow had to come with the fast. Understanding comes in flashes, and there must be intervals of silence for the flashes to take place; but the quick are too impatient to allow space for these flashes. Understanding is not verbal, nor is there such a thing as intellectual understanding. Intellectual understanding is only on the verbal level, and so no understanding at all. Understanding does not come as a result of thought, for thought after all is verbal. There is no thought without memory, and memory is the word, the symbol, the process of image-making. At this level there is no understanding. Understanding comes in the space between two words, in that interval before the word shapes thought. Understanding is neither for the quick-witted nor for the slow, but for those who are aware of this measureless space.

"What is disintegration? We see the rapid disintegration of human relationship in the world, but more so in ourselves. How can this falling apart be stopped? How can we integrate?"

There is integration if we can be watchful of the ways of disintegration. Integration is not on one or two levels of our existence, it is the coming together of the whole. Before that can be, we must find out what we mean by disintegration, must we not? Is conflict an indication of disintegration? We are not seeking a definition, but the significance behind that word.

"Is not struggle inevitable? All existence is struggle; without struggle there would be decay. If I did not struggle towards a goal, I would degenerate. To struggle is as essential as breathing."

A categorical statement stops all inquiry. We are trying to find out what are the factors of disintegration, and perhaps conflict, struggle, is one of them. What do we mean by conflict, struggle?

"Competition, striving, making an effort, the will to achieve, discontent, and so on."

Struggle is not only at one level of existence, but at all levels. The process of becoming is struggle, conflict, is it not? The clerk becoming the manager, the vicar becoming the bishop, the pupil becoming the Master—this psychological becoming is effort, conflict.

"Can we do without this process of becoming? Is it not a necessity? How can one be free of conflict? Is there not fear behind this effort?"

We are trying to find out, to experience, not merely at the verbal level, but deeply, what makes for disintegration, and not how to be free of conflict or what lies behind it. Living and becoming are two different states, are they not? Existence may entail effort; but we are considering the process of becoming, the psychological urge to be better, to become something, the struggle to change what *is* into its opposite. This psychological becoming may be the factor that makes everyday living painful, competitive, a vast conflict. What do we mean by becoming? The psychological becoming of the priest who wants to be the bishop, of the disciple who wants to be the Master, and so on. In this process of becoming there is effort, positive or negative; it is the struggle to change what *is* into something else, is it not? I am *this*, and I want to become *that*, and this becoming is a series of conflicts. When I have become *that*, there is still another *that*, and so on endlessly. The *this* becoming *that* is without end, and so conflict is without end. Now, why do I want to become something other than what I am?

"Because of our conditioning, because of social influences, because of our ideals. We cannot help it, it is our nature."

Merely to say that we cannot help it puts an end to discussion.

It is a sluggish mind that makes this assertion and just puts up with suffering, which is stupidity. Why are we so conditioned? Who conditions us? Since we submit to being conditioned, we ourselves make those conditions. Is it the ideal that makes us struggle to become *that* when we are *this*? Is it the goal, the Utopia, that makes for conflict? Would we degenerate if we did not struggle towards an end?

"Of course. We would stagnate, go from bad to worse. It is easy to fall into hell but difficult to climb to heaven."

Again we have ideas, opinions about what would happen, but we do not directly experience the happening. Ideas prevent understanding, as do conclusions and explanations. Do ideas and ideals make us struggle to achieve, to become? I am *this,* and does the ideal make me struggle to become *that*? Is the ideal the cause of conflict? Is the ideal wholly dissimilar from what *is*? If it is completely different, if it has no relationship with what *is,* then what *is* cannot become the ideal. To become, there must be relationship between what *is* and the ideal, the goal. You say the ideal is giving us the impetus to struggle, so let us find out how the ideal comes into being. Is not the ideal a projection of the mind?

"I want to be like you. Is that a projection?"

Of course it is. The mind has an idea, perhaps pleasurable, and it wants to be like that idea, which is a projection of your desire. You are *this,* which you do not like, and you want to become *that,* which you like. The ideal is a self-projection; the opposite is an extension of what *is*; it is not the opposite at all, but a continuity of what *is,* perhaps somewhat modified. The projection is self-willed, and conflict is the struggle towards the projection. What *is* projects itself as the ideal and struggles towards it, and this struggle is called becoming. The conflict between the opposites is considered necessary, essential. This conflict is the what *is* trying to become what it is not; and what it is not is the ideal, the self-projection. You are struggling to become something, and that something is part of yourself. The ideal is your own projection. See how the mind has played a trick upon itself. You are struggling after words, pursuing your own projection, your own shadow. You are violent, and you are struggling to become non-violent, the ideal; but the ideal is a projection of what *is*, only under a different name. This struggle is considered necessary, spiritual, evolutionary, and so on; but it is wholly within the cage of the mind and only leads to illusion.

When you are aware of this trick which you have played upon yourself, then the false as the false is seen. The struggle towards an illusion is the disintegrating factor. All conflict, all becoming is disintegration. When there is an awareness of this trick that the mind has played upon itself, then there is only what *is*. When the mind is stripped of all becoming, of all ideals, of all comparison and condemnation, when its own structure has collapsed, then the what *is* has undergone complete transformation. As long as there is the naming of what *is*, there is relationship between the mind and what *is*; but when this naming process—which is memory, the very structure of the mind—is not, then what *is* is not. In this transformation alone is there integration.

Integration is not the action of will, it is not the process of becoming integrated. When disintegration is not, when there is no conflict, no struggle to become, only then is there the being of the whole, the complete.

FEAR AND ESCAPE

WE WERE STEADILY climbing, without any perceptible movement. Below us was a vast sea of clouds, white and dazzling, wave upon wave as far as the eye could see. They looked so astonishingly solid and inviting. Occasionally, as we climbed higher in a wide circle, there were breaks in this brilliant foam, and far below was the green earth. Above us was the clear blue sky of winter, soft and immeasurable. A massive range of snow-covered mountains stretched from north to south, sparkling in the brilliant sun. These mountains reached an elevation of over fourteen thousand feet, but we had risen above them and were still climbing. They were a familiar range of peaks, and they looked so near and serene. The higher peaks lay to the north, and we shot off to the south, having reached the required altitude of twenty thousand feet.

The passenger in the next seat was very talkative. He was unfamiliar with those mountains, and had dozed as we climbed; but now he was awake and eager for a talk. It appeared that he was going out on some business for the first time; he seemed to have many interests, and spoke with considerable information about them. The sea was now below us, dark and distant, and a few ships were dotted here and there. There was not a tremor of the wings, and we passed one lighted town after another along the coast. He was saying how difficult it was not to have fear, not particularly of a crash, but of all the accidents of life. He was married and had children, and there was always fear—not of the future alone, but of everything in general. It was a fear that had no particular object, and though he was successful, this fear made his life weary and painful. He had always been rather apprehensive, but now it had become extremely persistent and his dreams were of a frightening nature. His wife knew of his fear, but she was not aware of its seriousness.

Fear can exist only in relation to something. As an abstraction, fear is a mere word, and the word is not the actual fear. Do you know specifically of what you are afraid?

"I have never been able to lay my finger on it, and my dreams too are very vague; but threading through them all there is fear. I have talked to friends and doctors about it, but they have either laughed it off or otherwise not been of much help. It has always eluded me, and I want to be free of the beastly thing."

Do you really want to be free, or is that just a phrase?

"I may sound casual, but I would give a great deal to be rid of this fear. I am not a particularly religious person, but strangely enough I have prayed to have it taken away from me. When I am interested in my work, or in a game, it is often absent; but like some monster it is ever waiting, and soon we are companions again."

Have you that fear now? Are you aware now that it is somewhere about? Is the fear conscious or hidden?

"I can sense it, but I do not know whether it is conscious or unconscious."

Do you sense it as something far away or near—not in space or distance, but as a feeling?

"When I am aware of it, it seems to be quite close. But what has that got to do with it?"

Fear can come into being only in relation to something. That something may be your family, your work, your preoccupation with the future, with death. Are you afraid of death?

"Not particularly, though I would like to have a quick death and not a long-drawn-out one. I don't think it is my family that I have this anxiety about, nor is it my job."

Then it must be something deeper than the superficial relationships that is causing this fear. One may be able to point out what it is, but if you can discover it for yourself it will have far greater significance. Why are you not afraid of the superficial relationships?

"My wife and I love each other; she wouldn't think of looking at another man, and I am not attracted to other women. We find completeness in each other. The children are an anxiety, and what one can do, one does; but with all this economic mess in the world, one cannot give them financial security, and they will have to do the best they can. My job is fairly secure, but there is the natural fear of anything happening to my wife."

So you are sure of your deeper relationship. Why are you so certain?

"I don't know, but I am. One has to take some things for granted, hasn't one?"

That's not the point. Shall we go into it? What makes you so sure of your intimate relationship? When you say that you and your wife find completeness in each other, what do you mean?

"We find happiness in each other: companionship, under-standing, and so on. In the deeper sense, we depend on each other. It would be a tremendous blow if anything happened to either of us. We are in that sense dependent."

What do you mean by "dependent"? You mean that without her you would be lost, you would feel utterly alone, is that it? She would feel the same; so you are mutually dependent.

"But what is wrong with that?"

We are not condemning or judging, but only inquiring. Are you sure you want to go into all this? You are quite sure? All right, then let's go on.

Without your wife, you would be alone, you would be lost in the deepest sense; so she is essential to you, is she not? You depend on her for your happiness, and this dependence is called love. You are afraid to be alone. She is always there to cover up the fact of your loneliness, as you cover up hers; but the fact is still there, is it not? We use each other to cover up this loneliness; we run away from it in so many ways, in so many different forms of relationship, and each such relationship becomes a dependence. I listen to the radio because music makes me happy, it takes me away from myself; books and knowledge are also a very convenient escape from myself. And on all these things we depend.

"Why should I not escape from myself? I have nothing to be proud of, and by being identified with my wife, who is much better than I am, I get away from myself."

Of course, the vast majority escape from themselves. But by escaping from yourself, you have become dependent. Dependence grows stronger, escapes more essential, in proportion to the fear of what *is*. The wife, the book, the radio, become extraordinarily important; escapes come to be all-significant, of the greatest value. I use my wife as a means of running away from myself, so I am attached to her. I must possess her, I must not lose her; and she likes to be possessed, for she is also using me. There is a common need to escape, and mutually we use each other. This usage is called love. You do not like what you are, and so you run away from yourself, from what *is*.

"That is fairly clear. I see something in that, it makes sense. But why does one run away? What is one escaping from?"

From your own loneliness, your own emptiness, from what you are. If you run away without seeing what *is*, you obviously cannot understand it; so first you have to stop running, escaping, and only then can you watch yourself as you are. But you cannot observe what *is* if you are always criticizing it, if you like or dislike it. You call it loneliness and run away from it; and the very running away from what *is* is fear. You are afraid of this loneliness, of this emptiness, and dependence is the covering of it. So fear is constant; it is constant as long as you are running away from what *is*. To be completely identified with something, with a person or an idea, is not a guarantee of final escape, for this fear is always in the background. It comes through dreams, when there is a break in identification; and there is always a break in identification, unless one is unbalanced.

"Then my fear arises from my own hollowness, my insufficiency. I see that all right, and it is true; but what am I to do about it?"

You cannot do anything about it. Whatever you do is an activity of escape. That is the most essential thing to realize. Then you will see that you are not different or separate from that hollowness. You *are* that insufficiency. The observer is the observed emptiness. Then if you proceed further, there is no longer calling it loneliness; the terming of it has ceased. If you proceed still further, which is rather arduous, the thing known as loneliness is not; there is a complete cessation of loneliness, emptiness, of the thinker as the thought. This alone puts an end to fear.

"Then what is love?"

Love is not identification; it is not thought about the loved. You do not think about love when it is there; you think about it only when it is absent, when there is distance between you and the object of your love. When there is direct communion, there is no thought, no image, no revival of memory; it is when the communion breaks, at any level, that the process of thought, of imagination, begins. Love is not of the mind. The mind makes the smoke of envy, of holding, of missing, of recalling the past, of longing for tomorrow, of sorrow and worry; and this effectively smothers the flame. When the smoke is not, the flame is. The two cannot exist together; the thought that they exist together is merely a wish. A wish is a projection of thought, and thought is not love.

EXPLOITATION AND ACTIVITY

IT WAS EARLY in the morning and the cheerful birds were making an awful lot of noise. The sun was just touching the tree tops, and in the deep shade there were still no patches of light. A snake must recently have crossed the lawn, for there was a long, narrow clearing of the dew. The sky had not yet lost its colour, and great white clouds were gathering. Suddenly the noise of the birds stopped, then increased with warning, scolding cries as a cat came and lay down under a bush. A big hawk had caught a white-and-black bird, and was tearing at it with its sharp, curving beak. It held its prey with eager ferocity, and became threatening as two or three crows came near. The hawk's eyes were yellow with narrow black slits, and they were watching the crows and us without blinking.

"Why shouldn't I be exploited? I don't mind being used for the cause, which has great significance, and I want to be completely identified with it. What they do with me is of little importance. You see, I am of no account. I can't do much in this world, and so I am helping those who can. But I have a problem of personal attachment which distracts me from the work. It is this attachment I want to understand."

But why should you be exploited? Are you not as important as the individual or the group that is exploiting you?

"I don't mind being exploited for the cause, which I consider has great beauty and worth in the world. Those with whom I work are spiritual people with high ideals, and they know better than I do what should be done."

Why do you think they are more capable of doing good than you are? How do you know they are "spiritual," to use your own word, and have wider vision? After all, when you offered your services, you must have considered this matter; or were you attracted, emotionally stirred, and so gave yourself to the work?

"It is a beautiful cause, and I offered my services because I felt that I must help it."

You are like those men who join the army to kill or to be killed for a noble cause. Do they know what they are doing? Do you know what you are doing? How do you know that the cause you are serving is "spiritual"?

"Of course you are right. I was in the army for four years during the last war; I joined it, like many other men, out of a feeling of patriotism. I don't think I considered then the significance of killing; it was the thing to do, we just joined. But the people I am helping now are spiritual."

Do you know what it means to be spiritual? For one thing, to be ambitious is obviously not spiritual. And are they not ambitious?

"I am afraid they are. I had never thought about these things, I only wanted to help something beautiful."

Is it beautiful to be ambitious and cover it up with a lot of high-sounding words about Masters, humanity, art, brotherhood? Is it spiritual to be burdened with self-centredness which is extended to include the neighbour and the man across the waters? You are helping those who are supposed to be spiritual, not knowing what it is all about and willing to be exploited.

"Yes, it is quite immature, isn't it? I don't want to be disturbed in what I am doing, and yet I have a problem; and what you are saying is even more disturbing."

Shouldn't you be disturbed? After all, it is only when we are disturbed, awakened, that we begin to observe and find out. We are exploited because of our own stupidity, which the clever ones use in the name of the country, of God, of some ideology. How can stupidity do good in the world even though the crafty make use of it? When the cunning exploit stupidity, they also are stupid, for they too do not know where their activities are leading. The action of the stupid, of those who are unaware of the ways of their own thought, leads inevitably to conflict, confusion and misery.

Your problem may not necessarily be a distraction. Since it is there, how can it be?

"It is disturbing my dedicated work."

Your dedication is not complete since you have a problem which you find distracting. Your dedication may be a thoughtless action, and the problem may be an indication, a warning not to get caught up in your present activities.

"But I like what I am doing."

And that may be the whole trouble. We want to get lost in some form of activity; the more satisfying the activity, the more we cling to it. The desire to be gratified makes us stupid, and gratification at all levels is the same; there is no higher and lower gratification. Though we may consciously or unconsciously disguise our gratification in noble words, the very desire to be gratified makes us dull, insensitive. We get satisfaction, comfort, psychological security through some kind of activity; and gaining it, or imagining that we have gained it, we do not desire to be disturbed. But there is always disturbance—unless we are dead, or understand the whole process of conflict, struggle. Most of us want to be dead, to be insensitive, for living is painful; and against that pain we build walls of resistance, the walls of conditioning. These seemingly protecting walls only breed further conflict and misery. Is it not important to understand the problem rather than to find a way out of it? Your problem may be the real, and your work may be an escape without much significance.

"This is all very disturbing, and I shall have to think about it very carefully."

It was getting warm under the trees, and we left. But how can a shallow mind ever do good? Is not the doing of "good" the indication of a shallow mind? Is not the mind, however cunning, subtle, learned, always shallow? The shallow mind can never become the unfathomable; the very becoming is the way of shallowness. Becoming is the pursuit of the self-projected. The projection may be verbally of the highest, it may be an extensive vision, scheme or plan; yet it is ever the child of the shallow. Do what it will, the shallow can never become the deep; any action on its part, any movement of the mind at any level, is still of the shallow. It is very hard for the shallow mind to see that its activities are vain, useless. It is the shallow mind that is active, and this very activity keeps it in that state. Its activity is its own conditioning. The conditioning, conscious or hidden, is the desire to be free from conflict, from struggle, and this desire builds walls against the movement of life, against unknown breezes; and within these walls of conclusions, beliefs, explanations, ideologies, the mind stagnates. Only the shallow stagnate, die.

The very desire to take shelter through conditioning breeds more strife, more problems; for conditioning is separating, and the separate, the isolated cannot live. The separate, by joining itself to other separates, does not become the whole. The separate is always the isolated, though it may accumulate and gather, expand, include and identify. Conditioning is destructive, disintegrating; but the shallow mind cannot see the truth of this, for it is active in search of truth. This very activity hinders the receiving of truth. Truth is action, not the activity of the shallow, of the seeker, of the ambitious. Truth is the good, the beautiful, not the activity of the dancer, of the planner, of the spinner of words. It is truth that liberates the shallow, not his scheme to be free. The shallow, the mind can never make itself free; it can only move from one conditioning to another, thinking the other is more free. The more is never free, it is conditioning, an extension of the less. The movement of becoming, of the man who wants to become the Buddha or the manager, is the activity of the shallow. The shallow are ever afraid of what they are; but what they are is the truth. Truth is in the silent observation of what *is*, and it is truth that transforms what *is*.

THE LEARNED OR THE WISE?

THE RAINS HAD washed away the dust and heat of many months, and the leaves were sparklingly clean, with new leaves beginning to show. All through the night the frogs filled the air with their deep croaking; they would take a rest, and start again. The river was swift-flowing, and there was softness in the air. The rains were not over by any means. Dark clouds were gathering, and the sun was hidden. The earth, the trees and the whole of Nature seemed to be waiting for another purification. The road was dark brown, and the children were playing in the puddles; they were making mud-pies, or building castles and houses with surrounding walls. There was joy in the air after months of heat, and green grass was beginning to cover the earth. Everything was renewing itself.

This renewal is innocence.

The man considered himself vastly learned, and to him knowledge was the very essence of life. Life without knowledge was worse than death. His knowledge was not about one or two things, but covered a great many phases of life; he could talk with assurance about the atom and Communism, about astronomy and the yearly flow of water in the river, about diet and over-population. He was strangely proud of his knowledge and, like a clever showman, he brought it to impress; it made the others silent and respectful. How frightened we are of knowledge, what awesome respect we show to the knower! His English was sometimes rather difficult to understand. He had never been outside of his own country, but he had books from other countries. He was addicted to knowledge as another might be to drink or to some other appetite.

"What is wisdom, if it is not knowledge? Why do you say that one must suppress all knowledge? Is not knowledge essential? Without knowledge, where would we be? We would still be as the primitives, knowing nothing of the extraordinary world we live in. Without knowledge, existence at any level would be impossible. Why are you so insistent in saying that knowledge is an impediment to understanding?"

Knowledge is conditioning. Knowledge does not give freedom. One may know how to build an airplane and fly to the other end of the world in a few hours, but this is not freedom. Knowledge is not the creative factor, for knowledge is continuous, and that which has continuity can never lead to the implicit, the imponderable, the unknown. Knowledge is a hindrance to the open, to the unknown. The unknown can never be clothed in the known; the known is always moving to the past; the past is ever overshadowing the present, the unknown. Without freedom, without the open mind, there can be no understanding. Understanding does not come with knowledge. In the interval between words, between thoughts, comes understanding; this interval is silence unbroken by knowledge, it is the open, the imponderable, the implicit.

"Is not knowledge useful, essential? Without knowledge, how can there be discovery?"

Discovery takes place, not when the mind is crowded with knowledge, but when knowledge is absent; only then is there stillness and space, and in this state understanding or discovery comes into being. Knowledge is undoubtedly useful at one level, but at another it is positively harmful. When knowledge is used as a means of self-aggrandizement, to puff oneself up, then it is mischievous, breeding separation and enmity. Self-expansion is disintegration, whether in the name of God, of the State, or of an ideology. Knowledge at one level, though conditioning, is necessary: language, technique, and so on. This conditioning is a safeguard, an essential for outer living; but when this conditioning is used psychologically, when knowledge becomes a means of psychological comfort, gratification, then it inevitably breeds conflict and confusion. Besides, what do we mean by knowing? What actually do you know?

"I know about a great many things."

You mean you have lots of information, data about many things. You have gathered certain facts; and then what? Does information about the disaster of war prevent wars? You have, I am sure, plenty of data about the effects of anger and violence within oneself and in society; but has this information put an end to hate and antagonism?

"Knowledge about the effects of war may not put an immediate end to wars, but it will eventually bring about peace. People must be educated, they must be shown the effects of war, of conflict."

People are yourself and another. You have this vast information, and are you any less ambitious, less violent, less self-centred? Because you have studied revolutions, the history of inequality, are you free from feeling superior, giving importance to yourself? Because you have extensive knowledge of the world's miseries and disasters, do you love? Besides, what is it that we know, of what have we knowledge?

"Knowledge is experience accumulated through the ages. In one form it is tradition, and in another it is instinct, both conscious and unconscious. The hidden memories and experiences, whether handed down or acquired, act as a guide and shape our action; these memories, both racial and individual, are essential, because they help and protect man. Would you do away with such knowledge?"

Action shaped and guided by fear is no action at all. Action which is the outcome of racial prejudices, fears, hopes, illusions, is conditioned; and all conditioning, as we said, only breeds further conflict and sorrow. You are conditioned as a brahmin in accordance with a tradition which has been going on for centuries; and you respond to stimuli, to social changes and conflicts, as a brahmin. You respond according to your conditioning, according to your past experiences, knowledge, so new experience only conditions further. Experience according to a belief, according to an ideology, is merely the continuation of that belief, the perpetuation of an idea. Such experience only strengthens belief. Idea separates, and your experience according to an idea, a pattern, makes you more separative. Experience as knowledge, as a psychological accumulation, only conditions, and experience is then another way of self-aggrandizement. Knowledge as experience at the psychological level is a hindrance to understanding.

"Do we experience according to our belief?"

That is obvious, is it not? You are conditioned by a particular society—which is yourself at a different level—to believe in God, in social divisions; and another is conditioned to believe that there is no God, to follow quite a different ideology. Both of you will experience according to your beliefs, but such experience is a hindrance to the unknown. Experience, knowledge, which is memory, is useful at certain levels; but experience as a means of strengthening the psychological "me," the ego, only leads to illusion and sorrow. And what can we know if the mind is filled with experiences, memories, knowledge? Can there be experiencing if we know? Does not the known prevent experiencing? You may know the name of that flower, but do you thereby experience the flower? Experiencing comes first, and the naming only gives strength to the experience. The naming prevents further experiencing. For the state of experiencing, must there not be freedom from naming, from association, from the process of memory?

Knowledge is superficial, and can the superficial lead to the deep? Can the mind, which is the result of the known, of the past, ever go above and beyond its own projections? To discover, it must stop projecting. Without its projections, mind is not. Knowledge, the past, can project only that which is the known. The instrument of the known can never be the discoverer. The known must cease for discovery; the experience must cease for experiencing. Knowledge is a hindrance to understanding.

"What have we left if we are without knowledge, experience, memory? We are then nothing."

Are you anything more than that now? When you say, "Without knowledge we are nothing," you are merely making a verbal assertion without experiencing that state, are you not? When you make that statement there is a sense of fear, the fear of being naked. Without these accretions you are nothing—which is the truth. And why not be that? Why all these pretensions and conceits? We have clothed this nothingness with fancies, with hopes, with various comforting ideas; but beneath these coverings we are nothing, not as some philosophical abstraction, but actually nothing. The experiencing of that nothingness is the beginning of wisdom.

How ashamed we are to say we do not know! We cover the fact of not knowing with words and information. Actually, you do not know your wife, your neighbour; how can you when you do not know yourself? You have a lot of information, conclusions, explanations about yourself, but you are not aware of that which *is,* the implicit. Explanations, conclusions, called knowledge, prevent the experiencing of what *is.* Without being innocent, how can there be wisdom? Without dying to the past, how can there be the renewing of innocence? Dying is from moment to moment; to die is not to accumulate; the experiencer must die to the experience. Without experience, without knowledge, the experiencer is not. To know is to be ignorant; not to know is the beginning of wisdom.

STILLNESS AND WILL

THERE WAS HARDLY anyone on the long, curving beach. A few fishermen were going back to their village among the tall palms. As they walked they made thread, rolling the cotton on their naked thighs and winding it on the bobbin; it was a very fine thread, and strong. Some of them walked with ease and grace, and others with dragging feet. They were ill-fed, thin, and burnt dark by the sun. A boy passed by singing, with long, cheerful strides; and the sea came rolling in. There was no strong breeze, but it was a heavy sea, with thunderous waves. The moon, almost full, was just rising out of the blue-green water, and the breakers were white against the yellow sands.

How essentially simple life is, and how we complicate it! Life is complex, but we do not know how to be simple with it. Complexity must be approached simply, otherwise we shall never understand it. We know too much, and that is why life eludes us; and the too much is so little. With that little we meet the immense; and how can we measure the immeasurable? Our vanity dulls us, experience and knowledge bind us, and the waters of life pass us by. To sing with that boy, to drag wearily with those fishermen, to spin thread on one's thigh, to be those villagers and that couple in the car—to be all that, not as a trick of identity, needs love. Love is not complex, but the mind makes it so. We are too much with the mind, and the ways of love we do not know. We know the ways of desire and the will of desire, but we do not know love. Love is the flame without the smoke. We are too familiar with the smoke; it fills our heads and hearts, and we see darkly. We are not simple with the beauty of the flame; we torture ourselves with it. We do not live with the flame, following swiftly wherever it may lead. We know too much, which is always little, and we make a path for love. Love eludes us, but we have the empty frame. Those who know that they do not know are the simple; they go far, for they have no burden of knowledge.

He was a *sannyasi* of some repute; he had the saffron robe and the distant look. He was saying that he had renounced the world many years ago and was now approaching the stage when neither this world nor the other world interested him. He had practised many austerities, driven the body hard and fast, and had extra-ordinary control over his breathing and nervous system. This had given him a great sense of power, though he had not sought it.

Is not this power as detrimental to understanding as the power of ambition and vanity? Greed, like fear, breeds the power of action. All sense of power, of domination, gives strength to the self, to the "me" and the "mine"; and is not the self a hindrance to reality?

"The lower must be suppressed or made to conform to the higher. Conflict between the various desires of the mind and the body must be stilled; in the process of control, the rider tastes power, but power is used to climb higher or go deeper. Power is harmful only when used for oneself, and not when used to clear the way for the supreme. Will is power, it is the directive; when used for personal ends it is destructive, but when used in the right direction it is beneficial. Without will, there can be no action."

Every leader uses power as a means to an end, and so does the ordinary man; but the leader says that he is using it for the good of the whole, while the everyday man is just out for himself. The goal of the dictator, of the man of power, of the leader, is the same as that of the led; they are similar, one is the expansion of the other; and both are self-projections. We condemn one and praise the other; but are not all goals the outcome of one's own prejudices, inclinations, fears and hopes? You use will, effort, power, to make way for the supreme; that supreme is fashioned out of desire, which is will. Will creates its own goal and sacrifices or suppresses everything to that end. The end is itself, only it is called the supreme, or the State, or the ideology.

"Can conflict come to an end without the power of will?"

Without understanding the ways of conflict and how it comes into being, of what value is it merely to suppress or sublimate conflict, or find a substitute for it? You may be able to suppress a disease, but it is bound to show itself again in another form. Will itself is conflict, it is the outcome of struggle; will is purposive, directed desire. Without comprehending the process of desire, merely to control it is to invite further burning, further pain. Control is evasion. You may control a child or a problem, but you have not thereby understood either. Understanding is of far greater importance than arriving at an end. The action of will is destructive, for action towards an end is self-enclosing, separating, isolating. You cannot silence conflict, desire, for the maker of the effort is himself the product of conflict, of desire. The thinker and his thoughts are the outcome of desire; and without understanding desire, which is the self placed at any level, high or low, the mind is ever caught in ignorance. The way to the supreme does not lie through will, through desire. The supreme can come into being only when the maker of effort is not. It is will that breeds conflict, the desire to become or to make way for the supreme. When the mind which is put together through desire comes to an end, not through effort, then in that stillness, which is not a goal, reality comes into being.

"But is not simplicity essential for that stillness?"

What do you mean by simplicity? Do you mean identification with simplicity, or being simple?

"You cannot be simple without identifying yourself with that which is simple, externally as well as inwardly."

You *become* simple, is that it? You are complex, but you become simple through identification, through identifying yourself with the peasant or with the monk's robe. I am *this*, and I become *that*. But does this process of becoming lead to simplicity, or merely to the idea of simplicity? Identification with an idea called the simple is not simplicity, is it? Am I simple because I keep on asserting that I am simple, or keep on identifying myself with the pattern of simplicity? Simplicity lies in the understanding of what *is*, not in trying to change what *is* into simplicity. Can you change what *is* into something it is not? Can greed, whether for God, money or drink, ever become non-greed? What we identify ourselves with is always the self-projected, whether it is the supreme, the State or the family. Identification at any level is the process of the self.

Simplicity is the understanding of what *is*, however complex it may appear. The what *is* is not difficult to understand, but what prevents understanding is the distraction of comparison, of condemnation, of prejudice, whether negative or positive, and so on. It is these that make for complexity. What *is* is never complex in itself, it is always simple. What you are is simple to understand, but it is made complex by your approach to it; so there must be an understanding of the whole process of approach, which makes for complexity. If you do not condemn the child, then he is what he is and it is possible to act. The action of condemnation leads to complexity; the action of what *is* is simplicity.

Nothing is essential for stillness but stillness itself; it is its own beginning and its own end. No essentials bring it about, for it *is*. No means can ever lead to stillness. It is only when stillness is something to be gained, achieved, that the means become essential. If stillness is to be bought, then the coin becomes important; but the coin, and that which it purchases, are not stillness. Means are noisy, violent, or subtly acquisitive, and the end is of like nature, for the end is in the means. If the beginning is silence, the end is also silence. There are no means to silence; silence is when noise is not. Noise does not come to an end through the further noise of effort, of discipline, of austerities, of will. See the truth of this, and there is silence.

AMBITION

THE BABY HAD been crying all night, and the poor mother had been doing her best to quiet him. She sang to him, she scolded him, she petted and rocked him; but it was no good. The baby must have been teething, and it was a weary night for the whole family. But now the dawn was coming over the dark trees, and at last the baby became quiet. There was a peculiar stillness as the sky grew lighter and lighter. The dead branches were clear against the sky, slender and naked; a child called, a dog barked, a lorry rattled by, and another day had begun. Presently the mother came out carrying the baby, carefully wrapped, and walked along the road past the village, where she waited for a bus. Presumably she was taking him to the doctor. She looked so tired and haggard after that sleepless night, but the baby was fast asleep.

Soon the sun was over the tree tops, and the dew sparkled on the green grass. Far away a train whistled, and the distant mountains looked cool and shadowy. A large bird flew noisily away, for we had disturbed her brooding. Our approach must have been very sudden, for she hadn't had time to cover her eggs with dry leaves. There were over a dozen of them. Even though uncovered they were hardly visible, she had so cleverly concealed them, and now she was watching from a distant tree. We saw the mother with her brood a few days later, and the nest was empty.

It was shady and cool along the path, which led through the damp woods to the distant hill-top, and the wattle was in bloom. It had rained heavily a few days before, and the earth was soft and yielding. There were fields of young potatoes, and far down in the valley was the town. It was a beautiful, golden morning. Beyond the hill the path led back to the house.

She was very clever. She had read all the latest books, had seen the latest plays, and was well informed about some philosophy which had become the latest craze. She had been analysed and had apparently read a great deal of psychology, for she knew the jargon. She made a point of seeing all the important people, and had casually met someone who brought her along. She talked easily and expressed herself with poise and effect. She had been married, but had had no children; and one felt that all that was behind her, and that now she was on a different journey. She must have been rich, for she had about her that peculiar atmosphere of the wealthy. She began right away by asking, "In what way are you helping the world in this present crisis?" It must have been one of her stock questions. She went on to ask, more eagerly, about the prevention of war, the effects of Communism, and the future of man.

Are not wars, the increasing disasters and miseries, the outcome of our daily life? Are we not, each one of us, responsible for this crisis? The future is in the present; the future will not be very different if there is no comprehension of the present. But do you not think that each one of us is responsible for this conflict and confusion?

"It may be so; but where does this recognition of responsibility lead? What value has my little action in the vast destructive action? In what way is my thought going to affect the general stupidity of man? What is happening in the world is sheer stupidity, and my intelligence is in no way going to affect it. Besides, think of the time it would take for individual action to make any impression on the world."

Is the world different from you? Has not the structure of society been built up by people like you and me? To bring about a radical change in the structure, must not you and I fundamentally transform ourselves? How can there be a deep revolution of values if it does not begin with us? To help in the present crisis, must one look for a new ideology, a new economic plan? Or must one begin to understand the conflict and confusion within oneself, which, in its projection, is the world? Can new ideologies bring unity between man and man? Do not beliefs set man against man? Must we not put away our ideological barriers—for all barriers are ideological—and consider our problems, not through the bias of conclusions and formulas, but directly and without prejudice? We are never directly in relationship with our problems, but always through some belief or formulation. We can solve our problems only when we are directly in relationship with them. It is not our problems which set man against man, but our ideas about them. Problems bring us together, but ideas separate us.

If one may ask, why are you so apparently concerned about the crisis?

"Oh, I don't know. I see so much suffering, so much misery, and I feel something must be done about it."

Are you really concerned, or are you merely ambitious to do something?

"When you put it that way, I suppose I am ambitious to do something in which I shall succeed."

So few of us are honest in our thinking. We want to be successful, either directly for ourselves, or for the ideal, the belief with which we have identified ourselves. The ideal is our own projection, it is the product of our mind, and our mind experiences according to our conditioning. For these self-projections we work, we slave away and die. Nationalism, like the worship of God, is only the glorification of oneself. It is oneself that is important, actually or ideologically, and not the disaster and the misery. We really do not want to do anything about the crisis; it is merely a new topic for the clever, a field for the socially active and for the idealist.

Why are we ambitious?

"If we were not, nothing would get done in the world. If we were not ambitious we would still be driving about in horse-carriages. Ambition is another name for progress. Without progress, we would decay, wither away."

In getting things done in the world, we are also breeding wars and untold miseries. Is ambition progress? For the moment we are not considering progress, but ambition. Why are we ambitious? Why do we want to succeed, to be somebody? Why do we struggle to be superior? Why all this effort to assert oneself, whether directly, or through an ideology or the State? Is not this self-assertion the main cause of our conflict and confusion? Without ambition, would we perish? Can we not physically survive without being ambitious?

"Who wants to survive without success, without recognition?"

Does not this desire for success, for applause, bring conflict both within and without? Would being free of ambition mean decay? Is it stagnation to have no conflict? We can drug ourselves, put ourselves to sleep with beliefs, with doctrines, and so have no deep conflicts. For most of us, some kind of activity is the drug. Obviously, such a state is one of decay, disintegration. But when we are aware of the false as the false, does it bring death? To be aware that ambition in any form, whether for happiness, for God, or for success, is the beginning of conflict both within and without, surely does not mean the end of all action, the end of life.

Why are we ambitious?

"I would be bored if I were not occupied in striving to achieve some kind of result. I used to be ambitious for my husband, and I suppose you would say it was for myself through my husband; and now I am ambitious for myself through an idea. I have never thought about ambition, I have just been ambitious."

Why are we clever and ambitious? Is not ambition an urge to avoid what *is*? Is not this cleverness really stupid, which is what we are? Why are we so frightened of what *is*? What is the good of running away if whatever we are is always there? We may succeed in escaping, but what we are is still there, breeding conflict and misery. Why are we so frightened of our loneliness, of our emptiness? Any activity away from what *is* is bound to bring sorrow and antagonism. Conflict is the denial of what *is* or the running away from what is; there is no conflict other than that. Our conflict becomes more and more complex and insoluble because we do not face what *is*. There is no complexity in what *is*, but only in the many escapes that we seek.

SATISFACTION

THE SKY WAS heavy with clouds and the day was warm, though the breeze was playing with the leaves. There was distant thunder, and a sprinkling of rain was laying the dust on the road. The parrots were flying about wildly, screeching their little heads off, and a big eagle was sitting on the topmost branch of a tree, preening itself and watching all the play that was going on down below. A small monkey was sitting on another branch, and the two of them watched each other at a safe distance. Presently a crow joined them. After its morning toilet the eagle remained very still for a while, and then flew off. Except for the human beings, it was a new day; nothing was like yesterday. The trees and the parrots were not the same; the grass and the shrubs had a wholly different quality. The remembrance of yesterday only darkens today, and comparison prevents perception. How lovely were those red and yellow flowers! Loveliness is not of time. We carry our burdens from day to day, and there is never a day without the shadow of many yesterdays. Our days are one continuous movement, yesterday mingling with today and tomorrow; there is never an ending. We are frightened of ending; but without ending, how can there be the new? Without death, how can there be life? And how little we know of either! We have all the words, the explanations, and they satisfy us. Words distort ending, and there is ending only when the word is not. The ending that is of words we know; but the ending without words, the silence that is not of words, we never know. To know is memory; memory is ever continuous, and desire is the thread that binds day to day. The end of desire is the new. Death is the new, and life as continuance is only memory, an empty thing. With the new, life and death are one.

A boy was walking with long strides, singing as he walked. He smiled at all those he passed and seemed to have many friends. He was ill-clad, with a dirty cloth around his head, but he had a shining face and bright eyes. With his rapid strides he passed a fat man wearing a cap. The fat man waddled, head down, worried and anxious. He did not hear the song the boy was singing, nor even glance at the singer. The boy strode on through the big gates; passing the beautiful gardens and crossing the bridge over the river, he rounded a bend towards the sea, where he was joined by some companions, and as darkness gathered they all began to sing together. The lights of a car lit up their faces, and their eyes were deep with unknown pleasures. It was raining heavily now, and everything was dripping wet.

He was a doctor not only of medicine but also of psychology. Thin, quiet and self-contained, he had come from across the seas, and had been long enough in this country to be used to the sun and the heavy rains. He had worked, he said, as a doctor and psychologist during the war, and had helped as much as his capacity allowed, but he was dissatisfied with what he had given. He wanted to give much more, to help much more deeply; what he gave was so little, and there was something missing in it all.

We sat without a word for a long period while he gathered the pressures of his distress. Silence is an odd thing. Thought does not make for silence, nor does it build it up. Silence cannot be put together, nor does it come with the action of will. Remembrance of silence is not silence. Silence was there in the room with throbbing stillness, and the talk did not disturb it. The talk had meaning in that silence, and silence was the background of the word. Silence gave expression to thought, but the thought was not silence. Thinking was not, but silence was; and silence penetrated, gathered and gave expression. Thinking can never penetrate, and in silence there is communion.

The doctor was saying that he was dissatisfied with everything : with his work, with his capacities, with all the ideas he had so carefully cultivated. He had tried the various schools of thought, and was dissatisfied with them all. During the many months since he had arrived here, he had been to various teachers, but had come away with still greater dissatisfaction. He had tried many isms, including cynicism, but dissatisfaction was still there.

Is it that you are seeking satisfaction and have not so far found it? Is the desire for satisfaction causing discontent? Searching implies the known. You say you are dissatisfied, and yet you are searching; you are looking for satisfaction, and you have not yet found it. You want satisfaction, which means that you are not dissatisfied. If you were really dissatisfied with everything, you would not be seeking a way out of it. Dissatisfaction which seeks to be satisfied soon finds what it wants in some kind of relationship with possessions, with a person, or with some ism.

"I have been through all that, yet I am completely dissatisfied."

You may be dissatisfied with outward relationships, but perhaps you are seeking some psychological attachment that will give full satisfaction.

"I have been through that too, but I am still dissatisfied."

I wonder if you really are? If you were wholly discontented, there would be no movement in any particular direction, would there? If you are thoroughly dissatisfied with being in a room, you do not seek a bigger room with nicer furniture; yet this desire to find a better room is what you call dissatisfaction. You are not dissatisfied with all rooms, but only with this particular one, from which you want to escape. Your dissatisfaction arises from not having found complete satisfaction. You are really seeking gratification, so you are constantly on the move, judging, comparing, weighing, denying; and naturally you are dissatisfied. Is this not so?

"It looks that way, doesn't it?"

So you are really *not* dissatisfied; it is simply that you have not so far been able to find complete and lasting satisfaction in anything. That is what you want : complete satisfaction, some deep inner contentment that will endure.

"But I want to help, and this discontent prevents me from giving myself to it completely."

Your goal is to help and to find complete gratification in it. You really do not want to help, but to find satisfaction in helping. You look for gratification in helping, another looks for it in some ism, and yet another in some kind of addiction. You are looking for a completely satisfying drug which for the time being you call helping. In seeking to equip yourself to help, you are equipping yourself to be completely gratified. What you really want is lasting self-gratification.

With most of us, discontent finds an easy contentment. Discontent is soon put to sleep; it is soon drugged, made quiet and respectable. Outwardly you may have finished with all isms, but psychologically, deep down, you are seeking something that you can hold on to. You say you have finished with all personal relationship with another. It may be that in personal relationship you have not found lasting gratification, and so you are seeking relationship with an idea, which is always self-projected. In the search for a relationship that will be completely gratifying, for a secure refuge that will weather all storms, do you not lose the very thing that brings contentment? Contentment, perhaps, is an ugly word, but real contentment does not imply stagnation, reconciliation, appeasement, insensitivity. Contentment is the understanding of what *is*, and what *is* is never static. A mind that is interpreting, translating what *is*, is caught in its own prejudice of satisfaction. Interpretation is not understanding.

With the understanding of what *is* comes inexhaustible love, tenderness, humility. Perhaps that is what you are in search of; but that cannot be sought and found. Do what you will, you will never find it. It is there when all search has come to an end. You can search only for that which you already know, which is more gratification. Searching and watching are two different processes; one is binding, and the other brings understanding. Search, having always an end in view, is ever binding; passive watchfulness brings understanding of what *is* from moment to moment. In the what *is* from moment to moment there is ever an ending; in search there is continuity. Search can never find the new; only in ending is there the new. The new is the inexhaustible. Love alone is ever-renewing.

The cabin was high up in the mountains, and to get there one had to cross the wide desert by car, passing through many towns, and through luxuriant orchards and rich farms that had been reclaimed from the desert by irrigation and hard work. One town was especially pleasant with green lawns and big shady trees, for nearby was a river that came down from the distant mountains into the very heart of the desert. Beyond this town, following the cascading river, the road led on towards the snowy peaks. The earth was now rocky, bare and sunburnt, but there were many trees along the river's banks. The road curved in and out, rising higher and higher, and passing through forests of ancient pines with the scent of the sun among them. The air had become cool and fresh, and soon we arrived at the cabin.

After a couple of days, when it had got used to us, a red-and-black squirrel would come and sit on the window-sill and somewhat scold us. It wanted nuts. Every visitor must have fed it; but now visitors were few, and it was eager to store up for the coming winter. It was a very active, cheerful squirrel, and it was always ready to gather what it could for the many cold and snowy months ahead. Its home was in the hollow of a tree that must have been dead for many years. It would grab a nut, race across to the huge trunk, climb up it noisily, scolding and threatening, disappear into a hole, and then come down again with such speed that one thought it would fall; but it never did. We spent a morning giving it a whole bag of nuts; it became very friendly and would come right into the room, its fur shining and its large beady eyes sparkling. Its claws were sharp, and its tail very bushy. It was a gay, responsible little animal, and it seemed to own the whole neighbourhood, for it kept off all the other squirrels.

He was a pleasant man, and eager for wisdom. He wanted to collect it as that squirrel gathered nuts. Though he was not too well-to-do, he must have travelled a good bit, for he seemed to have met many people in many countries. He had apparently read very extensively also, for he would bring out a phrase or two from some philosopher or saint. He said he could read Greek easily and had a smattering of Sanskrit. He was getting old and was eager to gather wisdom.

Can one gather wisdom?

"Why not? It is experience that makes a man wise, and knowledge is essential for wisdom."

Can a man who has accumulated be wise?

"Life is a process of accumulation, the gradual building up of character, a slow unfoldment. Experience, after all, is the storing up of knowledge. Knowledge is essential for all understanding."

Does understanding come with knowledge, with experience? Knowledge is the residue of experience, the gathering of the past. Knowledge, consciousness, is always the past; and can the past ever understand? Does not understanding come in those intervals when thought is silent? And can the effort to lengthen or accumulate those silent spaces bring understanding?

"Without accumulation, we would not be; there would be no continuity of thought, of action. Accumulation is character, accumulation is virtue. We cannot exist without gathering. If I did not know the structure of that motor, I would be unable to understand it; if I did not know the structure of music, I would be unable to appreciate it deeply. Only the shallow *enjoy* music. To appreciate music, you must know how it is made, put together. Knowing is accumulation. There is no appreciation without knowing the facts. Accumulation of some kind is necessary for understanding, which is wisdom."

To discover, there must be freedom, must there not? If you are bound, weighed down, you cannot go far. How can there be freedom if there is accumulation of any kind? The man who accumulates, whether money or knowledge, can never be free. You may be free from the acquisitiveness of things, but the greed for knowledge is still bondage, it holds you. Is a mind that is tethered to any form of acquisition capable of wandering far and discovering? Is virtue accumulation? Can a mind that is accumulating virtue ever be virtuous? Is not virtue the freedom

223

from becoming? Character may be a bondage too. Virtue can never be a bondage, but all accumulation is.

"How can there be wisdom without experience?"

Wisdom is one thing, and knowledge another. Knowledge is the accumulation of experience; it is the continuation of experience, which is memory. Memory can be cultivated, strengthened, shaped, conditioned; but is wisdom the extension of memory? Is wisdom that which has continuance? We have knowledge, the accumulation of ages; and why are we not wise, happy, creative? Will knowledge make for bliss? Knowing, which is the accumulation of experience, is not experiencing. Knowing prevents experiencing. The accumulation of experience is a continuous process, and each experience strengthens this process; each experience strengthens memory, gives life to it. Without this constant reaction of memory, memory would soon fade away. Thought is memory, the word, the accumulation of experience. Memory is the past, as consciousness is. This whole burden of the past is the mind, is thought. Thought is the accumulated; and how can thought ever be free to discover the new? It must end for the new to be.

"I can comprehend this up to a point; but without thought, how can there be understanding?"

Is understanding a process of the past, or is it always in the present? Understanding means action in the present. Have you not noticed that understanding is in the instant, that it is not of time? Do you understand gradually? Understanding is always immediate, now, is it not? Thought is the outcome of the past; it is founded on the past, it is a response of the past. The past is the accumulated, and thought is the response of the accumulation. How, then, can thought ever understand? Is understanding a conscious process? Do you deliberately set out to understand? Do you choose to enjoy the beauty of an evening?

"But is not understanding a conscious effort?"

What do we mean by consciousness? When are you conscious? Is consciousness not the response to challenge, to stimulus, pleasant or painful? This response to challenge is experience. Experience is naming, terming, association. Without naming, there would be no experience, would there? This whole process of challenge, response, naming, experience, is consciousness, is it not? Consciousness is always a process of the past. Conscious effort, the will to understand, to gather, the will to be, is a continuation of the past, perhaps modified, but still of the past. When we make an effort to be or to become something, that something is the projection of ourselves. When we make a conscious effort to understand, we are hearing the noise of our own accumulations. It is this noise that prevents understanding.

"Then what is wisdom?"

Wisdom is when knowledge ends. Knowledge has continuity; without continuity there is no knowledge. That which has continuity can never be free, the new. There is freedom only to that which has an ending. Knowledge can never be new, it is always becoming the old. The old is ever absorbing the new and thereby gaining strength. The old must cease for the new to be.

"You are saying, in other words, that thought must end for wisdom to be. But how is thought to end?"

There is no ending to thought through any kind of discipline, practice, compulsion. The thinker is the thought, and he cannot operate upon himself; when he does, it is only a self-deception. He *is* thought, he is not separate from thought; he may assume that he is different, pretend to be dissimilar, but that is only the craftiness of thought to give itself permanency. When thought attempts to end thought it only strengthens itself. Do what it will, thought cannot end itself. It is only when the truth of this is seen that thought comes to an end. There is freedom only in seeing the truth of what *is*, and wisdom is the perception of that truth. The what *is* is never static, and to be passively watchful of it there must be freedom from all accumulation.

DISTRACTION

IT WAS A long, wide canal, leading from the river into lands that had no water. The canal was higher than the river, and the water which entered it was controlled by a system of locks. It was peaceful along that canal; heavy-laden barges moved up and down it, and their white triangular sails stood out against the blue sky and the dark palms. It was a lovely evening, calm and free, and the water was very still. The reflections of the palms and of the mango trees were so sharp and clear that it was confusing to distinguish the actual from the reflection. The setting sun made the water transparent, and the glow of evening was on its face. The evening star was beginning to show among the reflections. The water was without a movement, and the few passing villagers, who generally talked so loud and long, were silent. Even the whisper among the leaves had stopped. From the meadow came some animal; it drank, and disappeared as silently as it had come. Silence held the land, it seemed to cover everything.

Noise ends, but silence is penetrating and without end. One can shut oneself off from noise, but there is no enclosure against silence; no wall can shut it out, there is no resistance against it. Noise shuts all things out, it is excluding and isolating; silence includes all things within itself. Silence, like love, is indivisible; it has no division of noise and silence. The mind cannot follow it or be made still to receive it. The mind that is *made* still can only reflect its own images, and they are sharp and clear, noisy in their exclusion. A mind that is made still can only resist, and all resistance is agitation. The mind that *is* still and not *made* still is ever experiencing silence; the thought, the word, is then within the silence, and not outside of it. It is strange how, in this silence, the mind is tranquil, with a tranquillity that is not formed. As tranquillity is not marketable, has no value, and is not usable, it has a quality of the pure, of the alone. That which can be used is soon worn out. Tranquillity does not begin or end, and a mind thus tranquil is aware of a bliss that is not the reflection of its own desire.

She said she had always been agitated by something or other; if it was not the family, it was the neighbour or some social activity. Agitation had filled her life, and she had never been able to find the reason for these constant upheavals. She was not particularly happy; and how could one be with the world as it was? She had had her share of passing happiness, but all that was in the past and now she was hunting for something that would give a meaning to life. She had been through many things which at the time seemed worth while, but which afterwards faded into nothingness. She had been engaged in many social activities of the serious kind; she had ardently believed in the things of religion, had suffered because of death in her family, and had faced a major operation. Life had not been easy with her, she added, and there were millions of others in the world like herself. She wanted to go beyond all this business, whether foolish or necessary, and find something that was really worth while.

The things that are worth while are not to be found. They cannot be bought, they must happen; and the happening cannot be cunningly planned. Is it not true that anything that has deep significance always happens, it is never brought about? The happening is important, not the finding. The finding is comparatively easy, but the happening is quite another matter. Not that it is difficult; but the urge to seek, to find, must wholly stop for the happening to take place. Finding implies losing; you must have in order to lose. To possess or be possessed is never to be free to understand.

But why has there always been this agitation, this restlessness? Have you seriously inquired into it before?

"I have attempted it half-heartedly, but never purposively. I have always been distracted."

Not distracted, if one may point out; it is simply that this has never been a vital problem to you. When there is a vital problem, then there is no distraction. Distraction does not exist; distraction implies a central interest from which the mind wanders; but if there is a central interest, there is no distraction. The mind's wandering from one thing to another is not distraction, it is an avoidance of what *is*. We like to wander far away because the problem is very close. The wandering gives us something to do, like worry and gossip; and though the wandering is often painful, we prefer it to what *is*.

Do you seriously wish to go into all this, or are you merely playing around with it?

"I really want to go through to the very end of it. That is why I have come."

You are unhappy because there is no spring that keeps the well full, is that it? You may once have heard the whisper of water on the pebbles, but now the river-bed is dry. You have known happiness, but it has always receded, it is always a thing of the past. Is that spring the thing you are groping after? And can you seek it, or must you come upon it unexpectedly? If you knew where it was, you would find means to get to it; but not knowing, there is no path to it. To know it is to prevent the happening of it. Is that one of the problems?

"That definitely is. Life is so dull and uncreative, and if that thing could happen one wouldn't ask for anything more."

Is loneliness a problem?

"I don't mind being lonely, I know how to deal with it. I either go out for a walk, or sit quietly with it till it goes. Besides, I like being alone."

We all know what it is to be lonely : an aching, fearsome emptiness that cannot be appeased. We also know how to run away from it, for we have all explored the many avenues of escape. Some are caught in one particular avenue, and others keep on exploring; but neither are in direct relationship with what *is*. You say you know how to deal with loneliness. If one may point out, this very action upon loneliness is your way of avoiding it. You go out for a walk, or sit with loneliness till it goes. You are always operating upon it, you do not allow it to tell its story. You want to dominate it, to get over it, to run away from it; so your relationship with it is that of fear.

Is fulfilment also a problem? To fulfil oneself in something implies the avoidance of what one is, does it not? I am puny; but if I identify myself with the country, with the family, or with some belief, I feel fulfilled, complete. This search for completeness is the avoidance of what *is*.

"Yes, that is so; that is also my problem."

If we can understand what *is*, then perhaps all these problems will cease. Our approach to any problem is to avoid it; we want to do something about it. The doing prevents our being in direct relationship with it, and this approach blocks the understanding of the problem. The mind is occupied with finding a way to deal with the problem, which is really an avoidance of it; and so the problem is never understood, it is still there. For the problem, the what *is*, to unfold and tell its story fully, the mind must be sensitive, quick to follow. If we anæsthetize the mind through escapes, through knowing how to deal with the problem, or through seeking an explanation or a cause for it, which is only a verbal conclusion, then the mind is made dull and cannot swiftly follow the story which the problem, the what *is*, is unfolding. See the truth of this, and the mind is sensitive; and only then can it receive. Any activity of the mind with regard to the problem only makes it dull and so incapable of following, of listening to the problem. When the mind is sensitive—not *made* sensitive, which is only another way of making it dull—then the what *is*, the emptiness, has a wholly different significance.

Please be experiencing as we go along, do not remain on the verbal level.

What is the relationship of the mind to what *is*? So far, the what *is* has been given a name, a term, a symbol of association, and this naming prevents direct relationship, which makes the mind dull, insensitive. The mind and what *is* are not two separate processes, but naming separates them. When this naming ceases, there is a direct relationship : the mind and the what *is* are one. The what *is* is now the observer himself without a term, and only then is the what *is* transformed; it is no longer the thing called emptiness with its associations of fear, and so on. Then the mind is only the state of experiencing, in which the experiencer and the experienced are not. Then there is immeasurable depth, for he who measures is gone. That which is deep is silent, tranquil, and in this tranquillity is the spring of the inexhaustible. The agitation of the mind is the usage of word. When the word is not, the measureless is.

TIME

HE WAS AN oldish man, but well preserved, with long, grey hair and a white beard. He had lectured about philosophy at universities in different parts of the world. He was very scholarly and quiet. He said he did not meditate; nor was he religious in the ordinary sense. He was concerned with knowledge only; and though he lectured on philosophy and religious experiences, he hadn't any of his own nor was he looking for any. He had come to talk over the question of time.

How difficult it is for the man of possessions to be free! It is a great hardship for a rich man to put aside his wealth. Only when there are other and greater inducements will he forgo the comforting realization that he is a rich man; he must find the fulfilment of his ambition at another level before he will let go the one he has. To the rich man, money is power, and he is the wielder of it; he may give away large sums, but he is the giver.

Knowledge is another form of possession, and the man of knowledge is satisfied with it; for him it is an end in itself. He has a feeling—at least this one had—that knowledge will some-how solve our problems if only it can be spread, thick or thin, around the world. It is much more difficult for the man of know-ledge to be free from his possessions than for the man of wealth. It is strange how easily knowledge takes the place of understand-ing and wisdom. If we have information about things, we think we understand; we think that knowing or being informed about the cause of a problem will make it non-existent. We search for the cause of our problems, and this very search is the post-ponement of understanding. Most of us know the cause; the cause of hate is not very deeply hidden, but in looking for the cause we can still enjoy its effects. We are concerned with the reconciliation of effects, and not with the understanding of the total process. Most of us are attached to our problems, without them we would be lost; problems give us something to do, and the activities of the problem fill our lives. We *are* the problem and its activities.

Time is a very strange phenomenon. Space and time are one; the one is not without the other. Time to us is extraordinarily important, and each one gives to it his own particular significance. Time to the savage has hardly any meaning, but to the civilized it is of immense significance. The savage forgets from day to day; but if the educated man did that, he would be put in an asylum or would lose his job. To a scientist, time is one thing; to a layman, it is another. To an historian, time is the study of the past; to a man on the stock market, it is the ticker; to a mother, it is the memory of her son; to an exhausted man, it is rest in the shade. Each one translates it according to his particular needs and satisfactions, shaping it to suit his own cunning mind. Yet we cannot do without time. If we are to live at all, chronological time is as essential as the seasons. But is there psychological time, or is it merely a deceptive convenience of the mind? Surely, there is only chronological time, and all else is deception. There is time to grow and time to die, time to sow and time to reap; but is not psychological time, the process of becoming, utterly false?

"What is time to you? Do you think of time? Are you aware of time?"

Can one think of time at all except in the chronological sense? We can use time as a means, but in itself it has little meaning, has it not? Time as an abstraction is a mere speculation, and all speculation is vain. We use time as a means of achievement, tangible or psychological. Time is needed to go to the station, but most of us use time as a means to a psychological end, and the ends are many. We are aware of time when there is an impediment to our achievement, or when there is the interval of becoming successful. Time is the space between what *is* and what might, should, or will be. The beginning going towards the end is time.

"Is there no other time? What about the scientific implications of time-space?"

There is chronological and there is psychological time. The

chronological is necessary, and it is there; but the other is quite a different matter. Cause-effect is said to be a time process, not only physically but also psychologically. It is considered that the interval between cause and effect is time; but is there an interval? The cause and the effect of a disease may be separated by time, which is again chronological; but is there an interval between psychological cause and effect? Is not cause-effect a single process? There is no interval between cause and effect. Today is the effect of yesterday and the cause of tomorrow; it is one movement, a continuous flowing. There is no separation, no distinct line between cause and effect; but inwardly we separate them in order to become, to achieve. I am *this,* and I shall become *that.* To become *that* I need time—chronological time used for psychological purposes. I am ignorant, but I shall become wise. Ignorance becoming wise is only progressive ignorance; for ignorance can never become wise, any more than greed can ever become non-greed. Ignorance is the very process of becoming.

Is not thought the product of time? Knowledge is the continuation of time. Time is continuation. Experience is knowledge, and time is the continuation of experience as memory. Time as continuation is an abstraction, and speculation is ignorance. Experience is memory, the mind. The mind is the machine of time. The mind is the past. Thought is ever of the past; the past is the continuation of knowledge. Knowledge is ever of the past; knowledge is never out of time, but always in time and of time. This continuation of memory, knowledge, is consciousness. Experience is always in the past; it *is* the past. This past in conjunction with the present is moving to the future; the future is the past, modified perhaps, but still the past. This whole process is thought, the mind. Thought cannot function in any field other than that of time. Thought may speculate upon the timeless, but it will be its own projection. All speculation is ignorance.

"Then why do you even mention the timeless? Can the timeless ever be known? Can it ever be recognized as the timeless?"

Recognition implies the experiencer, and the experiencer is

always of time. To recognize something, thought must have experienced it; and if it has experienced it, then it is the known. The known is not the timeless, surely. The known is always within the net of time. Thought cannot know the timeless; it is not a further acquisition, a further achievement; there is no going towards it. It is a state of being in which thought, time, is not.

"What value has it?"

None at all. It is not marketable. It cannot be weighed for a purpose. Its worth is unknown.

"But what part does it play in life?"

If life is thought, then none at all. We want to gain it as a source of peace and happiness, as a shield against all trouble, or as a means of uniting people. It cannot be used for any purpose. Purpose implies means to an end, and so we are back again with the process of thought. Mind cannot formulate the timeless, shape it to its own end; it cannot be used. Life has meaning only when the timeless is; otherwise life is sorrow, conflict and pain. Thought cannot solve any human problem, for thought itself is the problem. The ending of knowledge is the beginning of wisdom. Wisdom is not of time, it is not the continuation of experience, knowledge. Life in time is confusion and misery; but when that which *is* is the timeless, there is bliss.

SUFFERING

A LARGE DEAD animal was floating down the river. On it there were several vultures, tearing away at the carcass; they would fight off the other vultures till they had their fill, and only then would they fly away. The others waited on the trees, on the banks, or hovered overhead. The sun had just risen, and there was heavy dew on the grass. The green fields on the other side of the river were misty, and the voices of the peasants carried so clearly across the water. It was a lovely morning, fresh and new. A baby monkey was playing around the mother among the branches. It would race along a branch, leap to the next one, and race back again, or jump up and down near the mother. She was bored by these antics, and would come down the tree and go up another. When she began to climb down, the baby would run and cling to her, getting on her back or swinging under her. It had such a small face, with eyes that were full of play and frightened mischief.

How frightened we are of the new, of the unknown! We like to remain enclosed in our daily habits, routines, quarrels and anxieties. We like to think in the same old way, take the same road, see the same faces and have the same worries. We dislike to meet strangers, and when we do we are aloof and distraught. And how frightened we are to encounter an unfamiliar animal! We move within the walls of our own thought; and when we do venture out, it is still within the extension of those walls. We have never an ending, but always nourish the continuous. We carry from day to day the burden of yesterday; our life is one long, continuous movement, and our minds are dull and insensitive.

He could hardly stop weeping. It was not controlled or restrained weeping, but a sobbing that shook his whole body. He was a youngish man, alert, with eyes that had seen visions. He was unable to speak for some time; and when at last he did, his voice shook and he would burst into great sobs, unashamed and free. Presently he said:

"I haven't wept at all since the day of my wife's death. I don't know what made me cry like that, but it has been a relief. I have wept before, with her when she was alive, and then weeping was as cleansing as laughter; but since her death everything has changed. I used to paint, but now I can't touch the brushes or look at the things I have done. For the last six months I also have seemed to be dead. We had no children, but she was expecting one; and now she is gone. Even now I can hardly realize it, for we did everything together. She was so beautiful and so good, and what shall I do now? I am sorry to have burst out like that, and God knows what made me do it; but I know it is good to have cried. It will never be the same again, though;

something has gone out of my life. The other day I picked up the brushes, and they were strangers to me. Before, I didn't even know I held a brush in my hand; but now it has weight, it is cumbersome. I have often walked to the river, wanting never to come back; but I always did. I couldn't see people, as her face was always there. I sleep, dream and eat with her, but I know it can never be the same again. I have reasoned about it all, tried to rationalize the event and understand it; but I know she is not there. I dream of her night after night; but I cannot sleep all the time, though I have tried. I dare not touch her things, and the very smell of them drives me almost crazy. I have tried to forget, but do what I will, it can never be the same again. I used to listen to the birds, but now I want to destroy everything. I can't go on like this. I haven't seen any of our friends since then, and without her they mean nothing to me. What am I to do?"

We were silent for a long time.

Love that turns to sorrow and to hate is not love. Do we know what love is? Is it love that, when thwarted, becomes fury? Is there love when there is gain and loss?

"In loving her, all those things ceased to exist. I was completely oblivious of them all, oblivious even of myself. I knew such love, and I still have that love for her; but now I am aware of other things also, of myself, of my sorrow, of the days of my misery."

How quickly love turns to hate, to jealousy, to sorrow! How deeply we are lost in the smoke, and how distant is that which was so close! Now we are aware of other things, which have suddenly become so much more important. We are now aware that we are lonely, without a companion, without the smile and the familiar sharp word; we are aware of ourselves now, and not only of the other. The other was everything, and we nothing; now the other is not, and we are that which *is*. The other is a dream, and the reality is what we are. Was the other ever real, or a dream of our own creation, clothed with the beauty of our own joy which soon fades? The fading is death, and life is what we are. Death cannot always cover life, however much we may desire it; life is stronger than death. The what *is* is stronger than what is not. How we love death, and not life! The denial of life is so pleasant, so forgetting. When the other is, we are not; when the other is, we are free, uninhibited; the other is the flower, the neighbour, the scent, the remembrance. We all want the other, we are all identified with the other; the other is important, and not ourselves. The other is the dream of ourselves; and upon waking, we are what *is*. The what *is* is deathless, but we want to put an end to what *is*. The desire to end gives birth to the continuous, and what is continuous can never know the deathless.

"I know I cannot go on living like this, a half-death. I am not at all sure that I understand what you are saying. I am too dazed to take anything in."

Do you not often find that, though you are not giving your full attention to what is being said or to what you are reading, there has nevertheless been a listening, perhaps unconsciously, and that something has penetrated in spite of yourself? Though you have not deliberately looked at those trees, yet the image of them suddenly comes up in every detail—have you never found that happening? Of course you are dazed from the recent shock; but in spite of that, as you come out of it, what we are saying now will be remembered and then it may be of some help. But what is important to realize is this : when you come out of the shock, the suffering will be more intense, and your desire will be to escape, to run away from your own misery. There are only too many people who will help you to escape; they will offer every plausible explanation, conclusions which they or others have arrived at, every kind of rationalization; or you yourself will find some form of withdrawal, pleasant or unpleasant, to drown your misery. Till now you have been too close to the event, but as the days go by you will crave for some kind of consolation : religion, cynicism, social activity, or some ideology. But escapes of any kind, whether God or drink, only prevent the understanding of sorrow.

Sorrow has to be understood and not ignored. To ignore it is to give continuity to suffering; to ignore it is to escape from suffering. To understand suffering needs an operational, experimental approach. To experiment is not to seek a definite result. If you seek a definite result, experiment is not possible. If you know what you want, the going after it is not experimentation. If you seek to get over suffering, which is to condemn it, then you do not understand its whole process; when you try to overcome suffering, your only concern is to avoid it. To understand suffering, there must be no positive action of the mind to justify or to overcome it : the mind must be entirely passive, silently watchful, so that it can follow without hesitation the unfolding of sorrow. Mind cannot follow the story of sorrow if it is tethered to any hope, conclusion or remembrance. To follow the swift movement of what *is*, the mind must be free; freedom is not to be had at the end, it must be there at the very beginning.

"What is the meaning of all this sorrow?"

Is not sorrow the indication of conflict, the conflict of pain and pleasure? Is not sorrow the intimation of ignorance? Ignorance is not lack of information about facts; ignorance is unawareness of the total process of oneself. There must be suffering as long as there is no understanding of the ways of the self; and the ways of the self are to be discovered only in the action of relationship.

"But my relationship has come to an end."

There is no end to relationship. There may be the end of a particular relationship; but relationship can never end. To be is to be related, and nothing can live in isolation. Though we try to isolate ourselves through a particular relationship, such isolation will inevitably breed sorrow. Sorrow is the process of isolation.

"Can life ever be what it has been?"

Can the joy of yesterday ever be repeated today? The desire for repetition arises only when there is no joy today; when today is empty, we look to the past or to the future. The desire for repetition is desire for continuity, and in continuity there is never the new. There is happiness, not in the past or in the future, but only in the movement of the present.

SENSATION AND HAPPINESS

WE WERE HIGH up over the green sea, and the noise of the
propellers beating the air and the roar of the exhaust made
talking difficult. Besides, there were some college boys going to
an athletic meet on the island; one of them had a banjo, and
he played upon it and sang for many hours. He egged on the
others, and they all joined in singing together. The boy with the
banjo had a good voice, and the songs were American, songs of
the crooners and the cowboys, or jazz. They did it all very well,
just like the gramophone records. They were an odd group,
concerned only with the present; they had not a thought of
anything but immediate enjoyment. Tomorrow held all the
troubles : job, marriage, old age and death. But here, high over
the sea, it was American songs and picture papers. The lightning
among the dark clouds they ignored, and they never saw the
curve of the land as it pursued the sea, nor the distant village in
the sun.

The island was almost below us now. It was green and
sparkling, freshly washed by the rains. How neat and orderly
everything was from that altitude ! The highest hill was flattened,
and the white waves had no movement. A brown fishing boat
with sails was hurrying before the storm; she would reach safety,
for the port was in sight. The winding river came down to the
sea, and the soil was golden brown. At that height one saw what
was happening on both sides of the river, and the past and the
future met. The future was not hidden, though it lay around
the bend. At that height there was neither the past nor the
future; curving space did not conceal either the time of sowing
or the time of reaping.

The man in the next seat began to talk of the difficulties of
life. He complained of his job, the incessant travelling, the in-
considerateness of his family, and the futility of modern politics.
He was on his way to some far-off place, and was rather sad at
leaving his home. As he talked he became more and more serious,

more and more concerned about the world and particularly about himself and his family.

"I would like to go away from it all to some quiet place, work a little, and be happy. I don't think I have been happy in all my life, and I don't know what it means. We live, breed, work and die, like any other animal. I have lost all enthusiasm, except for making money, and that too is becoming rather boring. I am fairly good at my job and earn a good salary, but what it is all about I haven't the vaguest idea. I would like to be happy, and what do you think I can do about it?"

It is a complex thing to understand, and this is hardly the place for a serious talk.

"I am afraid I have no other time; the moment we land I must be off again. I may not sound serious, but there are spots of seriousness in me; the only trouble is, they never seem to get together. I am really quite serious at heart. My father and my older relations were known for their earnestness, but the present economic conditions don't allow one to be completely serious. I have been drawn away from all that, but I would like to get back to it and forget all this stupidity. I suppose I am weak and grumbling about circumstances; but all the same, I would like to be really happy."

Sensation is one thing, and happiness is another. Sensation is always seeking further sensation, ever in wider and wider circles. There is no end to the pleasures of sensation; they multiply, but there is always dissatisfaction in their fulfilment; there is always the desire for more, and the demand for more is without end. Sensation and dissatisfaction are inseparable, for the desire for more binds them together. Sensation is the desire for more and also the desire for less. In the very act of the fulfilment of sensation, the demand for more is born. The more is ever in the future; it is the everlasting dissatisfaction with what has been. There is conflict between what has been and what will be. Sensation is always dissatisfaction. One may clothe sensation in religious garb, but it is still what it is : a thing of the mind and a source of conflict and apprehension. Physical sensations are always crying for more; and when they are thwarted, there is anger, jealousy, hatred. There is pleasure in hatred, and envy is satisfying; when one sensation is thwarted, satisfaction is found in the very antagonism that frustration has brought.

Sensation is ever a reaction, and it wanders from one reaction to another. The wanderer is the mind; the mind is sensation. The mind is the storehouse of sensation, pleasant and unpleasant, and all experience is reaction. The mind is memory, which after all is reaction. Reaction or sensation can never be satisfied; response can never be content. Response is always negation, and what is not can never be. Sensation knows no contentment. Sensation, reaction must always breed conflict, and the very conflict is further sensation. Confusion breeds confusion. The activity of the mind, at all its different levels, is the furthering of sensation; and when its expansion is denied, it finds gratification in contraction. Sensation, reaction, is the conflict of the opposites; and in this conflict of resistance and acceptance, yielding and denying, there is satisfaction which is ever seeking further satisfaction.

Mind can never find happiness. Happiness is not a thing to be pursued and found, as sensation. Sensation can be found again and again, for it is ever being lost; but happiness cannot be found. Remembered happiness is only a sensation, a reaction for or against the present. What is over is not happiness; the experience of happiness which is over is sensation, for remembrance is the past, and the past is sensation. Happiness is not sensation.

Have you ever been aware of being happy?

"Of course I have, thank God, otherwise I would not know what it is to be happy."

Surely, what you were aware of was the sensation of an experience which you call happiness; but that is not happiness. What you know is the past, not the present; and the past is sensation, reaction, memory. You remember that you were happy; and can the past tell what happiness is? It can recall but it cannot be. Recognition is not happiness; to know what it is to be happy, is not happiness. Recognition is the response of memory; and can the mind, the complex of memories, experiences, ever be happy? The very recognition prevents the experiencing.

When you are aware that you are happy, is there happiness? When there is happiness, are you aware of it? Consciousness comes only with conflict, the conflict of remembrance of the more. Happiness is not the remembrance of the more. Where there is conflict, happiness is not. Conflict is where the mind is. Thought at all levels is the response of memory, and so thought invariably breeds conflict. Thought is sensation, and sensation is not happiness. Sensations are ever seeking gratifications. The end is sensation, but happiness is not an end; it cannot be sought out.

"But how can sensations come to an end?"

To end sensation is to invite death. Mortification is only another form of sensation. In mortification, physical or psychological, sensitivity is destroyed, but not sensation. Thought that mortifies itself is only seeking further sensation, for thought itself is sensation. Sensation can never put an end to sensation; it may have different sensations at other levels, but there is no ending to sensation. To destroy sensation is to be insensitive, dead; not to see, not to smell, not to touch is to be dead, which is isolation. Our problem is entirely different, is it not? Thought can never bring happiness; it can only recall sensations, for thought is sensation. It cannot cultivate, produce, or progress towards happiness. Thought can only go towards that which it knows, but the known is not happiness; the known is sensation. Do what it will, thought cannot be or search out happiness. Thought can only be aware of its own structure, its own movement. When thought makes an effort to put an end to itself, it is only seeking to be more successful, to reach a goal, an end which will be more gratifying. The more is knowledge, but not happiness. Thought must be aware of its own ways, of its own cunning deceptions. In being aware of itself, without any desire to be or not to be, the mind comes to a state of inaction. Inaction is not death; it is a passive watchfulness in which thought is wholly inactive. It is the highest state of sensitivity. When the mind is completely inactive at all its levels, only then is there action. All the activities of the mind are mere sensations, reactions to stimulation, to influence, and so not action at all. When the mind is without activity, there is action; this action is without cause, and only then is there bliss.

To see the False as the False

IT WAS A beautiful evening. The sky was flaming red behind the rice fields, and the tall, slender palms were swaying in the breeze. The bus loaded with people was making a lot of noise as it climbed the little hill, and the river wound round the hill as it made its way to the sea. The cattle were fat, the vegetation was thick, and there was an abundance of flowers. Plump little boys were playing in a field, and the little girls looked on with astonished eyes. There was a small shrine nearby, and someone was lighting a lamp in front of the image. In a solitary house the evening prayers were being said, and the room was lighted by a lamp which was not too bright. The whole family had gathered there, and they all seemed to be enjoying their prayers. A dog was fast asleep in the middle of the road, and a cyclist went round it. It was getting dark now, and the fireflies lit up the faces of the people who silently passed by. One was caught in a woman's hair, giving her head a soft glow.

How kind we naturally are, especially away from the towns, in the fields and the small villages! Life is more intimate among the less educated, where the fever of ambition has not yet spread. The boy smiles at you, the old woman wonders, the man hesitates and passes by. A group stops its loud talk and turns to look with surprised interest, and a woman waits for you to pass her. We know so little of ourselves; we know, but we do not understand; we know, but we have no communion with another. We do not know ourselves. And how can we know another? We can never know another, we can only commune with another. We can know the dead, but never the living; what we know is the dead past, not the living. To be aware of the living, we must bury the dead in ourselves. We know the names of trees, of birds, of shops, but what do we know of ourselves beyond some words and appetites? We have information, conclusions about so many things; but there is no happiness, no peace that is not stagnant. Our lives are dull and empty, or so full of words and activity that it blinds us. Knowledge is not wisdom, and without wisdom there is no peace, no happiness.

He was a young man, a professor of some kind, dissatisfied, worried and burdened with responsibilities. He began by narrating his troubles, the weary lot of man. He had been well educated, he said—which was mostly a matter of knowing how to read and gathering information from books. He stated that he had been to as many of the talks as he could, and went on to explain that for years he had been trying to give up smoking, but had never been able to give it up entirely. He wanted to give it up because it was expensive as well as stupid. He had done everything he could to stop smoking, but had always come back to it. This was one of his problems, among others. He was intense, nervous and thin.

Do we understand anything if we condemn it? To push it away, or to accept it, is easy; but the very condemnation or acceptance is an avoidance of the problem. To condemn a child is to push him away from you in order not to be bothered by him; but the child is still there. To condemn is to disregard, to pay no attention; and there can be no understanding through condemnation.

"I have condemned myself for smoking, over and over again. It is difficult not to condemn."

Yes, it is difficult not to condemn, for our conditioning is based on denial, justification, comparison and resignation. This is our background, the conditioning with which we approach every problem. This very conditioning breeds the problem, the conflict. You have tried to rationalize away the smoking, have you not? When you say it is stupid, you have thought it all out and come to the conclusion that it is stupid. And yet rationalization has not made you give it up. We think that we can be free from a problem by knowing its cause; but the knowing is merely information, a verbal conclusion. This knowledge obviously prevents the understanding of the problem. Knowing the cause of a problem and understanding the problem are two entirely different things.

"But how else can one approach a problem?"

That is what we are going to find out. When we discover what the false approach is, we shall be aware of the only approach. The understanding of the false is the discovery of the true. To see the false as the false is arduous. We look at the false through comparison, through the measure of thought; and can the false be seen as the false through any thought process? Is not thought itself conditioned and so false?

"But how can we know the false as the false without the thought process?"

This is our whole trouble, is it not? When we use thought to solve a problem, surely we are using an instrument which is not at all adequate; for thought itself is a product of the past, of experience. Experience is always in the past. To see the false as the false, thought must be aware of itself as a dead process. Thought can never be free, and there must be freedom to discover, freedom from thought.

"I don't quite see what you mean."

One of your problems is smoking. You have approached it with condemnation, or you have tried to rationalize it away. This approach is false. How do you discover that it is false? Surely, not through thought, but by being passively watchful of how you approach the problem. Passive watchfulness does not demand thought; on the contrary, if thought is functioning there can be no passivity. Thought functions only to condemn or justify, to compare or accept; if there is a passive watchfulness of this process, then it is perceived as what it is.

"Yes, I see that; but how does this apply to my smoking?"

Let us experiment together to find out if one can approach the problem of smoking without condemnation, comparison, and so on. Can we look at the problem afresh, without the past over-shadowing it? It is extremely difficult to look at it without any reaction, is it not? We seem unable to be aware of it passively, there is always some kind of response from the past. It is interesting to see how incapable we are of observing the problem as though it were new. We carry along with us all our past efforts, conclusions, intentions; we cannot look at the problem except through these curtains.

No problem is ever old, but we approach it with the old formulations, which prevent our understanding it. Be passively watchful of these responses. Just be passively aware of them, see that they cannot solve the problem. The problem is real, it is an actuality, but the approach is utterly inadequate. The inadequate response to what *is* breeds conflict; and conflict is the problem. If there is an understanding of this whole process, then you will find that you will act adequately with regard to smoking.

SECURITY

THE SMALL STREAM was flowing very gently beside the path that wound round the rice fields, and it was crowded with lotuses; they were dark violet with golden hearts, and they were clear of the water. Their scent remained close to them, and they were very beautiful. The sky was overcast; it was beginning to drizzle, and there was thunder among the clouds. The lightning was still far away, but it was coming towards the tree under which we were sheltering. It began to rain heavily, and the lotus leaves were collecting drops of water; when the drops became too large, they slipped off the leaves, only to form again. The lightning was now above the tree, and the cattle were frightened and straining at their ropes. A black calf, wet and shivering, was calling piteously; it broke its rope and ran towards a nearby hut. The lotuses were closing themselves tightly, shutting their hearts against the gathering darkness; one would have had to tear the violet petals to get at the golden hearts. They would remain tightly closed till the coming of the sun. Even in their sleep they were beautiful. The lightning was moving towards the town; it was now quite dark, and one could just hear the murmur of the stream.

The path led past the village to the road which took us back to the noisy town.

He was a young man, in his twenties; he was well fed, had travelled a little and been to college. He was nervous and there was anxiety in his eyes. It was late, but he wanted to talk; he wanted someone to explore his mind for him. He exposed himself very simply, without any hesitation or pretension. His problem was clear, but not to him; he went groping about.

We do not listen and discover what *is*; we foist our ideas and opinions on another, trying to force the other into the frame of our thought. Our own thoughts and judgments are so much more important to us than to find out what *is*. The what *is* is always simple; it is we who are complex. We make the simple, the what *is*, complex, and we get lost in it. We listen only to the increasing noise of our own confusion. To listen, we must be free. It is not that there must be no distractions, for thinking itself is a form of distraction. We must be free to be silent, and only then is it possible to hear.

He was saying that just as he was going off to sleep he would sit up with a start of naked fear. Then the room would lose its proportions; the walls would go flat, there would be no roof, and the floor would disappear. He would be frightened and sweating. This had been going on for many years.

What are you frightened of?

"I don't know; but when I wake up with fear, I go to my sister, or to my father and mother, and talk with them for some time to calm myself, and then go off to sleep. They understand, but I am in my twenties and it is getting rather silly."

Are you anxious about the future?

"Yes, somewhat. Though we have money, I am still rather anxious about it."

Why?

"I want to marry and provide comfort for my future wife."

Why be anxious about the future? You are quite young, and you can work and give her what is necessary. Why be so preoccupied with this? Are you afraid of losing your social position?

"Partly. We have a car, some property and reputation. Naturally I don't want to lose all this, which may be the cause of my fear. But it isn't quite this. It is the fear of not being. When I wake up with fear, I feel I am lost, that I am nobody, that I am falling to pieces."

After all, a new government may come in and you may lose your property, your holdings; but you are quite young, and you can always work. Millions are losing their worldly goods, and you too may have to face that. Besides, the things of the world are to be shared and not to be exclusively possessed. At your age, why be so conservative, so afraid of losing?

"You see, I want to marry a particular girl, and I am anxious that nothing should stop it. Nothing is likely to stop it, but I miss her and she misses me, and this may be another cause of my fear."

Is that the cause of your fear? You say that nothing out of the ordinary is likely to happen to prevent your marrying her, so why this fear?

"Yes, it is true that we can marry whenever we decide to, so that cannot be the cause of my fear, at least not now. I think I am really frightened of not being, of losing my identity, my name."

Even if you did not care about your name, but had your property and so on, would you not still be afraid? What do we mean by identity? It is to be identified with a name, with property, with a person, with ideas; it is to be associated with something, to be recognized as this or that, to be labelled as belonging to a particular group or country, and so on. You are afraid of losing your label, is that it?

"Yes. Otherwise, what am I? Yes, that is it."

So you *are* your possessions. Your name and reputation, your car and other property, the girl you are going to marry, the ambitions that you have—you *are* these things. These things, together with certain characteristics and values, go to make up what you call "I"; you are the sum total of all this, and you are afraid of losing it. As with everyone else, there is always the possibility of loss; a war may come, there may be a revolution or a change in government towards the left. Something may happen to deprive you of these things, now or tomorrow. But why be afraid of insecurity? Is not insecurity the very nature of all things? Against this insecurity you are building walls that will protect you; but these walls can be and are being broken down. You may escape from it for a time, but the danger of insecurity is always there. That which *is,* you cannot avoid; insecurity is there, whether you like it or not. This does not mean that you must resign yourself to it, or that you must accept or deny it; but you are young, and why be afraid of insecurity?

"Now that you put it this way, I don't think I am afraid of insecurity. I really don't mind working; I work over eight hours a day at my job, and though I don't particularly like it, I can carry on. No, I am not afraid of losing property, the car, and so on; and my fiancée and I can marry whenever we want to. I see now that it is none of this that is making me fearful. Then what is it?"

Let us find out together. I might be able to tell you, but it would not be your discovery; it would only be on the verbal level, and so utterly useless. The finding of it will be your own experiencing of it, and it is this that is really important. Discovering is experiencing; we will discover it together.

If it is none of these things that you are frightened of losing, if you are not afraid of being insecure outwardly, then of what are you anxious? Don't answer right away; just listen, be watchful to find out. Are you quite sure it is not physical insecurity that you are frightened of? As far as one can be sure of such things, you say that you are not frightened of it. If you are sure that this is not a mere verbal assertion, then of what are you afraid?

"I am quite sure I am not frightened of being physically insecure; we can marry and have what we need. It is something more than the mere loss of things that I am afraid of. But what is it?"

We will find out, but let us consider it quietly. You really want to find out, don't you?

"Of course I do, especially now that we have gone as far as this. What is it that I am frightened of?"

To find out we must be quiet, watchful, but not pressing. If you are not frightened of physical insecurity, are you frightened of being inwardly insecure, of being unable to achieve the end which you have set for yourself? Don't answer, just listen. Do you feel incapable of becoming somebody? Probably you have a religious ideal; and do you feel you have not the capacity to live up to or achieve it? Do you feel a sense of hopelessness about it, a sense of guilt or frustration?

"You are perfectly right. Ever since I heard you some years ago as a boy, it has been my ideal, if I may say so, to be like you. It's in our blood to be religious, and I have felt I could be like that; but there has always been a deep fear of never coming near it."

Let us go slowly. Though you are not frightened of being outwardly insecure, you are frightened of being insecure inwardly. Another man makes himself secure outwardly with a reputation, with fame, with money, and so on, while you want to be secure inwardly with an ideal; and you feel you have no capacity to become that ideal. Why do you want to become or achieve an ideal? Isn't it only to be secure, to feel safe? This refuge you call an ideal; but actually you want to be safe, protected. Is that it?

"Now that you point it out, that is exactly it."

You have discovered this now, have you not? But let us proceed further. You see the obvious shallowness of outward security; but do you also see the falseness of seeking inward security through becoming the ideal? The ideal is your refuge, instead of money. Do you really see this?

"Yes, I really do."

Then be what you are. When you see the falseness of the ideal, it drops away from you. You are what *is*. From there proceed to understand what *is*—but not towards any particular end, for the end, the goal is always away from what *is*. The what *is* is yourself, not at any particular period or in any given mood, but yourself as you are from moment to moment. Do not condemn yourself or become resigned to what you see, but be watchful without interpreting the movement of what *is*. This will be arduous, but there is delight in it. Only to the free is there happiness, and freedom comes with the truth of what *is*.

WORK

ALOOF AND INCLINED to be cynical, he was some kind of minister in the Government. He had been brought along, or more probably dragged, by a friend, and seemed rather surprised at finding himself there. The friend wanted to talk something over and evidently thought that the other might as well come along and hear his problem. The minister was curious and rather superior. He was a big man, sharp of eye and a facile talker. He had arrived in life, and was settling back. To travel is one thing, and to arrive is another. Travelling is constant arriving, and arrival that has no further travelling is death. How easily we are gratified, and how quickly discontent finds contentment! We all want a refuge of some kind, a haven from all conflict, and we generally find it. The clever, like the foolish, find their haven and are alert within it.

"I have been trying to understand my problem for a number of years, but I haven't been able to get to the bottom of it. In my work I have always brought about antagonism; enmity has somehow crept in amongst all the people I have tried to help. In helping some, I sow opposition among others. With one hand I give, and with the other I seem to injure. This has been going on for more years than I can remember, and now a situation has arisen in which I have to act rather decisively. I really don't want to hurt anyone, and I am at a loss what to do."

Which is more important: not to hurt, not to create enmity, or to do some piece of work?

"In the course of my work I do hurt others. I am one of those people who throw themselves into their work; if I undertake something, I want to see it through. I have always been that way.

I think I am fairly efficient, and I hate to see inefficiency. After all, if we undertake some kind of social work, we must go through with it, and those who are inefficient or slack naturally get hurt and become antagonistic. The work of bringing help to others is important, and in helping the needy I hurt those who come in the way. But I really don't want to hurt people, and I have begun to realize that I must do something about it."

Which to you is important: to work, or not to hurt people?

"When one sees so much misery and plunges into the work of reform, in the course of that work one hurts certain people, though most unwillingly."

In saving one group of people, others are destroyed. One country survives at the expense of another. The so-called spiritual people, in their ardour for reform, save some and destroy others; they bring blessings and also curses. We always seem to be kind to some and brutal to others. Why?

Which to you is important: to work, or not to hurt people?

"After all, one has to hurt certain people, the slovenly, the inefficient, the selfish, it seems inevitable. Don't you hurt people by your talks? I know a rich man who has been very hurt by what you say about the wealthy."

I do not want to hurt anyone. If people are hurt in the process of certain work, then to me that work has to be put aside. I have no work, no schemes for any kind of reform or revolution. With me work is not first, but not to hurt others. If the rich man feels hurt by what is said, he is not hurt by me, but by the truth of what *is*, which he dislikes; he doesn't want to be exposed. It is not my intention to expose another. If a man is temporarily exposed by the truth of what *is* and gets angry at what he sees, he puts the blame on others; but that is only an escape from the fact. It is foolish to be angry with a fact. Avoidance of a fact through anger is one of the commonest and most thoughtless reactions.

But you have not answered my question. Which to you is important: to work, or not to hurt people?

"Work has to be done, don't you think?" put in the minister.

Why should it be done? If in the course of benefiting some you hurt or destroy others, what value has it? You may save your particular country, but you exploit or maim another. Why are you so concerned about your country, your party, your ideology? Why are you so identified with your work? Why does work matter so much?

"We have to work, be active, otherwise we might as well be dead. When the house is burning, we cannot for the moment be concerned with fundamental issues."

To the merely active, fundamentals are never the issue; they are only concerned with activity, which brings superficial benefits and deep harms. But if I may ask our friend: why is a certain kind of work so important to you? Why are you so attached to it?

"Oh, I don't know, but it gives me a great deal of happiness."

So you are really not interested in the work itself, but in what you get out of it. You may not make money at it, but you derive happiness from it. As another gains power, position and prestige in saving his party or his country, so you gain pleasure from your work; as another finds great satisfaction, which he calls a blessing, in serving his saviour, his *guru,* his Master, so you are satisfied by what you call altruistic work. Actually it is not the country, the work, or the saviour that is important to you, but what you get out of it. Your own happiness is all-important, and your particular work gives you what you want. You are really not interested in the people you are supposed to be helping; they are only a means to your happiness. And obviously the inefficient, those who stand in your way, get hurt; for the work matters, the work being your happiness. This is the brutal fact, but we cunningly cover it with high-sounding words like service, country, peace, God, and so on.

So, if one may point out, you really do not mind hurting people who hinder the efficiency of the work that gives you happiness. You find happiness in certain work, and that work, whatever it be, is you. You are interested in getting happiness, and the work offers you the means; therefore the work becomes very important, and then of course you are very efficient, ruthless, dominating for the sake of that which gives you happiness. So you do not mind hurting people, breeding enmity.

"I have never seen it that way before, and it is perfectly true. But what am I to do about it?"

Is it not important to find out also why you have taken so many years to see a simple fact like this?

"I suppose, as you say, I really didn't care whether I hurt people or not so long as I got my way. I generally do get my way, because I have always been very efficient and direct—which you would call ruthlessness, and you are perfectly right. But what am I to do now?"

You have taken all these years to see this simple fact because until now you have been unwilling to see it; for in seeing it you are attacking the very foundation of your being. You have sought happiness and found it, but it has always brought conflict and antagonism; and now, perhaps for the first time, you are facing facts about yourself. What are you going to do? Is there not a different approach to work? Is it not possible to be happy and work, rather than to seek happiness in work? When we use work or people as a means to an end, then obviously we have no relationship, no communion either with the work or with people; and then we are incapable of love. Love is not a means to an end; it is its own eternity. When I use you and you use me, which is generally called relationship, we are important to each other only as a means to something else; so we are not important to each other at all. From this mutual usage, conflict and antagonism must inevitably arise. So what are you going to do? Let us both discover what to do rather than seek an answer from another. If you can search it out, your finding of it will be your experiencing of it; then it will be real and not just a confirmation or conclusion, a mere verbal answer.

"What, then, is my problem?"

Can we not put it this way? Spontaneously, what is your first reaction to the question: Does the work come first? If it does not, then what does?

"I am beginning to see what you are trying to get at. My first response is shock; I am really appalled to see what I have been doing in my work for so many years. This is the first time I have faced the fact of what *is*, as you call it, and I assure you it is not very pleasant. If I can go beyond it, perhaps I shall see what is important, and then the work will naturally follow. But whether the work or something else comes first is still not clear to me."

Why is it not clear? Is clarity a matter of time, or of willingness to see? Will the desire not to see disappear by itself in the course of time? Is not your lack of clarity due to the simple fact that you don't want to be clear because it would upset the whole pattern of your daily life? If you are aware that you are deliberately postponing, are you not immediately clear? It is this avoidance that brings confusion.

"It is all becoming very clear to me now, and what I shall do is immaterial. Probably I shall do what I have been doing, but with quite a different spirit. We shall see."